DAVID G. ROSKIES

YIDDISHLANDS

David G. Roskies is a native of Montreal, where his home was a salon for writers, actors, and artists, and where he came under the spell of Yiddish culture. Educated at Brandeis and the Hebrew University, Mr. Roskies is the Sol and Evelyn Henkind Professor of Yiddish Literature at the Jewish Theological Seminary.

A former Guggenheim recipient, Mr. Roskies was also awarded the Ralph Waldo Emerson Prize from Phi Beta Kappa for his book *Against the Apocalypse*. *Yiddishlands* is his first book without footnotes.

Mr. Roskies lives with his wife and son on the Upper West Side of Manhattan. Most mornings he can be seen riding to work on his bicycle. Other times, he resides in Old Katamon, Jerusalem, where he goes on foot.

ALSO BY DAVID G. ROSKIES

The Jewish Search for a Usable Past
A Bridge of Longing
Against the Apocalypse
Nightwords

EDITED BY DAVID G. ROSKIES

Everyday Jews by Yehoshue Perle
Scribblers on the Roof (with Melvin Jules Bukiet)
The World According to Itzik (with Leonard Wolf)
The Dybbuk and Other Writings by S. Ansky
The Literature of Destruction
The Shtetl Book (with Diane K. Roskies)

YIDDISHLANDS

The World of
Mother's Youth

BALTIC SEA

GERMANY

Berlin

St. Petersburg

U.S.S.R. Border
(ca. 1921)

Riga

Moscow

Kovno

Vilna

Lita
(Lithuanian
Jewish culture)

Bialystok

Minsk

Warsaw

RUSSIA

Gomel

Kraków

Tarnow

Zakopane

Krosno

Vienna

Kharkov

Czernowitz

Yekaterinoslav

AUSTRO-
HUNGARY

0   75
miles

Bucharest

BLACK   SEA

Rutgers Cartography 2007

YIDDISHLANDS

A MEMOIR

David G. Roskies

WAYNE STATE UNIVERSITY PRESS

Detroit

12 11 10 09 08   5 4 3 2 1

Library of Congress Cataloging-in-Publication Data
Roskies, David G., 1948—
Yiddishlands : a memoir / David G. Roskies.
p. cm.
The Rebbe Elimeylekh — The Dybbuk — Cafe Rudnitsky — Bread — Prayer for
the Tsar — Scribal errors — Malvina's roses — The watercarrier — Yeast —
Beloved fatherland — The black canopy — May day — The wooden box — The
last Seder night — Lisbon — Playing solitaire — The soirée — Cape Cod —
Double feature — Male bonding — Etudes — Sutzkever's address — Leybl's
ark — Between two mountains — Kotsk — The sale of Joseph — The two
bulvanes — Yom Kippur — New York Jew — Partisans' hymn — The menorah —
Dream house.
ISBN-13: 978-0-8143-3397-6 (cloth : alk. paper)
ISBN-10: 0-8143-3397-4 (cloth : alk. paper)
1. Roskies, David G., 1948–   2. Roskies, Masha, 1906–   3. Jews—Québec—
Montreal—Biography.   4. Yiddishists—United States—Biography.   5. Jewish
scholars—United States—Biography.   6. Mothers and sons.   7. Montréal
(Québec)—Ethnic relations.   I. Title.
F1054.5.M853R678 2008
974.7'10049240092—dc22

∞

Portions of this manuscript have appeared in *Commentary, Maggid:
A Journal of Jewish Literature,* and *The Pakn Treger.*

Publication of this book was made possible through the generosity of
the Bertha M. and Hyman Herman Endowed Memorial Fund.

Designed by Isaac Tobin
Typeset by The Composing Room of Michigan, Inc.
Composed in Farnham

אריה-לייבן אַ מתנה —

זאָלסט באַגערן צו לייענען,

און צו פֿאַרצײַלן מעשׂיות.

Our Rabbis taught: Thirteen things were said of the morning bread: It is an antidote against heat and cold, winds and demons; instills wisdom into the simple, causes one to triumph in a lawsuit, enables one to study and teach the Torah, to have his words heeded, and retain scholarship; he [who partakes thereof] does not perspire, lives with his wife and does not lust after other women; and it kills the worms in one's intestines. Some say, it also expels jealousy and induces love.

—BABYLONIAN TALMUD, *Baba Metsia* 107b

Der iker iz der pas-shákharis.
The most important thing in life is your morning bread.

—MASHA WELCZER ROSKIES

CONTENTS

I

TABLE TALK

YIDDISHLANDS

I

TABLE TALK

3

J. Chonovitz   à Vilna.

4

1

A portrait of Odl and Dovid Roskes, my paternal grandparents. Photographed in their kitchen on Polna Street 20, Bialystok, Poland, ca. 1930.

2

Formal portrait of my maternal grandmother, Fradl Matz. Vilna, ca. 1890. She wears a tiara of her own hair and the diamond earrings she would later sell to buy a grand piano. This photo is a copy of the life-size portrait of Fradl that hung over my parents' bed. Mother also wore a miniature thereof in a locket around her neck.

3

Studio portrait of my mother, Masha Welczer, Vilna, ca. 1918.

4

Studio portrait of my maternal grandparents, Yisroel Welczer and Fradl Matz. Having cast off his Hasidic gabardine, this is how Yisroel may have appeared when he came to ask for Fradl's hand in marriage. Taken at the Chonovitz Studio on Bolshoya Ul. (Breyte Gas), Vilna, ca. 1903.

1

The Rebbe Elimeylekh

The first thing I heard when I entered this world was my mother singing. It must have been a command performance. Given her rich past, her gift for languages, and her tenacious memory, she might have sung to me in Russian, Polish, Hebrew, Yiddish, or Ukrainian; but given our recent and decisive move to the Yiddish-speaking part of Montreal, away from the assimilated Jews of Westmount, it behooved her to sing only in Yiddish, the consecrated mother tongue.

Because March 2, 1948, the day of my birth, happily coincided with the festival of Purim, the most obvious song for her to sing was "Hop, mayne homentashn." Set to a Ukrainian folk melody, it memorialized the mock-heroic efforts of a housewife named Yakhne Dvoshe to bake a batch of three-cornered Purim cookies. Mother, who always "prayed from her own siddur," that is, marched to her own drummer, replaced the song with another that better fit her mood; she would no more be bound by the Jewish calendar than link her joy to a shtetl half-wit.

And didn't she have reason enough to celebrate? While Purim merely commemorated our rescue from the hands of wicked Haman, Mother had beaten the odds twice over, having escaped from Europe with her husband and children, and now, eight years later, was about to give birth to a healthy, adorable boy at the age of forty-two. Only a song from her rich repertoire could mark the present moment; therefore she chose a *tishlid,* one of the lively sing-alongs that she would orchestrate while seated around the table or *tish* at the end of a satisfying evening.

Just as she had done so many times before, singing a song, whether solo or in chorus, would help her when the going got rough, as when she was forced to undergo inner ear surgery in a Warsaw hospital when she was seven months pregnant with my brother, Benjamin. If she survived that, it was only thanks to the hymn she had instructed those assembled around her hospital bed to sing. So the moment she went into labor with me, Mother launched into a solo rendition of the triumphant "Az der Rebbe Elimey-lekh."

What a great song to choose! To the untrained ear of her obstetrician, this was an Old Country song about a wonder-working Hasidic rabbi named Elimeylekh who in a crescendo of religious ecstasy at the conclusion of the Sabbath called for his fiddlers, then for his cymbalists, and finally for his drummers to play. Mother knew full well that this was not your standard Hasidic folk song, first because she had learned it from her sister Annushka, who in turn had heard it sung on a train by two Yiddish actors visiting from America; moreover, the lyrics played fast and loose with Jewish sancta. As for the refrain, which mimicked the sound of each group of musicians playing his instrument, such a display of virtuosity was a perfect way to banish the excruciating pain.

Taken together, the dance tempo, the parodic lyrics, and the simulated orchestration worked their magic. No sooner did the good Rebbe Elimey-lekh have his whole klezmer band fiddling, cymbaling, and drumming away, than I poked my slimy head into the world; whereupon Mother was never heard to sing "Az der Rebbe Elimeylekh" again. No reason to worry, though. The song lives on in my classroom repertoire, where it deftly illustrates the "art of creative betrayal," as practiced by the American Yiddish poet Moyshe Nadir, who adapted the lyrics from "Ol' King Cole Was a Merry Ol' Soul."

Other unscripted things happened in the wake of my birth. The first person to show up in the maternity ward was not my father but my brother. When the nurse announced that "Mr. Roskies" was here to see her, Mother rushed out in her blue-green surgical gown and blushed scarlet at the sight of her seventeen-year-old son still carrying his school bag. The nurse had mistaken Ben for my father.

My birth, in short, was greeted with much joy. Papale, my father, she loved to remind me, burst out laughing when she announced that she was pregnant, and they should have named me Yitskhok, which means "he shall laugh"—like the patriarch Isaac, except that one Isaac in the Roskies family was more than enough. When she broke the news to Ben, he grabbed her in his arms and danced a jig. Then he took a calendar into the alcove where he slept (my sister Ruthie saw him do it) and tried to determine the day of conception.

The choice of my name was similarly inspired. Dovid was the family pa-triarch, Papale's father, who died in the Bialystok ghetto, and the Second World War was still raw in everyone's mind. My sister Eva, born in Canada in wartime, was nearly named Victoria, to honor Montgomery's victory over Rommel in El Alamein; but Mother chose Eva instead, after the YIVO, the Yiddish Scientific Institute of Vilna, now based in New York. Just six weeks before my birth, however, cousins Nat and Sally had named their firstborn David, which ought to have been reason enough for Mother to look elsewhere. This time, it seems, the choice was not Mother's to make. Naming me for my father's father was more than an act of filial piety. It was nothing less than a redemptive act hearkening back to the last family seder in Bialystok. David was a good choice of name if you consider that over the years, as I grew a beard and started covering my head, I began to look just like the portrait of my grandfather commissioned from the Montreal artist Alexander Bercovitch, especially after I had my first detached retina sur-gery, the same operation my father had in Boston that saved him from going blind.

Now that I think of it, ushering in my birth by singing in Yiddish was Mother's subtle way of acknowledging the literary origins of my concep-tion. I wouldn't have been born at all, family lore will tell you, but for the Yiddish poet Leyb Feinberg. She was prepared to close her womb with Evale, lock it up and throw away the key, because of a whole series of mis-carriages she had due to a botched abortion on the eve of their escape from Europe. Then one day, she saw an article in *Der tog,* the Yiddish daily from New York, congratulating the poet Leyb Feinberg on the birth of his fourth child. "*Der alter kaker ken,*" she cried out, "*un ikh ken nit*?—If that old fart can do it, so can I!" (Leyb, as it happened, was my father's name too.) So certain was she of having a son that she bet Mitsia Hoffman a golden amulet of the Ten Commandments, which he very reluctantly had to forfeit. (She won the bet, but twelve years later I lost the prize while taking swimming lessons at Camp Massad.)

I learned at once my place in the family constellation. "Binyomin-Benjamin," she said, "is the crown on my head. Rutale-Ruthie is my good fortune. Evale is my joy. And you, Dodele, are my life. But you are more than that. You are my gift from God, *mayn óysgebetener bay got.*" This lineup, she hastened to assure me, would bring me no grief from my brothers and sisters, the way it had in her family back in Europe, where her mother, Fradl, so blatantly favored her Benjamin, "Nyonya," over all the rest.

Having ceded my first name to the Roskies side of the family, Mother insisted that my second name be Gregory, after her beloved brother Grisha. She kept his photo on her dresser, half of the prominent Matz nose hidden in shadow, the other giving out an aristocratic glow. He is sixteen years old, just the age at which Sophia Solomovna, founder and headmistress of the Sophia Kagan Russian-Jewish Gymnasium, whisked him off to Yekaterinoslav at the outbreak of the First World War, entrusting him with the evacuation of her entire school! Even more heroic was the way he rushed from Kharkov to his brother Nyonya's deathbed. When the train was stopped by the Bolsheviks, Grisha jumped onto the roof and shouted "Brothers!" to the ragtag army, to assure them of the solidarity of all suffering peoples. Sonia Tencer told her how later, during the Soviet occupation of 1940, Grisha singlehandedly organized a laundry for the flood of Jewish refugees pouring through Vilna from Nazi-occupied Poland.

My mother's firstborn, Benjamin, named after Nyonya, evinced musical talent virtually from the moment he was born. Rather than become a pianist, however, my brother went into textiles, later to save the family business, Huntingdon Woolen Mills. Ruth should have been named Helena, after one of her six half-sisters who had the chutzpah to debate at the dinner table about Jesus—why just to utter that name was an affront, rather than refer to him as Yoshke Pandre, let alone to sing his praises—which was no surprise coming from Helena. Fradl's first husband, Judah Leib Matz, turned to his wife and said, "Fradl, how did such a chastising rod end up in our home?" He said it in Yiddish, and her Russian-speaking sisters memorized these words and taught them to my mother, their youngest sibling, as a lesson on how parents ought to keep their children within the fold. Helena later caught the revolutionary bug in 1934, divorced her husband, Samuil Vilinsky, and took their three children, Ifa, Vera, and Arkady, to the Jewish

Autonomous Region of Birobidjan, where, as "Commissar Vilinskaya," she persecuted the Yiddish writers who had come there to build a new Soviet Zion. Ruth, my sister, outspoken and single-minded in pursuit of her dreams, could never beat that, not even by leaving for Israel at the peak of her career with her husband and three children in tow. If only Grisha had finished medical school in Kharkov, Mother would still lament. Absent a medical degree, he still landed a terribly responsible job running the TOZ Colony for undernourished and tubercular children after its founder-director, Dr. Zemach Szabad, died—Szabad, who idolized Fradl Matz. And if only Grisha hadn't showered roses on Malvina Rappel after every performance of the Yiddish cabaret, roses paid for from *her* dowry!—A good thing Grisha never sired any children with his beautiful wife, Nadianka; he was much too busy, not just running TOZ, the Society for the Protection of Health, but also as the chairman of the Yiddish Theater Society. Still, Papale never forgave him for squandering Mother's dowry. When they bumped into him at the Paris World's Fair—Grisha had a boxed seat at the Follies Bergères—Father gave him the cold shoulder. Did she ever tell me, no she never told me, that Sophia Solomovna Kagan had not just adopted Grisha as her son, she took him as her lover. She a woman of forty and he only sixteen! Yes, each one of us had been suitably named, especially me, with my twin legacy: David, after the patriarch, and Gregory, after the man-about-town. Naming me after Grisha would serve for years to come as a subtle warning not to follow my own eyes and my own heart, by which I am so easily seduced.

With the names that she named me and her exuberant song, Mother ushered me into the world of Yiddish—a world that was already built, abandoned, and remade before I got there. *Gey shoyn, mayn gelibter,* now go, my beloved, she said, *un farges kholile nit,* and don't ever forget, *ver s'hot di ershte tsu dir gezungen,* who first sang to you.

2

The Dybbuk

Born between the fifth and sixth Hanukkah candles in 1906, Mother belonged to a new generation of Lithuanian Jews. The first of her many siblings to attend a kindergarten instead of the traditional *heder*, she was instructed in Russian instead of Yiddish and was the first to grow up with a grand piano in her own home, a Royale that her mother Fradl bought at Barski Dom by selling her diamond earrings following the death of her first husband, the pious and imperious Judah Leib Matz. He died at the age of seventy-one on Tisha b'Av, a symbolic coincidence, if you consider that on this day the Temple in Jerusalem was destroyed, whereupon a new culture was created, sans prophets and priests; and with Judah Leib's passing, in 1902, Fradl, his widow, became the chief repository of time, the source of revelation, moral instruction, and music. The chain of transmission now began with her, the matriarch who anchored all the generations.

I who was born into yet another generation, on Purim day, 1948, understood from an early age that time was riven in two: Time Before/Time After. When Mother said, "*dos iz geshén in fertsikstn yor*, such-and-such took place in the fortieth year," I knew she was referring not just to 1940 but to an entire Red Sea of circumstances by which the Old World stood divided from the New. Because everything of lasting value had been destroyed, because the letters stored away in her carved wooden box were mostly written in

Russian, which I still cannot read, and because I wasn't old enough to remember the one time she left for New York and my sister Eva prevailed
upon Father to tell his side of the story, Mother was the only link across the
abyss of time. Like Moses on Mount Nebo.

To receive such knowledge was a fearful inheritance. We children might
have compared notes, if we weren't spaced so many years apart, two born in
Europe and two in Canada, each seemingly to a different set of parents. We
certainly knew enough not to tell secrets out of *heder,* and even Khaskl, my
best friend since the age of twelve, was not a good sounding board, because
he also had a surfeit of stories, from his own mother.

So we went into the theater. On stage we tried to perform as well as
Mother, in front of a larger audience, and with equally memorable lines.
Ruth was the most dedicated. Eva and I would listen for her voice on Children's Theater every Saturday morning on the radio, directed by the legendary Dorothy Davis and Violet Walters. I never saw Ruth perform her
most fabled role, as the bereaved mother, in Moshe Shamir's *He Walked in the
Fields,* which should have led to her marrying Jerry Levin, who played her
kibbutz husband—or so Mother always claimed. Eva's best role was as Leah
in Khayele Grober's English-language production of *The Dybbuk.* How did
Grober ever suspect that my quiet, bookish sister Eva could bring that dybbuk to life, speak in his voice, rail and blaspheme? As for me, a performer of
magic and parlor tricks, my strength lay not in Hebrew, not in English, but
in Yiddish theater. The obstacles were manifold: mastering the Yiddish r's;
getting the vowels clear of diphthongs; distinguishing between a soft and
hard *lamed.* But my formal debut as Shloymele in Dora Wasserman's production of *Kiddush Hashem* made the next day's *Jewish Eagle,* Canada's only
Yiddish daily. The veteran editor, Israel Rabinovitsh, wrote that there on
stage "Roskies was like a fish in water."

Mother alone appeared not to be impressed. For one thing, she feared an
evil eye. Having labored so hard to maintain a metaphysical balance among
her living children and the dead who never died, she could not risk that
equanimity being toppled by a stray remark, a casual compliment: Masha,
such a talented daughter (or son) you have! For another thing, no performance could ever match the ones of her youth. Nothing could have kept her
from attending the original Vilna Troupe production of Ansky's *The Dybbuk,*
directed by her former gym teacher, Mordecai Mazeh, who perished in Treblinka: not the fact of her mother's death, which occurred but thirty-plus

days before the performance; not her father's reprimand not to go. "Father," she said to him in Russian, "if I were to know that a year from now my sorrow will vanish, I certainly would not have gone. But my sorrow will stay with me all through my life." A relative by marriage with the beautiful stage name of Leah Naomi, who played in the production, took pity on the young orphan, letting her in free of charge. From that day on, the Yiddish theater became Masha's true home, and her sanctuary.

The Dybbuk is the drama of two star-crossed lovers, Khonon and Leah. Khonon dies under mysterious circumstances because Leah is betrothed to another. When the spirit of Khonon possesses the bride under the wedding canopy, two older men are called in to set things right: the Zaddik of Mirópolye, who comes from a long line of exorcists, and the local rabbi, who convenes a rabbinical court. Meanwhile, a mysterious messenger flits in and out, acting as a Greek chorus. Which of these roles most impressed itself upon my bereaved, fifteen-year-old mother? To judge from old photos that show a slim, brooding girl still in possession of her beautiful black braids, she could have passed for Leah any day. Yet she identified with the Messenger instead.

And I believed her. Mother alone could negotiate between this world and the next. Her oracles invariably came true. She appeared to be a supertemporal being. Today, to be sure, I see things differently and would say that she had learned all the parts, had learned to play all the characters.

Like the Zaddik, she felt her painful insufficiency vis-à-vis the founding generation of miracle workers. It was thanks to modern medicine, not through any merit of hers, that Masha had surpassed her saintly mother in age. Did she or did she not possess Fradl's power to withstand the forces of evil? That was the question.

A too-easy fit for Reb Shimshon, the rabbi, she recited and enforced our code of behavior, but she was also no doubt the wealthy Reb Sender, like him trapped in a world of bourgeois appearances, a woman whose morning toilette took upward of an hour, who treated her taxi driver like a private chauffeur, who kept Madame Lafleur employed year in, year out, producing a fantastic array of hats at the sight of which all five tellers at the Canadian Imperial Bank of Commerce would stop whatever they were doing; yet like Reb Sender, she feared that someday, somehow, for some long-forgotten misdeed, her wealth and security might vanish. Which perhaps explained how she could also play Khonon, the ascetic young kabbalist who flirted with danger and would enter into a pact with Satan if that was what it would take to get her way.

Most profoundly, most terrifyingly, Mother was the dybbuk. In a moment of domestic tranquility, she could erupt in apocalyptic rage, rip asunder the fabric of falsehood and hypocrisy with thunderous, blasphemous fury. "*Svoletsh!*" she would scream in Russian, the language of obscenity. To exorcise that demon was impossible. The only way to respond was to flee the house.

Normally, I could head off or defuse the impending outburst by coming up to her, caressing her arm and saying, "I'm your cavalier, Mother, am I not?" saying it in Yiddish, of course, a trick that never worked with any other woman or in any other language—God knows how many times I've tried.

Yet was it also not the case that the dybbuk, her unalloyed and unallayed anger at the manifold sins that had gone unpunished, was precisely what signaled that the past was still potent and demanded its due? For the chief offenders were never the generation born in innocence, but rather their parents and their parents before them: those of her contemporaries now resettled in Montreal, who thought that with their outward piety and extravagant philanthropy, and worse yet, their refusal to speak anything but English, they could fool the whole world. Hah! Since no one in Montreal still remembered that Dr. Professor Samuel Weininger had left a bastard son behind in Warsaw, then at least her Dovidl would know. At least he would know that to harness the anarchic power of memory you needed to impose a binary structure—Time Before/Time After, This World and the Next, Tranquility and Rage—adopt a trope of generational decline, and learn how to sing.

3

Café Rudnitsky

So why *didn't* she marry Boris Seidman, the great love of her life? He was tall, spoke fluent Russian, and owned one of the largest dry goods stores in Vilna. When it was just the two of us, Mother and I, at my lunch break from school, there was an even chance of finding out.

The last time they met on European soil was at Café Rudnitsky, on the corner of Trocka and German Street. Every detail was carefully planned. Of two Cafés Rudnitsky in Vilna, men and women in their social position would normally meet at the one located on Mickiewicz. There were good reasons, however, to choose the Trocka location, at the heart of the old neighborhood, instead. Just up the block, at 28/30 Zawalna, was the court-yard where Mother was born, and around the corner stood the chestnut tree where she and Seidman had first met, sometime after the death of her mother when she was forced to live alone with her father. Another reason for choosing this spot was that Boris needed an alibi, and since the store of Seidman & Freidberg was located but a block away in the opposite direc-tion, it would seem as if he were taking his lunch break. Don't forget that Masha had not come alone, but with my six-year-old brother in tow, not that the lovers had any chance of hiring a droshky to take them up to Castle Hill with its commanding view of the Old Town and the New, for what if they were seen together by a member of the Matz Family—her half-brother

Grisha was at work in the TOZ Colony outside of town, but at this very moment his wife, Nadianka, sporting a pale blue parasol might be out window shopping on Mickiewicz. So the best that could be hoped for was to sit down at one of the marble-and-wrought-iron tables and order a pastry with a cup of tea or perhaps a glass of cognac, while Benjamin her firstborn was kept busy as long as possible choosing a box of Wedel's, for Café Rudnitsky sold a fine array of chocolate—Mother's favorites were called *Provençalkes*.

Wedel's are still sold in a red tin box in the shape of a heart. How perfect, Benjamin must have thought, for storing the spare parts of his new electric train—the envy of his best friend, Didi. Back in Romania, so Mother always said, the only other kid to own an electric train was the son of King Carol II. The box of Wedel's in hand, I imagined little Benjamin already babbling away in Polish with the waitress at the cash register. In her white lace apron over a black tunic and blouse, she may have reminded him of Zosia, their maid, and he smiled, thinking of the way Zosia shook her ample tits whenever she polished their parquet floors, wearing buffing cloths tied to her naked feet, and how she sometimes danced with him on the slippery floor until one day Mother caught them at it. Lost in thought, Benjamin never suspected that the tall Russian-speaking gentleman with the receding hairline his mother bumped into had specifically asked to meet him: the son they would never have together.

How my family got to Czernowitz, then a part of Romania, is another story, divulged at other meals. I only bring it up because back home in Czernowitz my father was busy all day at the rubber factory and Mother had a governess named Peppi for her newborn daughter, which left Mother plenty of time to correspond with Seidman. Someone acted as the go-between—maybe it was her niece Salla, someone who was beholden to Mother and therefore would not give her away. In Montreal, ten and twenty years later, on the far side of the great divide, the same role would be played by her manicurist—let's call her Margaret, since the "real" Margaret is still alive. So in the guise of visiting her family in Vilna, my mother met Seidman at Café Rudnitsky. What a long trip for so brief a rendezvous, even with fewer borders to cross in 1937 than there are today.

Boris Seidman is the name I've given him, for Boris sounds properly Russian, remembering Boris Godunov, my favorite LP from the age of three, and Seidman in Yiddish signifies his trade. He appears under an alias because Monica, his granddaughter, who lives in Newton, Massachusetts, doesn't want the whole world to know, while Mother would have appreciated the way an alias adds to his luster. Nowhere in our two-story house on Pagnuelo Street did Mother keep a photograph of Seidman, neither in the treasured albums, numbered 1–4, nor tucked away in an envelope inside her carved wooden box. Monica's father, for reasons of his own, was reluctant to release the two photos in his possession. They show a balding man with an apache-style haircut and very broad shoulders. Back in Europe, the ideal of male beauty must have been quite different if a man like that could make a girl get tingles down her spine every time she caught sight of him on the street.

The official reason why she broke up with Seidman before marrying my father was a story any of us could recite. One evening, out on a date, they passed a beggar in front of the Maccabi Rowing Club. Mother, always impulsive, gave him what she had, but Seidman refused to cough up even a zloty. Such a stingy man, Mother decided then and there, she could not, would not marry.

Eva and I, her captive audience most lunchtimes, accepted the story at face value, and understood the implication to be that our father, in contrast to Boris, was generous to a fault and therefore worthy of her love. I had no reason to doubt this, because every Saturday morning I saw Father sitting in his study writing out checks to every charity that solicited funds, from the local Lubavitch yeshiva to the Canadian Cancer Society. If Seidman were my father, the charities would have had to look elsewhere. But my brother-in-law, a lay analyst, has a different spin on Seidman's stinginess. Mother, he says, was much too insecure to marry a man she couldn't control.

But what exactly had Seidman done to forfeit her love? Once, just before the honk of the school bus roused me from my reverie, Mother recalled something that Boris had told her: When they got married and she was with child, he would have to fulfil his sexual needs by visiting a prostitute. So his cards were on the table. And in none of the stories was he guilty of prevaricating. It was Seidman, after all, who informed her that Leybele Roskes was in love with her, though a student wearing elbow patches on his jacket didn't seem like much of a catch, while with Seidman she could live in the arms of luxury, even if he was a tightwad.

Isn't it, rather, I now ask myself, that she never recovered from the loss of her mother and therefore needed above all a man she could depend on? If

Seidman would have left her during each pregnancy, when else would he have seen fit to leave? Suddenly realizing that she couldn't depend on him, and with the same impulse that she gave away her pocket money, she broke off the relationship for good.

Gleaned over a lifetime of lunches was the counter-analogy to her many sisters. One after the other, each of her half-sisters had taken up with a married man, this despite my grandmother Fradl's stern warning: "A man may possess a thousand fine qualities, daughter of mine. He can be handsome, rich, and refined. Just beware of one tiny flaw: he already has a wife." The message was clear, never to be guilty of stealing another woman's joy, and while her sisters had failed the ultimate test, Masha could not afford to slip, because, as she explained to me over compote one day, "*ikh bin a gezalbte*—I was an anointed one—*ikh tor nit shlofn mit keyn man*—and I must not sleep with a man out of wedlock." Men, in short, were not to be trusted either, for life was a battlefield, and it was up to women like Fradl Matz and her youngest daughter, Masha, to draw the line.

Soon after their rendezvous in Café Rudnitsky, Seidman married Judith Krensky, much older than Mother, a physician who was also from the Russian-speaking elite, and together they had a daughter, Frieda, who grew up knowing, as we did, that Masha was the real love of his life.

Seidman himself never gave up hope. Once he invited Aunt Mina, Mother's half-sister, to a café, and asked her to pass on this message: "Tell Masha that I still love her." And in the Vilna ghetto, he sought out Uncle Grisha's wife, Nadia, and paid her well to do a pedicure, wondering out loud if she happened to have Masha's new address in Canada. That is how he found her, after the war, and began his first letter to her from Sweden with the words: "I am Onegin writing to his Tatiana." (If I ever learn Russian, that's the first letter *I'll* read.)

Only one of Mother's siblings survived, our Uncle Alexander, who had fled his dental practice and his wife, six years his senior, and taken ship to America, where he lived incognito so as not to grant her a divorce, until fourteen years later Uncle Grisha gave her *ḥalitsah*, a release from her *agunah* status (see Deut. 25:7–9), whereupon she finally remarried and promptly died of cancer. Under the pretext of visiting Alexander in New York, Mother once again began to rendezvous with Seidman, now in Manhattan. It was during one of those visits that Eva prevailed upon Father, who stayed home, to do some storytelling of his own—but at Seidman's deathbed, Father insisted on being present.

If she had married Seidman, I would have lost a father a whole lot sooner than I did, and probably wouldn't have been born in the first place, because Mother wouldn't have needed a child in her middle age, and I would never have grown up believing that what is lost forever is what you love the most.

4

Bread

"In wartime, even rabbis abandon their flock."

Across from her at the dining room table in our spacious Montreal home sat Mother's confidant, Rabbi Baron. What startled him was not her sudden and seemingly random association of Montreal in peacetime with Vilna during the First World War or the fact that the illustrious Rabbi Chaim Ozer Grodzenski, the subject of Mother's pronouncement, had lived just across the street from her, on the corner of Zawalna and Trocka. Rather, it was her claim that by the time the Germans entered Vilna, on Yom Kippur day, 1915, Rabbi Grodzenski had already fled eastward, leaving Vilna without a guardian. Rabbi Baron, who knew full well that our kitchen was categorically *treyf*—Mother was fond of saying that *treyf* is not what you put into your mouth, but what comes out of it—but could nevertheless not refuse a glass of hot tea, abruptly stopped sipping through his neatly trimmed beard to shake his head.

"Mrs. Roskies, that cannot be. His saintly bones were just reinterred by the Soviets in the new Vilna cemetery, after much money traded hands."

Mother was so insulted by Rabbi Baron's skepticism, his lack of faith in her, so shocked by his naiveté in matters pertaining to the past, that she refused to invite him back for the next six months, and I, then ten years old, became the sole repository not only of this story but of the whole family chronicle of the first German occupation.

"How could she have left all that behind?" Mother asked rhetorically a week later, as if surveying the kitchen, her back to the sink. She meant my grandmother Fradl Matz, of course, who had already, by the time of the German occupation, spent forty years of her life in the courtyard at Zawalna 28/30, and by "that" Mother meant the vast inventory of Hebrew prayer books, Bibles, and Yiddish penny dreadfuls published by the Matz Press.

Unlike Rabbi Baron, I had no need of explanatory notes. If Fradl was being spoken of, then what followed would surely track her everyday acts of heroism. And indeed, "were it not for the women," she said, "the menfolk would have no home to come back to. Take a look, why don't you, at how wives pursue their profligate passions nowadays! Where's love? Where's loyalty?" And as for the rabbis, well "Dovidl, just last week we saw what rabbis are really made of"—by which she meant the whole lot of them, from Vilna to Montreal.

Nyonya, or Benjamin, Fradl's favorite, who played the balalaika like a real Gypsy, had already signed up for the tsarist army in July. Her sixteen-year-old son, Grisha, was soon to leave, too. For the Vilna schools were beginning to evacuate, first Kochanovsky's Kindergarten located in their courtyard, then Sophia Kagan's Gymnasium. Sophia came to Fradl and pleaded with her to let young Grisha accompany her to Yekaterinoslav, deep inside Russia, where she promised to take good care of him. Fradl agreed. Just when she thought there would be two fewer mouths to feed, her married daughters, Mina and Anna, came home to roost with their children, and Vilna fell to the Germans.

Bread became the currency that could save you from death.

"Not Canadian bread, to be sure," she laughed a theatrical laugh. I nodded.

Upon their arrival in Canada, in the autumn of 1940, Mother was invited to a meal at her sister-in-law's, where only Wonder Bread was served, the fluffy white stuff. When Mother asked for a piece of real bread, Aunt Mandy curtly replied that this was what one ate in Canada, and she might as well get used to it, whereupon Mother burst out crying. Mandy's version of the story, which we were to hear at Mother's shivah, is of course very different. According to Aunt Mandy, it was Father who spat out the Wonder

Bread, having ordered his first Canadian sandwich at a restaurant in Quebec City.

In the terrible winter of 1916, bread was strictly rationed and the lines were very long. Once, Mother continued, now joining me at the table, after sister Lisa (was she sixth in line or seventh?) returned home empty-handed and so famished that she devoured a whole plateful of drippings from the cast-iron pot, my ten-year-old mother came up with a plan. The bakery was located in their courtyard, and Badaness the Baker had a daughter about her own age. It was just before Purim. From the warehouse of the Matz Printing Press, Mother extracted a beautiful *Megilas Esther* and a *birkas-hamózndl,* a tiny edition of the Blessing After Meals, in return for which Badaness's daughter let Mother receive the family's bread ration without ever again having to wait on line.

How else women managed to forage for bread during wartime was a story that would have to wait, another story reserved for my ears alone. And not at one meal but doled out in morsels, or during one of my periodic colds when I stayed home from school altogether, the better to learn exactly what happened to Aunt Annushka when her husband was off serving at the front.

Her parents had been very modern, said Mother, as I lay in the sun porch wrapped in my comforter. They sent her to Kochanovsky's Kindergarten, where she was taught by trained Froebelistines, specialists in early childhood education, including the music teacher, her very own sister Annushka. When Glasha Kochanovsky became engaged to be married, Annushka was of course invited to the party, held in the spacious hall of the kindergarten, just across the courtyard, and here she danced the night away with Glasha's fiancé, the incredibly virile Warshawsky. But before the wedding could take place, Glasha was evacuated along with her parents. With the terrible bread shortage in Vilna, Annushka went off to the Committee to see if she could pull strings, and whom should she meet there but Warshawsky, the newly appointed Director of the Bread Supply. Fradl, who had an unerring eye for such things, forbade her daughter from accepting Warshawsky's invitation to a café. How and where the lovers met, my mother never learned.

So in wartime bread was also the currency of love. And now we come to the main story, a story that could accompany any meal, because it tells of a love that was absolute, the love of Fradl for her beloved son Nyonya.

CHAPTER FOUR

As a volunteer and graduate of a gymnasium, a Russian high school, Nyonya was jumped to the rank of officer and served as a medic with Red Cross. As soon as the Germans arrived, there was no more news from the front. So Fradl Matz took a vow: if God would return her beloved son to her, first thing, even before putting her arms around him, she would take him into the Matz Press and place him, in full uniform—boots, greatcoat, ammunition belt and all—onto the huge industrial scale. She would donate his weight in bread to the Jewish orphans.

Nyonya and his surviving regiment were captured by the Germans. As the ranking officer, he surrendered his papers to the German commandant who, taking one look at the name Venyamin Levovich Matz, shouted *"verflüchter Jude!"* and slapped Nyonya twice across the face, drawing blood. That night, they arrived at a village inn. Nyonya and his men were locked up in a barn while the Germans went in for a drink. Nyonya, who also did reconnaissance, still had the relevant maps, and he calculated how far they were from the front. Under cover of darkness, he and his men broke down the barn door, commandeered a few horses and carts, drove them to the nearest railroad tracks, flagged down a military supply train, and were rescued. The tsar awarded him a medal for his bravery.

In Vilna, Fradl continued to hope. Then came the revolution, Russia sued for peace, and Nyonya was demobilized. He returned, just as Fradl had envisioned, in full gear. His sisters came to greet him at the train station, and the youngest, my Mother, once again reliving the moment for my benefit, found him looking "pale, exalted, full of longing." Together, they marched him between the two *bulvanes*, the half-naked male torsos that held up the balcony at the palatial entrance to the courtyard. True to her promise, Fradl led him straightaway to the packing area and placed him on the scale. He weighed four and a half *pood,* a hundred eighty pounds. Fradl ordered that the same weight in bread be donated immediately to the children of the Talmud Torah. It took some doing, but so it was done.

Nyonya's stay was short. First there was the episode of the conman, who claimed to be his army buddy from Kazan. Late one night, holding a knife to Nyonya's throat, he stole his gold watch and all his new clothes and ran off. Worse yet was the presence of Germans in his own home. No matter that these officers were Jews or that they were smitten with his sisters. Nyonya could not forgive the two slaps he had received at the hands of the German commandant. The blood on his face, he said, had not yet congealed. Without warning, Nyonya returned to the Russian interior.

Eating her favorite pumpernickel smeared with butter, the closest thing you could get in Montreal to the tart black bread that I first tasted in Moscow, Mother rehearsed what happened next. Nyonya headed for Yekaterinoslav, where Grisha had gone earlier with Sophia Kagan. Sophia had also kept her promise, to take good care of Grisha, sending him off to study medicine in Kharkov, so he was not in Yekaterinoslav when Nyonya returned. It was from old Mrs. Kagan that Nyonya contracted influenza. Maybe, being a medic, he had tried to attend to her himself. When Grisha got word, he rushed to his brother's deathbed, arriving just in time to hear Nyonya say in Russian: "Mother sends her regards."

Grisha was so shaken by Nyonya's death (old Mrs. Kagan recovered) that he decided to return home without completing his studies. Everyone was sworn to secrecy, never to reveal the fact of Nyonya's death to Fradl, for fear that it might kill her. One time, when Fradl walked into Grisha's room and saw a portrait of Nyonya hanging over his bed, Grisha quickly explained: "It's a sign of how much I miss him." There was every reason to fear for Fradl's health. She was coughing blood, and Mother never knew when she returned home from school whether she would find her mother alive or dead. Once, in 1920, Mother came home to find Fradl so sick that it was only by screaming at the top of her lungs that Mother scared off the Angel of Death. (That Mother could so frighten the sword-bearing angel with her screams that he would abandon his mission and come back some other time is something that I never doubted.)

They kept the secret of Nyonya's death for three years. Until, one day, Fradl happened to be walking along German Street when she overheard a woman whisper to her daughter: "You see, my dear? There goes Fradl Moiseyevna, whose son died so tragically during the great epidemic." That night Fradl's first husband, Judah Leib Matz, appeared to her in a dream. ("I didn't see his face," she explained to Mother, "because I now lived with another man," her second husband Yisroel Welczer.) "Benjamin is still alive," said Judah Leib in Yiddish.

Soon thereafter Fradl died of tuberculosis, and for seventy-eight years her daughter would go on eating black bread three times a day.

5

Prayer for the Tsar

Speakers of Yiddish never confuse a *seyfer* with a *bukh*. A *bukh* they can read in the bathroom and a *seyfer* they can't. That's because a *seyfer* is written in the Sacred Tongue, about sacred matters, while a *bukh* is neither. As for Yiddish itself, Yiddish can be invested with sanctity so long as it fulfills its original promise, to bridge the cosmic and the mundane, God's word and life as we live it. How? By providing a *taytsh,* an accurate translation, usually printed on the very same page. That way, the men can learn what's on top of the page and the women can read what's on the bottom. In between a *seyfer* and a *bukh* is a hybrid called a *mayse-bukh,* a Yiddish storybook, a book for everyone, rendered kosher so long as its stories purport to derive from traditional sources.

A *seyfer* is always judged by its cover. The title page of a prayer book, for example, will tell you whether it follows the Ashkenazi or Sephardi rite, another crucial distinction, because it separates a Litvak from a Polish Hasid. Whosoever prays according to the Ashkenazi rite is by definition a coldhearted rationalist who eats gefilte fish seasoned with pepper, as opposed to a "Sephardi," a passionate mystic who eats his gefilte fish sweet. And of course, neither is to be confused with *real* Sephardim, Jews who hail from the Iberian peninsula and view all recipes of gefilte fish with revulsion.

Mother's family was Litvak to the core, claiming as its progenitor the type-founder and printer Eliezer Lipmann Matz, a direct descendant, according to Mother, of the great Gaon of Vilna himself, while his son Judah Leib built up the Matz Press into one of the largest in town, second only to the famed publishing house of the Widow Rom and her sons. Judah Leib, she told us, was a strict man, so strict that he forbade the use of soap on the Sabbath and divorced his first wife for being deficient in piety. (Their only daughter converted to Christianity.) You can't get more Litvak than that.

Now, the story I am about to tell will give some Litvaks a bad name, and it sounds in part like the penny dreadfuls that the Matz Press produced for servant girls to buy on Friday afternoons at the Fish Market, the kind of storybook that has no chance in hell of achieving cosanctification. So be it, if my "traditional sources" demand that it be so.

For Judah Leib was left a widower at forty-five with two children of marriageable age from his second marriage.

And Fradl Polachek was a fifteen-year-old beauty from Minsk with a phenomenal singing voice, recently discovered by an impecunious young impresario from St. Petersburg, who wanted to take her back with him as both wife and protégée and make her a second Adelina Patti, the famous coloratura singer whom the British loved so much they called her "Patty," and she would have made it, with proper training and the help of her natural beauty, were it not for—

Grune Soltz, her evil stepmother. Grune had a passion for cards, and one night she lost a bundle. Casting around for the most valuable asset she could pawn (assuming her jewels had long since been gambled away), she remembered her stepdaughter. So Grune headed for her native Vilna to see about arranging a match, and it didn't take long for her to get wind of the wealthy widower Judah Leib Matz, who offered Grune an impressive sum.

The wily stepmother returned to Minsk, and knowing that her husband, Moyshe, would never agree to his beautiful daughter marrying a man his own age, she introduced him to the prospective groom's younger brother, "a slim, chestnut-haired bachelor of thirty" (according to my sister Ruth, the first family chronicler).

Imagine, then, Fradl's surprise when standing under the wedding canopy her veil was lifted, just high enough for her to consecrate the wine, and she caught her first glimpse of the stern and substantial gentleman who was now to be her husband.

What happened next? Fradl cried for three days and three nights, until Judah Leib took pity on her and said, "Fradele, if you're so unhappy with me, I'm ready to dissolve the [as yet unconsummated] marriage and send you home," whereupon she realized that she had no real home to go back to, made her peace, and bore him fourteen or fifteen children, some stillborn. Fradl also became his trusted partner.

Unlike a *bukh*, a *seyfer* never lies, never makes things up just to bring the reader pleasure. So what were we children to do with the stories of Fradl Matz, whose regal portrait hung over our parents' bed and whose words of wisdom guided our every action? The moment we were old enough, we set out into the world looking for a *seyfer* to corroborate the stories.

That is how my twenty-one-year-old sister Ruth—on her honeymoon, no less—ended up one sweltering day in a bookstore on Allenby Street in Tel Aviv, talking to an old man with an unkempt tobacco-stained beard, a black suit and an ancient black fedora. They spoke in Yiddish, of course, and she asked him whether he had for sale any *sforim* published by Fradl Matz.

"Fradl Matz?" he replied. "She was the most beautiful woman in Vilna."

So there it was: her name alone could turn an ancient relic of a man into an unrequited lover. In return, my sister bought a *Korbn minkhe*, the all-purpose Hebrew-Yiddish prayer book for women, published in 1909. This hefty tome, which roughly translates as "meal offering," was both a votive offering to propitiate my mother and proof positive of Fradl's storybook romance, because it carried the imprimatur of Y. Welczer and F. Matz.

Yisroel Welczer was a handsome wholesaler of sacred books from the town of Józefów Lubelski, who had often done business with Fradl. After Judah Leib died, on Tisha b'Av, 1902, Fradl vowed never again to marry for money, but she was not to remain a widow for long. For Yisroel had been biding his time, and the moment he learned that she was available, my grandfather trimmed his beard, replaced his Hasidic gabardine with a stylish jacket, and offered his hand in marriage, claiming to be a childless widower. The attraction must have been mutual, for Fradl said yes, whereupon Yisroel returned home, divorced his wife, and arranged for the care of his four children, a son and three daughters. Here, on the inside cover of the *Korbn minkhe* that Ruth just brought back from Israel, the book-crossed lovers Yisroel and Fradl had affixed their names.

As the youngest and most expert at making Mommy happy, I was determined to outdo my sister, and because I had honed my observational skills under the tutelage of the Hardy Boys, I noticed that when Ruth presented her prayer book to Mother, Mother flipped through the pages as if she were looking for something. Was it something hidden or printed inside? I couldn't tell. Whatever it was, she hadn't found it. Until one day at lunch break from school, when Mother had returned from a particularly rewarding shopping expedition at Ogilvy's, I asked her what she had been hoping to find.

Life wasn't so bad, she said with that faraway look that presaged a long story, when the Germans occupied Vilna; in some ways, better than it had been under the tsar. Why, her first solo performance was singing in the park with Slepp's Choir, she sang "They Call Me Zhamele," and the audience was studded with those funny spiked helmets worn by German soldiers. Never before had Yiddish been sung in a public space.

But the Germans were much harder to bribe than the Russians, and were fanatics when it came to censorship. The Germans wouldn't let anything be published until military-appointed censors arrived who could read Hebrew and Yiddish, and no prayer book could be sold that contained the once-obligatory prayer for the welfare of the tsar. Meanwhile, debts were piling up. One day, when Mademoiselle Cahan, mother's French tutor, remarked on Fradl's ample household, Fradl brought out her blue leather briefcase and displayed packets of promissory notes tied up with string, not one of which had been collected since the war began. Even when the two Jewish censors Erlich and Kornicker arrived from Berlin, and more or less billeted themselves in Fradl's home—so enamored were they of the five Matz sisters who sang and accompanied themselves on the piano, a Royale that Fradl had bought at Barski Dom by pawning her diamond earrings, because now that Judah Leib no longer ruled over her she could return to a life of music, if not for herself then for her talented daughters, especially Rosa, a drop-dead beauty of a woman, who performed duets with Sergeant Kornicker—even Erlich could not risk a court-martial and allow the sale of books that contained the prayer for the welfare of the tsar. This contraband lay just across the courtyard, stored in the basement of the Matz Press.

Fradl and Yisroel agonized over what to do. To tear out the offending page meant to risk the charge of sedition when the Russians returned, which was punishable by death. Not to tear out the page meant certain starvation. And to whom to entrust this dangerous task? That was easy enough to decide. The only one of their children who could be trusted to help get the job done as fast and as skillfully as possible was nine-year-old Masha, the child born out of love.

I imagined the three of them working in the dead of night, beneath kerosene lamps, each one armed with a razor blade. Since they lived on the top floor of the fancy side of the courtyard, I further imagined the three of them sneaking down three flights of stairs, silently crossing the yard, and stealing into the basement of the press on the opposite side. Some books, I knew for a fact, were untouchable, like the merchandise Romelgolski, the bookseller from Homel, had purchased that last July for ten thousand gold rubles. Those books were to lie packed and ready, for the duration of the war, and would eventually outlive the tsar. So they must have followed some kind of order, beginning, perhaps, with the prayer book for every day of the year, then maybe the *Korbn minkhe* for women, and finally, the *maḥzor* for each of the festivals: Rosh Hashanah, Yom Kippur, Sukkos, Pesach, and Shavuos. When they finished cutting out the offending page, the Matz Press and Publishing House was ready to reopen for business.

My big chance to bring home the prize came in 1993, a mere thirty-six years later, during my teaching stint in Moscow. In the Marina Roshcha synagogue where we *davened* every Shabbes, I found a huge pile of Hebrew and Yiddish books. Where else could Soviet Jews deposit their dead books, if not here, in what for seventy years was Moscow's only true synagogue? The *sforim* were much older than the books in Yiddish, and their torn bindings were so utterly indistinguishable that I gave up looking after two weeks, but my friend Yale Reisner kept digging away until he struck paydirt: a *Beys Yisroel,* "House of Israel" *maḥzor* for Pesach, and another for Shavuos, published by the Matz Press in 1911. First thing, I started flipping through the pages, found the Service for Taking Out the Torah, turned the page, and there, alas, in big print, was the Prayer for the Welfare of the Tsar, the Tsarina, and the Heir Apparent—fully intact.

I dared not betray my disappointment, for fear of offending Yale, who returned with me the next day to ask that Rabbi Lazar waive the strict rule against removing any books. Thanks to Yale, I was given the two *maḥzorim* in exchange for a modest donation.

Were this a *bukh,* designed merely to bring the reader pleasure, I would pretend to have discovered the evidence of excised pages I was looking for, return in triumph to Montreal, and outdo my sister for Mother's love. And who would be the wiser? Come the day of reckoning, I myself could cut out the incriminating page, and my story, long enough as it is, would now come to a satisfying closure.

There's more to a title page, however, than first meets the eye.

On the plane ride home from Moscow, I noticed something peculiar about the two salvaged *maḥzorim*. Not only did the names of Fradl Matz and Yisroel Welczer appear on the cover, but these were preceded by the name of Alexander, son of the printer Judah Leib Matz of blessed memory. I couldn't just hop a plane to Montreal after a semester-long absence from New York, so I waited another two months for an answer.

"Look what I brought back from Moscow," I almost shouted when I made the presentation, and to hide my disappointment at having found the *maḥzor* intact, made the pile of books in the Marina Roshcha Synagogue even bigger than it was. I got what I wanted, a big smile, for the memento itself and a sign of her forgiveness for having stayed away from her so long. When I asked her, by-the-way, how it was that Alexander's name appeared on the covers, she suddenly became very agitated.

Yes, she said, angrily buttering her piece of black bread, it must have been around that time. She was just getting over scarlet fever and her head was still in a cloud when she heard terrible shouts coming from the dining room. She could see what was going on because Fradl had relocated her bed, the better to keep an eye on her. "I'll kill you, son-of-a-bitch!" her eldest brother Alexander was screaming. Wielding a *kotshere,* an iron poker, he looked as if he meant it. "I'll smash your head in!" He was chasing her father. Fradl too was yelling "Sashinka! Sashinka!" in an effort to stop her son.

Of course, I already knew the background to this story, the prelude to Mother's precarious existence. The Matz-Welczer residence in Vilna was a house divided. So great was their contempt for their stepfather that when Yisroel Welczer entered the room, her siblings would say, in a stage whisper, "*Zhid idiot,* the Kike is coming." Early on, Masha was given the choice: either their love, or his. She chose theirs. They spoke to him, if at all, in Russian, a language he barely knew, and Masha, his flesh and blood, called him Uncle and used the second person plural when addressing him. (Only in the dead of night, then, away from their prying eyes, could she sit next to her father, sharing the clandestine work of razor blades, in total silence.) Why did they hate him so? Because he was a Hasid from the backwaters of Poland;

because Fradl had married him out of love; and because he had rescued the Matz Press from bankruptcy.

The proof of her father's business acumen was this very *House of Israel* prayer book that I had brought back from Moscow. The *House of Israel* must have stood for him, Yisroel-Israel Welczer! She couldn't have been more than a year or two old—anyway, it was soon after he had taken over the press that he saw how low it had fallen, so he got on a boat bound for America and returned six months later with a king's ransom. The Hebrew Publishing Company of New York had agreed to lease the lead plates of this best-selling prayer book for the High Holy Days and Festivals. With the fifty thousand rubles, the printing presses were mechanized, a telephone was installed—theirs was the first indoor telephone in all of Vilna—and business picked up dramatically. Her father was now entitled to full ownership, yet imagine that, he refused to take more than a 25 percent share. All he wanted, her father, all he ever dreamed of, was to have his name appear alongside that of Fradl Matz.

Until that bang-up fight with his stepson, Alexander, over exclusive rights to the Matz imprimatur.

As a peacemaking gesture, her father agreed to place Alexander's name first. How many books were published this way she didn't know, but it couldn't have been many, for soon thereafter, Alexander ran off to America.

The scene of Alexander wielding an iron poker was hard for me to reconcile with the way I remembered him from my trips to New York. When my parents introduced him to me as my *feter Aleksander,* I replied, "*Aza darer feter?*" i.e., how could he be my uncle if he was so skinny, *feter* meaning both uncle and fat man. It was my first Yiddish pun. So I shared my surprise with Mother, whose voice dropped to that ominous register I had learned to fear.

"You remember," she said, "how much he loved Benjamin, his *beloved* nephew." Her voice was starting to shake and any minute now she would explode. "Even published a poem, one of his stupid poems, in the *Voice of Bialystok.* 'For My Nephew, Upon His Bar Mitzvah.' He thought that would do the trick, get him invited to Montreal for Binyomin's bar mitzvah. But I forbade Alexander from coming to the bar mitzvah. He wrote to me, pleaded with me to change my mind. He had no telephone, so I called him up at the Bialystok Benevolent Society in New York City.

"'Alexander,' I said," and now she began to scream, "'I'm paying you back for what you did to my father!'" She grabbed the *maḥzor* and started shaking it in the air, as if getting ready to throw it at Alexander's ghost.

"*Oy, hob ikh im batsolt,*" she screamed, "Oh, but I paid him back! Once and for all! *Shoyn eyn mol batsolt!*"

A year later, the Marina Roshcha synagogue in Moscow was burned down by vandals, and the library went with it. Other trips followed, and with my wife, Shana, taking up the challenge: in each place, no matter how unlikely, she went snooping through piles of old books. That's how we returned home from Poland with a *Mayne-loshn* (Judah Leib Matz, 1887), petitionary prayers to recite when visiting the dead, from a mad collector of Jewish relics who lived in a forest outside of Łańcut, and found a Leviticus and Numbers with the standard commentaries (Fradl Matz, 1906–9) in the Women's Section of the Bukharian Synagogue in Samarkand—Uzbekistan being a place of refuge for 250,000 Yiddish-speaking Jews during the last war—and finally, in the summer of 2003, in Berdichev, on an academic tour of Jewish Ukraine, the big prize.

I have forty-one witnesses to prove it, plus the *seyfer* itself, a *maḥzor* for Yom Kippur with a translation into Russian by Pirozhnikov and Pass (Matz and Welczer, 1909), given to me by the rabbi in return for an even smaller donation than the one I gave in Moscow, there being a plethora of new prayer books around with a more modern Russian translation.

Disappointed so often, Shana and I at first refused to believe what we weren't finding.

"Maybe the prayer isn't recited on Yom Kippur?" she asked.

This fancy *maḥzor,* however, for speakers of Russian, had the pagination in Roman numerals, and at last, where there ought to have been a Prayer for the Welfare of the Tsar, we found the telltale signs of Mother's handiwork, a clean cut that neither jeopardized the binding nor called attention to itself: pages 391–94 were missing.

And so, dear reader, in recompense for reading such a long story, we take away two lessons instead of just one. Even though title pages remain paramount, the inside matter of a *seyfer* also tells a story. And a Litvak is a person with passions, too.

6

Scribal Errors

Aunt Ánnushka was a graduate of the Berlin Conservatory of Music. She settled in Kovno with her second husband, Lyova Warshawsky, ran a kindergarten there, and performed Yiddish songs both as a soloist and member of Engel's Choir. Deported with her family from the Kovno ghetto on October 26, 1943, she perished in one of those Estonian labor camps reserved for the last remnants of Lithuanian Jewry.

Yet such horrors were never part of Mother's story, not because she censored the past, as if knowing how they were hunted down and butchered, thrown from moving trains, buried in anonymous graves, asphyxiated and ground into ashes, or neatly arrayed in a pyre, a row of logs, a row of bodies, the way it was done in Estonia, would corrupt me for life. Learning from her in the course of the usual banter that Madame Kagan became my uncle Grisha's lover in Yekaterinoslav, the real reason she needed him, and not some other sixteen-year-old, to help her evacuate the Sophia Kagan Gymnasium, was far more difficult to swallow, especially since the G. in my name stands for Gregory = Grisha. If Mother expunged their manner of death, it was in order to hold them accountable for their lives, to keep the ledger open.

A human life, she might have said, is like a Torah scroll. If a Torah scroll is letter perfect, it's perfect. No single scroll is more sacred than another, but the tiniest error in a Torah scroll renders it *posl*, ritually unfit. A Torah scroll, moreover, if you believe in it, can protect you and your family from harm. That is just one episode in the story of my aunt Annushka, which I'll pretend was told to me in logical, rather than analogical, order. What I ask in return is that you not get up from the table before the meal is done and Mother has finished speaking.

Mushroom-barley soup, nicknamed Soupy-Soupy for the sake of her English-speaking grandchildren, is the first course, which opens with Glasha Kochanóvsky's engagement party held in the kindergarten, where her beloved sister Annushka taught music. Located in their courtyard, you could hear the waltzes and foxtrots playing all night. There Annushka dances the night away with Glasha's fiancé, the incredibly virile Warshawsky, her dreamy eyes fixed on his, and the moment Glasha is evacuated to the interior of Russia, conveniently out of the way, very far away, he's itching to marry Annushka, only Annushka still has a husband named Samuíl Isakovitsh, who is sitting out the rest of the war with his parents in Homel, across enemy lines. Warshawsky gets hold of a military *Schein*, or pass, and bravely appears before Isakovitsh, incognito, to sound him out about granting Annushka a Jewish divorce. (For all that they were so emancipated, says Mother, still they went by the Book.)

"I know why she wants a divorce!" shouts Isakovitsh to the messenger from Vilna. "She has a lover. If I ever lay my hands on the guy, I'll shoot him like a dog!"

Mother interrupts to ask if I would like another piece of bread, which tells me that the punch line is coming. First in Yiddish, then, as if to vouch for its accuracy, she delivers the line in the Russian original.

"When her little red cheeks turn pale, and her beautiful locks turn gray, that's when I'll give her a divorce!"

Mother and I burst out laughing.

Another year passes, and it's Annushka's turn to make the perilous trip into the Russian interior. Her stated purpose is to bring brother Nyonya back from Russia, and Sophia Gurevitsh is also tagging along, attached to Annushka's pass as a fictitious aunt. (Now just because Nyonya died in one story doesn't mean he can't be alive in another, but without a single date to guide you, try to figure out that there's a war still being fought, and that Nyonya has an important role to play.)

Why did Annushka feel the sudden urge to retrieve her long-lost brother? Because only Nyonya can rescue her from her husband. The reason two elegantly dressed ladies are escorting a demobilized Russian soldier home is that along the way they have to stop in Homel. Here Annushka will try again, this time sending Nyonya as her emissary. And the maneuver works! Isakovitsh rejoices to see his brother-in-law, with whom he served as a medic at the beginning of the war. Then Nyonya raises the question of a *get,* a divorce, and explains that Annushka is in town, at which point Isakovitsh jumps up from his chair and cries:

"*Eyb a get, iz shoyn!* If she wants a divorce, she's got to do it now!"

Why the sudden change of heart? Well, says Mother, in life it's all a matter of timing. Unbeknownst to them, Isakovitsh had taken up with another woman and had gotten her pregnant. Being an honorable man, he probably wanted to raise the child as his own. So Nyonya rushes back to his sister with the news, and she calls for the rabbi, who appoints a scribe to copy out the writ of divorce. It's getting late, and just as the scribe is about to finish, around midnight, he makes a tiny error, rendering the whole document void.

"I'm terribly sorry, Madame Isakovitsh," says the rabbi, "it'll have to wait until tomorrow."

Annushka is in a panic. She knows her husband all too well. It's now or never.

"Rabbi," she pleads, "my military pass is about to expire and I have to leave first thing in the morning. Here," she says, opening her purse, "here, take all I've got. Pay the scribe to write out a new *get.*"

The scribe sits there until daybreak, copying out a new writ of divorce, and Isakovitsh hands it to her in front of two witnesses.

When his parents hear about it, they come running and throw themselves on Annushka's neck. Why did he do it? they wail. They love Annushka so. But the ordeal is not yet over, because there is still the matter of Lyúbochka, their four-year-old daughter. In the rabbi's presence, Isakovitsh makes his ex-wife take a vow that when Lyubochka turns fourteen, she will be returned to her father in Homel.

The ten years pass, and Annushka, honoring her vow, sends her daughter off to Homel in the company of her older cousin Salla. What Mother, of course, neglects to mention is that in the meantime, the Bolsheviks have seized power, and following a doomed campaign to capture Poland, which we will always remember thanks to Babel's *Red Cavalry,* they drew a border between the two countries, establishing the Belorussian Soviet Socialist Republic to the east of that border. (Again, with no dates to guide me, it's my educated guess that this happened no later than 1929, during the so-called New Economic Policy, when the border between Poland and the Soviet Union was still permeable.) So at first, getting back to the story, letters arrive telling of Lyubochka's great accomplishments at school; then the letters become few and far between. At the end of 1938, Annushka crosses into the Soviet Union in search of her daughter. When she arrives in Leningrad, where Lyubochka has been studying at an institute, she is told that her daughter has been arrested as a Trotskyite agent and deported to the Far East, destination unknown.

While in Leningrad, Annushka is recognized by her Intourist guide, a woman named Goldberg, formerly from Vilna. "There's something I've got to show you, Anna Levovna," says the guide, and takes her to the magnificent Kazan Cathedral, transformed by the Soviet regime into the Museum of Atheism. There, among the arcane relics of the world's religions, in a glass vitrine, is a Torah scroll, identified as follows: "This scroll made of parchment and covered with a richly embroidered velvet mantle and precious stones was presented by the Jewish community as a bribe to Tsar Nicholas II during his visit to Vilna. Belonged to the Family Matz."

"You see," says Mother as she clears away the soup, "Annushka lost her child but found our mother's Torah scroll."

The Torah, Mother explains as she brings in the plated main course, breaded veal chops, my favorite dish, was an heirloom from Judah Leib Matz, epitome in all her stories of the strictest piety. On Mondays and Thursdays he convened a quorum of nine other men in his home rather than pray with hoi polloi. Even in Vilna, with its hundreds of synagogues and study houses large and small, this Torah scroll was unique, for in 1913 a delegation headed by Bunemóvitsh the banker came to see Fradl. His Imperial Highness Tsar Nicholas II was about to pay a royal visit and the elders were in search of a stupendous gift to present on behalf of the Jerusalem of Lithuania. What recommended Fradl's Torah scroll was its manageable size and exquisite mantle: two facing lions embroidered in pure silver with emerald eyes. Name your price, said Bunemovitsh.

The value of the scroll might also have been pegged to its magical powers, since the last time it was removed from its miniature ark was when

Fradl came down with pneumonia and would surely have died were it not for a quorum convened in her home and the *mi-sheberakh* blessing that was recited for her recovery during the reading from this very scroll. Perhaps one of the men now standing before her, frail but ever-stately, had witnessed the miracle.

Anyway, Fradl did not enter into long negotiations. The scroll, she said, was not for sale. It would be her gift to the community. In return, let them commission the writing of a new scroll from a venerable scribe, a man in his eighties renowned for his skill, and as for payment, let them compensate her just for the Torah mantle.

Knowing that a Torah scroll was perfect so long as it was letter perfect, Fradl insisted on hiring a venerable scribe, who would draw the crowns atop of every letter with absolute precision, and was satisfied to replace the precious Torah mantle with something plain and utilitarian. Besides, with such a large household to support, she could have used the money.

The Matz family took up a suite of apartments, each room, Mother demonstrates with a flourish after handing me the salad—serving salad as a separate course was introduced when my brother married into an aristocratic family from oil-rich Baku via Paris—twice the size of our dining room, with brass chandeliers and a grand piano greeting every visitor, as if Count Tyszkiewicz himself were still in residence, a suite big enough to accommodate Fradl, six of her daughters, and two granddaughters, Salla and Lyubochka, for when the Germans took Vilna, most able-bodied men were either away at the front or lying low, and the Matz residence became the province of women, with no one to protect them when the Germans began to go from house to house requisitioning anything made of copper: door knobs, utensils, pots and pans. Krupp and Co. needed the copper for the manufacture of arms. Of greatest value to the Germans was the huge copper vat in the kitchen, where the household supply of fresh water was kept, replenished three times a day by Todros the Watercarrier. The women heard the wagon pull into the courtyard and from their third-floor window could see it laden with copper booty. A knock on the door. Fradl ushers the German officer into the salon. He looks around.

"*Bitte sehr*," Fradl addresses him in German, "take whatever you need."

So nonplussed is he by her regal visage and courteous demeanor that he stammers, "*Genedige Frau*, please accept my apologies for troubling you and your daughter," and he leaves empty-handed.

"You see, my child," says Fradl turning to her youngest. "The Torah scroll protected us from harm."

The mnemonic for this part of the story is *kúperner yeytser-hóre*. Damned if I know what it means. A cuprous passion? A deep desire? A bronzed nostalgia? And whose passion was made out of copper? A simple-minded reading would point to the Germans. After all these years, I should know better. The true villain in Mother's stories is always immanent, the enemy within. So who will it be?

Reviewing the first course, the story that went with the soup, I note that Nyonya had only a walk-on role, and might have failed in his rescue mission if Isakovitsh had not been looking to secure his own future. Isakovitsh, vindictive and erratic? The virile Warshawsky? I think he deserved a woman of Annushka's talents, someone who could dance, sing, and play the piano. Poor Lyubochka, though. She had no say whether to move in with a father she barely remembered. That leaves Annushka as the most problematic character. Why did she have to honor her vow if all other vows were summarily broken? Was she still so afraid of Isakovitsh? Or did she want to get on with her own life, now that she had completed her studies at the Berlin Conservatory and had settled in Kovno with Lyova Warshawsky? There's still a chance to resolve these questions, because Mother comes from the kitchen bearing two glasses of tea.

Annushka didn't go straight home. On the way back from Leningrad she pays Mother a visit in Czernowitz. They haven't seen each other in sixteen years. Imagine, there's so much to catch up on! When last they saw each other, Mother was still single; now she has two children, and Father is running a factory with hundreds of workers. Annushka is all broken up about her daughter.

"Annushka," says Mother, trying to console her, "none of this would have happened if I had been married at the time. I would never have let you send Lyubochka back. I would have adopted her as my own."

This is where the story ends, timed, more or less, with the end of the meal. We go on talking about my plans for the evening. Outside, the lilacs are in bloom, and tomorrow I'll take her for a drive to Beaver Lake, something we haven't done since Father died. She'll wear her floppy orange hat, and as we walk arm in arm, I will marvel at the difference between the founding generation of the Matz Family and their offspring, who made such a mess of their lives. We started with a Torah scroll that belonged to the patriarch Judah Leib Matz, then to his wise and practical wife, Fradl, who in a moment of religious inspiration had it replaced with a scroll that could still protect her family from harm. Fradl had many daughters. One, named Annushka, was Mother's favorite, her music teacher in Kochanovsky's Kindergarten, her first piano instructor, yet Annushka allowed her child to perish in the Gulag. That left Masha, the youngest daughter, child of a different marriage, to save her own two children, and the sad tale of Annushka and Lyubochka, from oblivion.

At the risk of sounding repetitive, this story too has a postscript. In January 2006, walking back from the Kazan Cathedral in St. Petersburg, I learned from my friend Valery Dymshits that Fradl's Torah scroll is now in the permanent collection of the State Ethnographic Museum. The Torah mantle looks exactly as Mother described it. Next time, Valery promised, he would arrange for me to see it.

7

Malvina's Roses

The Eclaire on West 72nd Street was New York City's equivalent of Café Rudnitsky, the kind of place you might go on a first date, where by day the dozen or so round marble and wrought-iron tables were occupied by retired ladies with heavy make-up, some with nose jobs, others—not. It was Malvina's venue for showing me a good time, and with her bleached blond hair, cut stylishly short, still looking every inch the actress, she fit right in. On our first rendezvous, I ordered the Peach Melba, in order to judge if The Eclaire was any match for Rumplemeyer's on Central Park South where my parents took Eva and me twice in our life (it wasn't, and the strawberry jam was cloyingly sweet), and I learned that Malvina was now married to a former opera singer who had made it rich and forbade her from performing on the stage. Through Max, who owned antiquities from Moshe Dayan's private hoard and had gold in a Swiss bank, I later discovered the Boyaner *shtibl* on West 81st Street where, like some penitent from a novel by I. B. Singer, he prayed every Friday night, and it was because of him that Malvina kept a kosher home; her pre–Yom Kippur meal of steak and baked potatoes would sustain me through the fast for five or six years in a row.

Scooping the vanilla ice cream from the bottom of the fluted glass dish— pardon my mentioning meat and milk in two consecutive paragraphs—I asked Malvina about the roses, and she burst out laughing. Neither had she any recollection of ever having shared a bed with Mother. But the next time we met and were seated at her favorite table, she did produce from out of her suede handbag a studio photo of herself as the Young Hasid.

The group photos of The Strúgatsh Band—*Di Bande,* for short—the cabaret theater that had taken Vilna by storm, were the most raucous in mother's album. They crowded around Grisha's radio, each emoting a different look of rapture and astonishment. Their autographs appeared on the back of another picture, inscribed *"Mashen, der mamen fun der velt,* to Masha, Mother of the World."

Masha was their mascot, the theater her home. She put on a pretty good act herself, because by now she was both motherless and homeless, living first with her father, then with her half-sister Mina, and finally with her best friend, Rivele Amsterdam; this, despite a late-night visit by Mr. Amsterdam, who offered to "comfort" his daughter's girlfriend.

They were all her buddies: Zalmen Hirshfeld, Yoysef Kamien, his wife, Nadia Kareni (as extravagant as her stage name), and the sisters Esther and Malvina Rappel. Malvina somehow got the juiciest parts: a dervish, a clown, a young Hasid, and most famously, The Street Walker. Jewish Vilna nearly came to blows over this one, because Olla Lillis of the rival Ararat Troupe had introduced the song in a raunchy, Brechtian style, while Malvina performed it to melancholy perfection. The cabaret crowd was fiercely divided between the Ollalístn and the Malvinístn. Mother, of course, sided with Malvina, imitating her performance before the regulars who gathered each evening at Grisha's house.

The story of Grisha her half-brother might itself have been written for the stage. Upon returning from Kharkov, one year shy of receiving his medical degree, he was hired by Dr. Zemach Szabad as the assistant director of TOZ, the Society for the Protection of Health, and married the beautiful and talented Nadianka, the only daughter of the owner of Vinisky's Bank. They lived on Small Pogulanka, on the hill, and Nadia's collection of dolls appears in every group photo, taken with Grisha's Leica at what seems to be one endless party, especially the one in which Mother, Rivele, and all her student friends stage their own Troki Concert in makeshift costumes (Mother, in drag, has a cigarette dangling from her dark lips, with a man's arm draped over her left shoulder). "We never knew where the stage ended and life began," she said, flipping through the album, and because Di Bande refused to perform offstage, the crowd at Grisha's took up the challenge.

Mother made Malvina's repertoire her own. Once, just before a new show was about to open, Malvina was having trouble memorizing the lyrics of "*Kh'vil nit zayn keyn rebbe,* Save me from becoming a rebbe," which had been written out for her in Cyrillic letters, since she only spoke but couldn't read Yiddish, and the mock-learned style required a knowledge of Hebrew too, "*As Rashi says: Three who sit down at one table are required to recite the Grace After Meals* / But what is the rule if one man eats for two, eats for three?" So Mother with her exemplary Judaic training shared Malvina's bed in the hotel. The next night Malvina stole the show, looking comically forlorn with her two sensuous side-curls, a big black *yarmulke* slightly askew, and a long gabardine down to her boots, and Masha mastered the lyrics that her friend had "sung right into her."

Mother envied Malvina her freedom—husband and child left behind in some city somewhere—and envied the attention that Grisha paid her. After every performance, Grisha sent Malvina a bouquet of roses, and Mother was convinced that the roses were paid for with her dowry, three thousand rubles deposited in Vinisky's Bank after Grisha got married. Presumably the money would be safe in father-in-law's safe. That dowry was Masha's mark of shame.

By 1928, she and Leybl Roskes were already engaged to be married, but word came from my father's hometown of Bialystok that they had to wait for Aunt Perele to be married off first. That was the official reason. In point of fact, my grandparents were stalling for time. Odl had already lined up a fine upstanding young lady from Bialystok and was opposed to her Léybuchke taking an orphan girl from Vilna, and when Leybuchke preempted them by announcing his engagement, Grandfather gave a knowing smile from behind his dark glasses and said, "*Haynt hob ikh gehat a hezek fun tsen toyznt rubl,* today I sustained a ten thousand ruble loss. *Mayn zun hot khasene.* My son has decided to get married."

Three thousand of those rubles would have mitigated the loss, but Grisha refused to cough them up. The money, he felt, belonged to him, as did the whole inheritance of the Matz Press.

Grisha's hatred of Yisroel Welczer ran even deeper than Alexander's, for after Fradl died, Yisroel padlocked the press at night to prevent Grisha from stealing it blind. Grisha decided to get even. Invoking a clause in Judah Leib Matz's will that, should Fradl remarry, the money would belong to her children, and having no trust in Jewish courts, Grisha brought a civil suit against his mother in the name of his father, both parents deceased. Fradl won the case. Yisroel, as her husband, was awarded 18.5 percent, over and above his original 25 percent share in the partnership, 43.5 percent in all. Only after Yisroel's death in 1925 did Grisha take over, trying his own hand at publishing Yiddish sheet music before selling the whole inventory of *sforim* to the Gerer Rebbe.

Grisha held on to the dowry, despite vigorous interventions by the Roskies brothers. Enoch appealed to him in person, offering promissory notes in exchange for the dowry, while Shiye came up with a plan to offer Grisha expensive furniture. Grisha, said Enoch at my last fact-finding interview, was a real charmer, a sentiment I never heard echoed by Father.

Of the all-night crowd at Grisha's, some were already doctors, lawyers, and journalists. When they weren't performing the lament of a Jewish gangster from Warsaw, brought to them by the Ararat, or another spoof on the wonder-working rebbe, courtesy of Di Bande, they made up parodies about each other, and sang the latest Polish hits from the twenties translated into Yiddish by Leyb Stotsky, that Vunderkind who had translated Pushkin at the age of thirteen.

"Madness has taken hold of Vilna," they sang. "They've all gone crazy over Malvina."

The regulars included Grisha, Nadianka, and Rivele; Pinkhes Kon, the lawyer and local historian; Shmuel Dreyer, another lawyer and a leading journalist at the Vilna *Tog*; Shloyme Gittel, who worked for a time in the census bureau; Fima Kaplan; Kletzkin's nephew, Sasha Rosen; and Yoysef Teytel. Only Dr. Libo, the dashing captain of the Maccabi rowing team, survived, by hiding with his wife in a bunker, and Malvina, who just happened to be playing on Second Avenue when Hitler invaded Poland.

Toward the end of her life, she played the role of the rich widow, surrounding herself with dependents who took care of her. She aged so much more gracefully than Mother that her death in 1987 took me completely by surprise. The funeral at the Plaza where I delivered the eulogy was sparsely attended. Esther flew in from Israel, worried about her inheritance.

No one seemed overly impressed by my formal, literary Yiddish, except for Felix Fibich, with whom I shared the limousine to the cemetery. Fibich, born in the heart of Jewish Warsaw, as I learned in the course of that rainy afternoon, was the son of a Hasid who ran Simkhe's Restaurant and agreed to support his studies at the actors' studio of the Young Theater. Michal Weichert, a cold intellect, taught Felix how to breathe from the diaphragm. When the Young Theater broke up, having run afoul of the government, he took up dance, and ended up marrying his instructor, Judith Berg. (I too had fallen in love with her, after seeing her dance in the Yiddish film version of *The Dybbuk*.) When the Germans invaded, they ran off together to Soviet-occupied Bialystok. There they met the famed Shloyme Mikhoels, who was so taken with them that he decided to create a Jewish dance ensemble, the Jews being the only Soviet nationality not yet to have one. But really, what Mikhoels sought was some way to express his national sorrow, or to drown it in vodka; so too Peretz Markish, who, after performances, would declaim his verse to the dancers, among whose number was Felix's old flame, Ella Lubelska, formerly a member of the Bialystok Mini-Theater directed by Dzigan and Shumacher. Markish followed her everywhere. She was the love of his life, the "Jewish Dancer" of his great lament for Polish Jewry.

At the outbreak of the German-Soviet war, Ella was evacuated to Tashkent, where she walked thirty miles to enroll in a nursing school. It was not easy for a Polish Jew to gain admittance to the Red Army as a nurse, but she persevered until, disillusioned by what she saw there, she joined the Polish army in exile. When the war ended, Ella made her way back to Moscow, expecting to take up again with Markish. He did not ask her to stay. So she married a Polish Jew, was repatriated, had a daughter by him, and moved to New York. In 1956, when the news broke that Markish and the other Soviet-Yiddish writers had all been shot in the Lubianka on August 12, 1952, Ella committed suicide.

Ever since then, Ella's unrequited love for a great Yiddish poet has been linked in my mind to the lavish attention paid by Uncle Grisha to a Yiddish cabaret singer—the one thing that makes me feel more sympathetic toward him. Chiastically, Markish's cruel treatment of his lover prefigures what Malvina did to Felix. For as co-executor of Malvina's will, which included Max's sizable fortune, the Swiss gold, and the antiquities, donated as per his instructions to the Israel Museum, I had to sign off on Felix, who had done so much for her, being left a pittance. I never saw Felix Fibich again. The gold alone, meanwhile, ate up so much in legal fees that I was stunned when a check arrived for $30,000, my half of the executor's fee. Not Mother. She took it all in stride. I could see her smile even over the telephone.

"Use the money in good health," she said to me. "It's pay-back for Malvina's roses."

8

The Watercarrier

Uncle Grisha's table, laden with fruit, jam, and tea—the late-night crowd didn't drink, never used any external, artificial means of stimulation—was a place for songfest and protest. Vilna, after all, had been the birthplace (in 1897) of the Jewish Labor Bund of Russia and Poland, and some of its founding members, like Anna Rosental, still marched at the head of every May Day rally. Only those whom Mother and her circle protested against were not the class enemy from without but the Jewish enemy from within. This she explained to my friend Michael Stanislawski, who was hired to interview her on behalf of a research project on the Yiddish Folksong in its Social Context. Poland of the 1920s, she contended, was rife with Jewish self-hatred, with what she called *kompleksn*, neuroses, and the best way to fight back was by means of parodic Yiddish songs.

No set of interviews was ever conducted so effortlessly. He visited Mother twelve times, never left without being fed—if Xenia, our Ukrainian-born maid, wasn't cooking, even anchovy sandwiches counted for a meal—and only in the middle of session twelve did he remember to fill in the analytic questionnaire with her name, place of birth, years of schooling, etc. for could anyone imagine a single informant recording 127 songs in six languages: Yiddish, Hebrew, Polish, Russian, Ukrainian, and one song in Gypsy, heard when she was eight from a beggar in the courtyard of Zawalna 28/30?

Those she called her "Bundist" songs were the naughtiest—and most interactive, like "In a Shtetl Not Far from Here," an anti-Hasidic number punctuated by the assembly adding *oy* at the end of each line, and with a chorus half in Yiddish, half in Polish.

> In a shtetl not far from here, (oy)
> there lives a little Rebbe dear. (oy)
> A living he makes not by doing miracles, (oy)
> But from his dumb Hasidic animals (oy-oy-oy)!

Next stanza, when the Rebbe's son is caught behind the bushes with a shiksa, he attempts to justify himself with a last-minute defense:

> Daddy, daddy, don't you fret (oy),
> a shiksa is kosher, you bet (oy).
> Our son will grow up a Talmud scholar, yet, (oy)
> the good Lord be blessed! (oy-oy-oy)

Real Bundist songs, about the overthrow of the tsar, or seamstresses slaving away at the workbench, she almost never sang, although she harbored certain sympathies for the poor and downtrodden. To begin with, there was an orphanage in her courtyard on Zawalna 28/30, and she sometimes overheard the children playing and singing in Yiddish. During summer vacations, she hung out with the *knéytsherkes,* the women who fed the reams of paper through the folding machine at the press, and so enjoyed listening to their stories and songs that during their lunch break, when they sent someone out for herring, radishes, and strawberries, she ordered the same menu from the cook and ate alongside them.

If these sympathies did not extend to Bundists per se—and here we leave the researcher of Yiddish song armed with his Wollensak reel-to-reel tape recorder and revert back to more primitive means of biographical study—it was because of what they did to my grandmother Fradl in the summer of 1906, a time of revolutionary upheaval, when she was carrying Mother in her womb. Fradl was at the Rom Press on business when someone rushed in to say that a group of Bundist agitators had just tried to publish illegal proclamations but were stopped from doing so by the foreman. Most certainly they were heading next for the Matz Publishing House. Sure enough, by the time Fradl got there—it was a good twenty-minute walk for a woman in her condition—the printing presses had been requisitioned, every worker pressed into service, and a young man brandishing a pistol was in charge. Within the hour, they were raided by the police, and everyone made a run for it by jumping through the ground floor window. The only one who stood by Fradl, who obviously couldn't run anywhere, was Moyshe Kamermakher, as loyal to her as a son, having spent his whole life at the Press. The two of them were hauled off to the Lukishki Prison, where the most hardened criminals and political prisoners were kept. Fradl was in mortal terror. But along the way, they ran into a watercarrier *mit fule emers,* his buckets overflowing with water, which Fradl knew was the best of omens. How the buckets are wasted on me, she thought, now that I am being imprisoned for life. But the police had made such a clean sweep of the revolutionary underground that every cell at the huge Lukishki complex was already filled to capacity. So Fradl and Moyshe Kamermakher were dragged off to the central police station, where, for a few groschen they were provided with pillows and blankets, but days turned to weeks and Fradl despaired.

Her husband, Yisroel, meanwhile, had sent word of her arrest to her niece, Naomi, who ran Syrkin's Bookstore in St. Petersburg, and this young woman came running to the governor of the Vilna region who was both her customer and personal friend to appeal on behalf of her aunt. Imagine, he was so taken with Naomi that he looked into the matter himself, found Fradl's file in the relevant office for internal security and destroyed it.

"Tell your aunt," he said, "that she has you to thank for her life, because in the present political crisis, she probably would have died in prison before her case ever came to trial."

Fradl was freed but made her own release conditional on Moyshe Kamermakher's, her most loyal worker. The whole experience cost her two of her front teeth, which fell out either from fear or despair, and Masha, growing up, was surprised to see that her mother, so beautiful and perfect, was missing two of her teeth, which is how she found out about her mother's arrest and about Moyshe Kamermakher, whose loyalty and love Fradl reciprocated, modeling the greatest possible respect for her workers, whom Fradl would invite to the table whenever they came to the house on business, serving them tea from the samovar, with preserves, and sometimes with beer, such that long before the revolution Fradl made no distinction between herself and her workers, and how natural, then, for Masha to befriend the *kneytsherkes* in her mother's press and to eat what they ate, a practice she continued even in Canada, for whenever Palmer Hart came from Huntingdon to do odd jobs around the house, she would serve him the same meal she served us, veal chops and mashed potatoes, which even with his one hand he could eat as deftly as we with two.

Still, there was no love lost for the Bund. One day she was out taking a walk in St. Sauveur, where every summer the Montreal Yiddish colony rented bungalows. She bumps into Shloyme Abramson, a leader of the Warsaw Bund who escaped on the Gerer Rebbe's special train, and he introduces her to a former comrade named Shloyme-Fayvish Gilinsky.

"Meet Masha Roskies," says Abramson, "she's from Vilna."

"Vilna," says Gilinsky with a smile, "that was my very first assignment. The Central Committee sent me there to print up some Yiddish proclamations. Just as I took over the Matz Press the boss rushed in and I stopped her at gunpoint."

"The boss," says Mother, "whom do you mean?"

"Fradl Matz," he says. "The gun was loaded and I held it to her head until the job was done. Those Jewish bandits, you know, I had to stop her from screaming, and she kept fainting anyway, that's how much I managed to scare her, though I would never have pulled the trigger."

Mother shot Gilinsky a venomous look and continued on her way.

When Mother read his obituary in the *Jewish Daily Forward,* she threw a fit.

"He nearly killed my mother," she yelled, "nearly killed *me,* for that matter, in utero. Some hero! The real hero was my mother, and Moyshe Kamermakher, and the lone watercarrier, her *lamed-vóvnik,* her hidden saint."

9

Yeast

It takes twelve hours for yeast to complete its work. This I know not from taking science (my worst subject), but from my father, who wrote his master's thesis for Stefan Batory University on the properties of yeast. The worst part, he told us, was not the long wait so much as the overpowering aroma, which became as sickening to him as the taste of turnips, his staple diet in Moscow and Saratov during World War I. Father spent the better part of 1927 nauseated by the smell of yeast on the ground floor of the chemistry building located off-campus. I think I got a whiff of it when I posed in front of that building some fifty years later.

Bored beyond words, especially on Sundays, Father whiled away the twelve-hour stretch by singing to himself. What did he sing? Not revolutionary hymns (he might blow his cover), and not the latest cabaret hits (when did this student living hand-to-mouth ever see the inside of a cabaret?). Vilna had recently become part of the Polish Republic, so singing in Russian might brand him as a Bolshevik while Polish he had only learned of late by memorizing a Russian-Polish dictionary. Father came from a strictly observant home, and despite the years of war, exile, and revolution, all he had to do was close his eyes and the sacred tunes of early childhood came flooding back. So he passed his time in the chemistry lab singing snippets from the liturgy and cantorial favorites from the High Holy Days.

One Sunday morning he hears a knock on the door. In walks the janitor. *Prosze Pana,* says the janitor, using the polite form of address. The young gentlemen, he says, is kindly requested to keep his singing to himself, for just above on the second floor lives Herr Doktor Professor Eger, the chairman of the chemistry department, and the singing disturbs his work. The young gentlemen promises to keep mum and manages to do so for a while, at least until there's another knock on the door. This time the exchange is testier, but Father placates the janitor with his sincerity: he positively won't sing. The third time, dispensing with the niceties, the janitor tells Father to follow him upstairs. Father is ushered into Professor Eger's study. Seated behind his huge mahogany desk, Eger sizes up the short bespectacled Jew standing before him.

"As you can see, young man, I live directly above the laboratory. Your constant singing disturbs my concentration."

Father apologizes in his best Polish and is about to promise to stifle his singing once and for all when his scientific eye spots a portrait hanging to the left above the desk. Eger follows the direction of the young man's gaze and responds with the hint of a smile. There hangs a rabbi with a large *yarmulke* covering his head. The black skullcap contrasts sharply with the rabbi's full white beard that blends into the sumptuous white of his fur collar. Take away that beard and there is something familiar about the contemplative look in his eyes.

Now unlike Mother, whose stories were hardly age-appropriate, Father waited to tell us this story until we were old enough to savor its ironies. From Lerer Dunsky, our history teacher, we knew about the illustrious Rabbi Akiva Eger and his various descendants, rabbis and halakhists, legal scholars, all. Was this the last chapter, one branch of the Eger family that opted out and one of whose offspring had gone on to become the very model of a Polish professor? Then why was he so proud of his Jewish lineage? And if he was so proud, why all the fuss about Father's melancholy chanting? Or did Eger simply want to take a closer look at this new generation of Polish Jews?

Since hearing this story, I've done some further research on the historical properties of enzymes. So powerful, I learned, were the enzymes from those yeast cells of Father's that despite a worldwide depression, despite economic boycotts against the Jews, despite the rise of Hitler, they worked their organic magic: my father, Leybl Roskes, moved from his spartan student quarters on Zawalna Street in Vilna to a cottage on the factory compound in Krosno to a luxury apartment on the hill in Czernowitz, all in the span of six years. And even when everything was lost, in the summer of 1940, the tiny one-celled fungus proved eminently adaptable to the harsh climate of Canada and my father made a new start, albeit in textiles, not in rubber, and as junior partner, not as Herr Direktor.

Problem was, too many enzymes spoiled the bread, for Leybl was now reunited with his three older brothers who, according to the *Golden Jubilee Edition* of the Yiddish *Daily Eagle* (1957), exemplified the inseparable bond of Torah and textiles, of Lithuanian learning and Hasidic majesty, which together had withstood the successive onslaughts of communist aggression in Moscow, Bialystok, Czernowitz, and Budapest; and problem was, that while Leybl and his Vilna-born wife Masha, daughter of the well-known Matz Family of printers, did receive honorable mention, they came last, after the oldest brother Shiye and his Esther Malka, "a highly educated *laydee*," after their diplomaed sons, after his late brother Itshe (Isaac), who might have become a great talmudic scholar, had he so desired, after Enoch, who served as president of the Bialystok Center from 1943 to 1950, and after Enoch and Mandy's son Ralph, who this very year had placed first among "no fewer than 2,000 high school students in Quebec province," and was a brilliant pianist. Problem was, the war of the incompatible enzymes spilled over from one molecular environment to another, from the factory to the home, from the brothers to their wives.

Salvaged from the past was a piece of old dough, which bakers call a starter, a particularly successful strain of yeast that when added to the bread gives it a distinctive flavor, and when my parents discovered that by moving down from the English-speaking heights of Westmount to Outremont, where the masses of Yiddish-speaking immigrants lived, they could replicate the rich cultural melange that had brought them together in the first place, back in Vilna, and this piece of old dough, when added to the new, better controlled the fermentation process. In Outremont, where Leybl sired new children and learned new languages, Yiddish became the lingua franca of our home and the medium of Father's cultural activism after hours.

Even Monsieur Gagnon, owner of the Shell station on Van Horne and Bloomfield, would greet Father with his three words of Yiddish whenever we filled up with gas. "Mr. Leo," he would say, "you're *óngeshtopt mit gelt.*"

Mr. Leo was the name they called my father at Huntingdon Woolen Mills, to distinguish him from Mr. Isaac, Mr. Enoch, Mr. Henry, Mr. Nat, Mr. Ben, and so on down the line of Roskies, for Monsieur Gagnon had once worked at Huntingdon and now enjoyed poking fun at his former boss. What, I often wondered, did Father find more revolting: that the Yiddish was so vulgar or that he was thought of as "rolling in dough"?

At home, *gelt* was a four-letter word. A federal census taker once came by and when asked his annual income, Father answered in a whisper, as if he were revealing a dirty secret. Whenever we ate out, of a Sunday or on vacation, and the bill was presented, Father would raise his thick glasses, pretend to examine the bill very closely, and then pronounce: "*a metsiye,* what a bargain!" which always made us laugh, especially when the Pu-Pu platter alone cost more than two portions of spare ribs. And although he no longer wore patches on the elbows of his one-and-only jacket, sewn there by his mother to ward off an evil eye and the eyes of a predatory woman, he would have been happy nowadays to wear the same suit week in and week out, were it not that Mother oversaw his wardrobe and augmented his tie collection, purchased at the exclusive store of Brisson & Brisson, others on the Cape, later, in Miami Beach, and later still in Switzerland, ties that filled up his closet at the top of the stairs, for Father never came down to breakfast without a tie on, except on vacation, but seemed to prefer wearing the gray ones, some indelibly stained, and rarely went in for Mother's extravagant choice of colors, though he surely marveled at her alchemy and magic potions, thanks to which she kept her face so young, like rubbing her cheeks with cucumber rind, daily ablutions followed by an hour spent at her boudoir cluttered with creams and powders and costly colognes, which I alone could observe, as for example when she replaced her unruly eyebrows with a very thin line penciled in at a provocative angle, as I alone knew of secret purchases at Ogilvy's and Eaton's, not to speak of the fashionable dresses and fur-lined coats especially tailored by Madame Lafleur on Sherbrooke Street, and Mother's endless supply of hats, hats of every conceivable shape, material, and color, hats that spilled over into every spare closet, of which there were many, hats that were finally donated to the Montreal Yiddish Theatre and can be seen today whenever Dora Wasserman stages a musical comedy, while Father did his best to hide his constant physical discomforts and to hide from me the truss that he now wore on account of his hernia, by repeating his optimistic slogan, "*s'vet zayn gut,* not to worry, things will turn out for the best," which he always uttered with a re-assuring smile, except for once, when he presided over the merger between the Folkshule, the Jewish People's School from which all four of his children graduated with distinction, and the Peretz School, a long, contentious meet-ing that took place in our dining room, where Father, wearing a striped red-and-blue silk tie, was seated sternly at the head of the table.

With so much going on, Father had little time to dwell on the past, and the scene of him singing cantorial hits while dressed in his lab coat just hung there in limbo, given that we were thrice-a-year shul-goers, like most of the Jews in Montreal, and when I sat next to him in the Adath Israel he never seemed truly engaged. Then again, our Rabbi Bender maintained strict deco-rum and did not countenance displays of spiritual enthusiasm. It wasn't un-til my senior year in college, when my parents visited with me at Havurat Shalom Community Seminary, that I ever saw him really *daven*. Mother, ter-ribly put out, sat in the adjacent living room, but Father stayed with it, the only one in suit and tie, and to my utter joy and surprise, joined in the circle dance at the end. There was Hasidic blood in him, and I had never known.

So the supply of yeast was constantly being replenished, until Mr. Ben, my brother, died suddenly, at age forty-three. By the time Father rushed back from Huntingdon to the Jewish General, the body had already been taken down to the morgue. "Are you alone, Mr. Roskies?" asked the head nurse, to which Father replied by turning toward the wall and banging his head against it, in silence, which is how my brother-in-law found him a half hour later; and Father hung onto life, just long enough to take care of Ben's estate, and now spent his evenings at home, pacing up and down in the dark to Chopin's Funeral March playing on the hi-fi—so Mother once told me as I drove her to the Canadian Imperial Bank of Commerce. Never had she imagined there would come a time when a man, let alone her own husband, would find her company less than stimulating.

Because Father died on the first day of Rosh Hashanah, the funeral was postponed until after the holiday. The cortege took a detour on its way from Paperman's Funeral Home to the cemetery on de la Savane. The two limou-sines in the lead and the whole caravan of cars with their headlights on passed slowly along Van Horne Avenue, right in front of the Folkshule, where exactly at one o'clock, the entire school, all the children, teachers, and staff, were assembled in the yard to watch us go by.

The filial duty of reciting the Kaddish now fell to me.

Of the many places I might have chosen on the Upper West Side, where I moved in the summer of 1975, I chose to say Kaddish at the Lemberger shtibl on West End Avenue. In this three-story brownstone with the whole second floor turned into a chapel I could speak Yiddish with some of the old-timers. On most mornings, I was also custom-bound to lead the service. Tolerant of my modern Hebrew pronunciation, they initiated me into the bitter taste of schnapps.

For eleven months I recited the Kaddish, trying to ignore the impending anniversary, Father's *yortsayt,* which would fall not on some ordinary day of the week but on the first day of Rosh Hashanah, the New Year. The Lemberger Rebbe took me aside and informed me that to honor my father's memory I was expected to chant the haftarah for the first day of Rosh Hashanah. This would be a piece of cake for anyone raised in a traditional home, but Hazzan Goldberger of Adath Israel had taught me my bar mitzvah portion by rote. Why? Because it had made his work that much easier. To learn a new haftarah now would require weeks of memorization. So we compromised: I would learn the Opening Psalms to the High Holy Day chant. My performance was such a dismal failure that I resolved never to return. The very next day I joined a few refugees from the old Havurah who had formed their own congregation on the Upper West Side. We met in a crowded living room surrounded by bookcases made of plywood and red bricks and we could hear children running and laughing overhead but a woman named Arlene with an angelic soprano led a service unlike any I had ever heard.

With the support of my refound friends, I eventually mastered the entire morning service for Rosh Hashanah. It took me five years. The first year I was so frightened that I forgot everything but the melody for the Opening Psalms. By year two I had figured out the leitmotif. By year three I had the whole Leader's Repetition down pat. By year four I was comfortable enough to improvise. Today my hour-and-a-half-long morning service in Father's memory is considered a high point of the congregation's liturgical calendar. The fear and trembling that prefigure this moment are dispelled when I start belting out the codas, but make it difficult for me to modulate my voice. Sometimes I fail to get the transitions just right, so I throw in a Hasidic tune here and there, as if I too were born in Bialystok and had sung to a chemist and a rabbi's portrait on the floor just above.

10

Beloved Fatherland

Getting my first summer job at the Montreal office of Huntingdon Woolen Mills seemed like a giant step. Mornings I spent indentured to Mr. Goldberg, the chief salesman, who drilled me on what to charge different customers for the same fabric, in between his tales of the Warsaw ghetto. On August 11, the twentieth anniversary of the *Selektion* at the Kurt Rörlich Factory, when another Goldberg stepped forward to be sent to the Umschalgplatz instead of him, we came inches away from crashing into a lamp post. But that was nothing compared to the rare lunch break with Uncle Enoch when Mr. Goldberg was off on his own. Such a lunch, which we ordered out, was worth a dozen at home, because what Enoch drew from his archival memory bank was a competing, heretical source of family lore, a patriarchal narrative of my grandfather's daring and acerbic wit.

"That courtyard on Zawalna Street," said Uncle Enoch, relishing the opportunity to set me straight, "your mother's Holy of Holies? The place was a dump. People threw their garbage out the windows, like in the Middle Ages, and the children made *kakkie* out in the open."

"Those were children from the orphanage," I countered.

"It was a palace in name only—Tyszkiewicz's was it? Compared to the Branicki Palace in Bialystok, your mother's yard was nothing but a dog house."

"In Fradl's day the courtyard belonged to Count Bukowski," I corrected him, "who paraded around with a gold-tipped walking stick and had rouged cheeks, 'like a homosexual.'"

"Yes, yes, very piquant, the way Masha serves up all her stories, but I'm telling you something else. I'm telling you about the Roskies. Your grandfather Dovid lived by his wits. All of Jewish Bialystok quoted his expressions."

"Like what?"

"Like *a fete kotlet brent zikh nit tsu*—a greasy hamburger, yes? will never get burned. You know what it means?"

"Fat cats get away with murder."

"Very nice. A good translation. Anyway, thanks to your grandfather, the family always stayed one step ahead of starvation and death. First they fled the German advance and ended up in Pavlovski Passad, just outside of Moscow, where Dovid built a thriving textile factory, which he tried to hold on to after the Bolsheviks came to power. What do you think Dovid did when they finally expropriated the factory? He talked them into letting him manage it on behalf of the state. When things got really rough, he would elude the secret police by selling his remaindered cloth on the black market."

Enoch rarely spoke to me in Yiddish, maybe because he considered my great enthusiasm for Yiddish a form of over-identification with Mother— even though at home (I knew from Mother), he spoke only Yiddish to Aunt Mandy, who would reply in her impeccable Viennese German.

If I failed to draw Uncle Enoch out more about Grandfather Dovid, whose name I carry and whose portrait in oil made from a photograph by Alexander Bercovitch hangs to the left of my desk, it's because the only patriarch who interested me at the time was the man who never behaved like one.

"Is it true that my dad was a Communist?"

"Who told you that?"

"I overheard Ruthie mention it once to Harry Bracken."

Leybl was the youngest, he told me, Grandmother's favorite. In 1918, the year of his bar mitzvah, he heard Trotsky harangue the crowds in Red Square. Later he got swept up in the great experiment. So when the Roskies made it back to Bialystok, penniless, mind you, robbed cleaned at the Polish-Soviet border, on an island on the Berezina River, where Polish bandits stole their diamonds and jewelry, each of them went his own way. Uncle Itshe not only refused to become a rabbi. He also arranged his own marriage to the slim and educated Ida. As for him, Enoch was never very practical and decided to study philosophy, while Leybl headed for Kraków to train as an agronomist. Someday he would run a Jewish agricultural commune in the Ukraine or Crimea and show the world what miracles the Jews can work on the land. But agronomy was off limits to Jews, to prevent them, I should know, from further polluting Poland's soil, so Leybl moved to Vilna where he met a fellow student named Chaim, and this Chaim was a member of a communist cell, who planned to steal across the Polish-Soviet border on a Party mission carrying two hundred rubles in cash. A lot of money in those days.

"Yes," I interrupted him, "two hundred rubles was half the cost of tuition in the yeshiva that Grandfather sent you to."

Enoch smiled.

So Leybl, still loyal to the cause, helped Chaim raise the required sum and organized the illegal crossing. The two boys hired an experienced border-guide, gave him a down payment and promised the rest upon his return to Vilna. To complete the protocol, they came up with a secret password that Chaim would give the guide once he was safe on the other side. Since word games ran in the family, they chose *kim'at* as the password, which means "almost" both in Yiddish and Hebrew; spell it phonetically, you get an acronym for *Kush-Mir-In-Tukhes*, kiss my ass.

The mission succeeded all right, but Chaim disappeared, he was probably arrested on suspicion of being a Polish spy, and back in Bialystok, Chaim's mother began to hound the father of the boy she held responsible for her son's death. As a precaution, Dovid took to sleeping with a wad of rubles under his pillow, for the moment he would have to buy off an arresting policeman, and when Leybl came home at the end of the first year, Grandfather dubbed him Fishke the Red.

"Know where that comes from?" asked Enoch as he polished off his smoked meat sandwich.

"Yes, from Mendele's novel, *Fishke the Lame*."

"Someday, you'll be a Yiddish professor, just like your sister."

Before he rushed off to his meeting with UTEX, Huntingdon's biggest client, Uncle Enoch left me with one last tale from his secret archive. In 1938, when he brought his newly wedded wife to live in Czernowitz, Mother made friends with her maid. After surreptitiously inspecting Aunt Mandy's shopping lists, my mother showed up in their apartment and pronounced her sister-in-law an utter incompetent as a housewife.

Mother could give as good as she got. During lunch break from school she filled my ears with Enoch's love affairs, as if they happened yesterday. The Vera Hacken Episode was her favorite—I nearly burst out laughing when I beheld Ms. Hacken's large shapeless body and scraggly hair at a literary gathering in New York many years later—and Mother too remembered one of Grandfather's bon mots, ad-libbed at Enoch's expense. Returning from a tryst one early morning, Enoch found Grandfather waiting up for him.

"Good morning, Nisn!" he called out.

"Nisn?" asked Enoch. "Why are you calling me Nisn?" (Nisn is Yiddish for Nathan.)

"*Vayl Nisn iz nit vayt fun Iyer,*" an amazing pun, the innocent meaning of which is that the Jewish month of Nissan is not far from the month of Iyyar, and the not-so-innocent meaning is: "Because wherever Nathan is cannot be too far from HER."

Then what did it take to woo a woman, say, someone like my mother? To do it right, not through arranged marriages, or botched love affairs that got the whole family embroiled in scandal? One thing was clear. Enoch's disclaimers notwithstanding, Vilna was the city of romance.

A recurrent theme of Mother's at my thirty-five-minute lunch breaks, where no time was wasted talking about school, was that it helped to be very smart.

After Vilna became part of the new Polish Republic, the last city to do so, very few Jewish youths went on to university, first, because they weren't admitted, and second, because the new government refused to accept a Russian diploma. Mother, for example, had no desire to rematriculate from *gymnasium*. On account of her typhus she had missed taking her final exams and received her diploma only through special intervention. Then her mother died. But Papale, my father, all of sixteen years old, did the impossible. He taught himself Polish by memorizing the poetry of Mickiewicz (this is Mother's version) and sat for his Polish matriculation.

Did I know he was almost expelled for spotting a mistake in the math exam? "If you interrupt me one more time," the proctor warned him, "I'm kicking you out." He was rescued by a supervisor who rushed in to report on the error. Papale ended up getting the top grade. In Polish composition, that's where he received a mere Pass. The theme was "Our Fatherland," a very touchy subject. Poland, remember, had just been reborn and Papale was so taken with the poetry of Mickiewicz that he overdid it by using the phrase *kochana ojczyzna*, "beloved fatherland," three times. When you speak of your "fatherland," the professor lectured him, it is by definition "beloved." Never again, said Mother, would Papale be accused of playing the *mayófesnik*, the ass-licking Jew.

So mastering Polish if you were a Jew could make you seem too smart, opened you to abuse instead, rendered you vulnerable. You're trying way too hard, Mr. Jew. Don't be so eager to prove your usefulness, your loyalty, your love. We've seen your kind before. Now that we have finally achieved our hearts' desire, become free and reunited at last, we are no longer beholden to anyone. We shall henceforth decide who's in and who's out, thank you very much, and while you Jews may pull off the requisite grades, we reserve the right to treat you as equals.

Still, turn the story around and the key to impressing a woman might be the "never again" part, the very ability to fight back.

You'd never guess looking at Papale, always with his thick glasses, how fearless he was, said Mother launching into another lunchtime soliloquy. He and his buddies from Bialystok were taking a walk one day along Great Pogulanka when they ran into a Polish Legionnaire. Hearing them speak Yiddish, the officer threw his glove in Father's face, which Papale casually kicked into the gutter. This so enraged the officer that he pulled out his pistol. Go ahead and shoot, Father yelled, ripping open his shirt. The officer hesitated, then, nearly apoplectic, hauled Father and his friends off to the police station.

"What happened?"

"They were charged with unruly conduct and let go."

Undaunted, Papale continued to fight for the underdog. Once a fellow student, Beilinson by name, was brought before the Jewish Student Council on a trumped-up charge, for what she couldn't remember, and Papale rose to his defense. When the student was cleared of the charge, Rudnitsky, a classmate of Father's who appears in no other story, got up and shouted from the back of the hall, "If only we had a hundred such as Leybl Roskes!" Then he yelled out in Yiddish (the meetings were conducted in Polish), "*Leybke, hob gikher khasene!* Leybke, get yourself married one-two-three!"

They called her Słowik, Polish for "Nightingale," and the figure she cut in bloomers and athletic blouse as she worked out in the gymnastics section of ŻAKS, the Jewish Academic Sports Club, more than compensated for her masculine nose. Masha Welczer was essentially marking time now that her original plan, to emigrate to Palestine with a degree in early childhood education from Pestalozzi Froebelhausen in Berlin, had fallen through. Her father had already deposited the requisite sum for her upkeep with the Vilna Jewish Community when he suddenly had a near-fatal heart attack. No way she could leave Vilna now, so she signed up for courses as a nonmatriculated student at Stefan Batory University, and she joined ŻAKS.

Thanks to her singing and her Matz-family voice, she was constantly surrounded by a bevy of men. On the fateful twenty-first night of March 1925, when after a rigorous workout the members of ŻAKS decided to take a walk through the Zakret Forest, Meir Mirsky asked her to sing Julian Tuwim's romantic ballad "Bajki cudowne," which means "Tales of Wonder," in Leyb Stotsky's masterful translation into Yiddish. It was a logical choice, because Tuwim, a Jew, was all the rage. "Remind me of my golden childhood," she rhapsodized, "those years of long ago; / tales of wonder and enchantment / that Granny told us by the stove." She felt someone take her by the arm and they continued walking together for the rest of the night. Before they parted, Leybl said, "*Shrayb mir dos iber,* copy it out for me, why don't you."

Masha never came through, not because she didn't like him, but because she did, and took pity on him, such a naive boy, never knew a woman before, never even went out with a woman before, why get him tangled up with someone as complicated as her? She was still seeing Boris. Her father's heart condition had taken a turn for the worse. And here was Leybl, who needed more than anything else (she selflessly decided) to complete his studies at the university. And who, after all, had seduced whom? It was through her singing that she had drawn him into her net. Copy it out and Leybl would belong to her.

So Leybl learned to bide his time, sublimating his desire in the chemistry lab, where he sang cantorial pieces until Professor Eger put a stop to it, but by the time he graduated, in 1928, they were engaged to be married, just as he headed off to his first job in the distant factory town of Krosno, from which he sent her love letters in Yiddish addressed, provocatively, to

"*Obywatelka Masha Welczer,* Citizen Masha Welczer." I'm not marrying you for your pedigree, the envelope proclaimed, I'm marrying you because together we'll build a free Poland and a productive Jewish future.

"Merely a symbolic gesture," says Mother, "because in order to win me, he had to give up his dream of doing agronomy and get rich."

11

The Black Canopy

Whenever we'd drive by the Catholic cemetery on Mount Royal, the one that faces Beaver Lake, Father would say, "A cemetery—what a fine place to make out with a girl." That Eros and Thanatos made natural bedfellows was a startling observation coming from Father, because on no other occasion would he indulge in romantic reverie, and even more startling given what I now know about cemeteries in the compass of Mother's past. No way would she have made out with a man surrounded by gravestones, so if not with her, then with whom?

Mother became a cemetery-goer after Father died, not only in the month of Elul, the time that was sanctified for communing with our family dead, but whenever I happened to be in town. The drive to the cemetery on de la Savane was something of an outing, in view of the fact that after my brother died, Father sold his forty-year-old burial plot at the Adath Israel and secured as close a grave to Ben as he could in the new Jewish cemetery. Standing at Ben's graveside, either because the wound refused to heal or remained unacknowledged, Mother said little, and would grow more talkative when we reached her own grave, where Father's flamboyant epitaph, "*undzer eyntisker*, our one-and-only," had been inscribed as per her wish, and where her own epitaph, "*shma kolenu*, hear our voices," would some day be engraved on her side of the joint headstone. Hear our voices, O Lord, hear our outcry, our protest, we will not let Thee off the hook, O God of Vengeance, until Thy job be done.

One brisk Friday morning in September she wore her black and brown tweed suit with matching hat. From the jacket pocket she removed an almost pearl-white stone that she had saved especially for this pre–Rosh Hashanah visit.

"You know," she said, polishing the stone in her hand, "every Tisha b'Av, when I was growing up, on the anniversary of Judah Leib Matz's death, Fradl would hire three carriages to take all ten of the Matz children to his graveside in the Old Vilna Cemetery at Shnípeshik, there to recite the Kaddish. Mother herself always stayed home. Once, when I was old enough to ask why, she explained, *'ikh geher shoyn nit tsu im,* I don't belong to him anymore.'"

"Because she was now remarried to your father?"

"That's right. Judah Leib had no spiritual claims upon my mother. But Fradl's wayward offspring, they were still required to recite the proper Kaddish."

Looking around at the spare surroundings, Mother suddenly grew indignant.

"So how come Mrs. Oberman managed to get the cemetery to install a bench right next to her husband's grave, while we are forced to stand? I asked Rabbi Baron to intercede on my behalf, made a very handsome offer, but to no avail!"

Good and angry now, and perhaps in the face of her own mortality, Mother laid bare for me her self-defining moment, the untold story of her mother's unveiling.

The moment Fradl died, Masha was left in the care of the one man for whom she had cared the least. Her father, refusing all offers of marriage, also refused to move out of their suite of apartments at Zawalna 28/30. It was just the two of them now, plus the maid. Exactly what happened next is a bit sketchy, because the story picks up eleven months later when, according to Jewish custom, it was time for Fradl's tombstone to be unveiled, and Masha, instead of squeezing into the last carriage with her siblings, headed for the new Jewish cemetery at Zarecze in a separate carriage with her father. She didn't quite know what to expect, for all the arrangements had been made by sister Rosa, who was back in the wake of her affair with Sergeant Kornicker. Rosa had been freed to marry Kornicker, as I surely remember, because his wife had committed suicide during the war, and the engagement was to take place in Berlin, where Sergeant Kornicker was to have met her at the train station. And he was there all right, waiting at the Leipziger Bahnhof, only instead of the man she had fallen in love with, that dashing officer in full uniform, who had accompanied her so perfectly at the piano, she was met by your typical Jewish burgher, somewhat comical, in fact, in his tight-fitting vest and half-coat.

The Hebrew inscription on the black marble obelisk was simple and stark:

> The Beloved Mother
> of Great Eminence
> FRADL daughter of MOSHE
> MATZ
> *18.X.1921*

Masha could not believe her eyes. There they all stood—her half-brothers and sisters, for whose sake she had renounced her own father—and they had written her out of the family. "*Vos bin ikh epes, a mámzer,*" she cried, turning to Rosa, "what do you think I am, a bastard?" The Welczer name that Fradl carried for eighteen years was nowhere to be seen. Masha Welczer was now an orphan twice over.

By this time, we're ensconced on Mrs. Oberman's Bench, and Mother is breathing heavily.

"It was the most traumatic day of my life," she says, taking my hand in hers, and without her having to elaborate, I get it: The woman who bore me had been born right then and there, her sense of self defined by a clean break with the other children of Fradl Matz, with their vendetta against her father, with their dandified snobbery. I also get why Rosa's name is linked in her stories to Kornicker showing up at the train station in his city clothes. It was Mother's way of savoring the bitter fruits of Rosa's seduction by the slicker of the two officers who came round the house.

"My sisters, they never forgave Mother for marrying out of love. Their marital life? Don't ask. A swamp, not a life. Were it not for our sacred dead, who surround us at this moment, I would tell you about Surávich, the widower my sister Rosa finally agreed to marry. Suravich's wife, like Kornicker's, had committed suicide."

"What about Annushka and her second marriage to Warshawsky?"

"Yes, divorce was fairly common, not unlike today. [This last was for my benefit, my first marriage being on the verge of breaking up.] But in my circle, we resolved to do it right, once and for all, and the reason we succeeded where they failed is that we found a *lebns-bagléyter*, a true partner-in-life, not just a partner-in-bed."

Whom she meant by "her circle" was Zalmen Merkin, alias Max Erik, and his young bride, Ida Rosenshein. Vilna had seen any number of Maskilim, Jews of secular learning, but never a banker's son, a bemedaled Polish officer with a law degree who chucked it all to lead the charge for modernism and Yiddish literature. Every lecture of his on Mendele, Peretz, or Expressionism was a manifesto. Of the whole class, Erik picked out Idachka, not the brightest student but certainly the most beautiful, and the fact that she reciprocated his love proved that by intellect alone you could get your girl, because the teacher, prematurely bald and somewhat rotund, looked more the banker's son than the enfant terrible. And she also meant Shmuel Dreyer, who though himself not indifferent to my mother, married Rivtshe, by any measure an exemplary match between the lawyer and Yiddish journalist and she who later founded Maydim, Vilna's first Yiddish marionette theater.

And of course, last but not least, she meant Leybl, who had waited and waited, first for Masha to break up with Seidman, then for his older sister Perele to find a husband. A measure of Leybl's idealism was choosing February 13 as the wedding date, because thirteen he considered a lucky number, thirteen the age of bar mitzvah, and the date of Pilsudski's Miracle on the Vistula. Some of their friends had dispensed with *huppah* and *kiddushin*, but Masha had promised her mother before her death that she would have a religious ceremony with wedding canopy and cantor, and Leybl behaved quite dutifully at first toward his own parents, both of whom were still alive.

So if this story has a happy end, why is Mother's grip getting stronger by the minute? I have Father's delicate long fingers, and they're beginning to ache.

Leybl and his Orthodox father did not see eye to eye. When Leybl returned to Bialystok with his master's in chemistry, one of three Jews to receive a graduate degree from Stefan Batory that year, Dovid greeted him in rhyme: "*Sholem-aleykhem magíster, vos ba tog est er un ba nakht shist er*; why hello, Mr. Masters, who chows all day and screws all night."

Dovid knew full well that his son did nothing of the kind, which may, in fact, explain the antagonism, for as Mother recalls, Dovid liked a person *mit khesreynes,* with flaws, someone like Grisha, for example, or like Enoch, with his love affairs. Leybl's behavior, by contrast, was saintly to a fault, with the exception of that foolhardy episode of smuggling Chaim into Soviet Russia.

It was to be a do-it-yourself wedding, at the farthest remove from his son Shiye's seven-day-long extravaganza in Bialystok with hundreds of guests and dozens of rabbis. Dovid's blindness had set in by now and it was diffi-cult for him to travel, so with Perele's help, his mother Odl set out for Vilna. The women then sent word of a last-minute delay, which coincided with a telegram from Enoch, the only brother Leybl really cared for, saying that he was held up and couldn't come. Leybl cried the whole night through, con-vinced that Enoch had been forbidden to attend, and on the morrow sum-moned his bride to the graveside of her mother. Two corpses went dancing, says Mother, describing that cold February day, and calls it *a shvartse khupe,* a black canopy, of the kind once used to propitiate a plague.

The graveside! The very graveside where his bride had suffered that ter-rible betrayal at the hands of her sister Rosa and the rest of the illustrious Family Matz. Did Father know this? Was there some kind of symmetry he was trying to achieve, with his scientific thoroughness? Betrayed yet again, on her wedding day, only not as in 1921 by her half-brothers and sisters, but by her in-laws and the equally despicable Roskies clan?

In protest, there was to be a cantor all right, but no canopy, and this Haz-zan was brought along to intone the "El malei raḥamim" prayer for Fradl's soul. Leybl then betrothed his bride in front of two witnesses. The first wit-ness was FRADL daughter of MOSHE / MATZ, lying in her grave, and the sec-ond was the Hazzan, standing next to her grave. Though not a valid be-trothal by Jewish standards, so far as my parents were concerned, this was the ceremony that mattered.

Odl and Perele arrived on the fourteenth, and a kosher wedding was held for their benefit, in Grisha's house, at which Mother's svelte wedding gown of white silk made a striking contrast with the black, somewhat dowdy dresses worn by the Bialystok contingent.

Weighed down by this dirty secret and by Mother's substantial body pulling on my left arm, we finally headed back to the car. With too much on my mind that visit, I didn't think to take the story any further, and forgot about it when my life fell back into place, having found my very own partner-in-life, until one day, Enoch paid a brave solo visit to our home. Sitting in the green swivel chair in the living room and out of Mother's earshot, he told me that our parents' prenuptial "black canopy" was a figment of her febrile imagination, and that if Father had cried the whole night through, it was on account of his colitis, not because of any embargo. And that's where matters stood until the week of Mother's shivah, when we started going through the contents of her carved wooden box, and came upon a long letter from Enoch written in Yiddish from Rovno, in which he apologized profusely for missing the wedding, a belabored excuse about his constant state of distraction, and how some Jew nabbed him on the street and he missed the train to Vilna, and then, not knowing about the one-day postponement, he went about his business, and neglected to catch the next available train, and so on. Mother held on to this letter for the rest of her married life and beyond, Exhibit A in her relentless campaign against Enoch.

Even in the new world, then, she continued to fight Father's battles, as she fought so many others, with her divide-and-conquer strategy, though she did proclaim an annual one-day truce, on February 14, which she discovered was celebrated as Valentine's Day, a day of universal love and courtship, for every year, besides sending Mother a dozen long-stemmed roses and a love letter, Father would take her out to Lindy's on a triple date with the Kupfeszmidts and Rosenfelds, whose wedding anniversaries almost coincided, and my parents would entertain their friends with the "Song of MashLeyb," a duet written by one of their friends, in honor of their wedding day in Vilna on the fourteenth of February, nineteen hundred and thirty.

12

May Day

Ruth may have been the family chronicler, but it was my brother, Ben, who first defied Mother's embargo against going back. The war was over, he insisted, and the past was not an occupied country. His remarkable series of trips abroad, it later emerged, were acts of reconnaissance, which would culminate in the boldest maneuver of all—aliyah, immigration to Israel—making him the first among us to harness the past to some imagined future, and then to fail.

The inaugural trip was to Baku, in the USSR, to visit his wife's relatives, where they met her young cousin, Sasha Wexler. Sasha was a passionate Zionist, something so unique in the early sixties that Ben smuggled out his poem, "I Am a Jew," and read it aloud to us in English translation at our next family seder. While in Moscow, Ben also managed to track down (through Mother's friends in Warsaw) the address of Ida Erik.

From the photographs that Ben brought back there was no way of knowing how apprehensive Ida had been about their meeting, or how reluctant to speak about Erik's arrest and death in a Soviet prison camp (the word Gulag not having entered our lexicon). Mother took one look at Ben's photographs, gave a distant smile, and promptly conjured up her circle of friends, dwarfed by the massive Vilna train station, who had come to see them off: Erik, Ida, and their year-and-a-half-old daughter Nellie. Erik was heading for Minsk, to assume a professorship in the Belorussian Academy of Sciences, something messianic for a Polish Jew to attain in the late 1920s, the Soviet Union itself being the locus of unimagined dreams.

"The Soviet Union is truly wondrous," Erik wrote back. "The sign that greets you in the central train station reads MINSK in Yiddish and Cyrillic letters, and Leybl would have much to contribute. But it's too rugged a place for Masha."

In the world according to Mother, cities, like people, occupied a fixed place on the moral compass. Each human abode carried a divine imprimatur. There was Beth El and there was Sodom, the fleshpots of Egypt and the lost Temple of Jerusalem. In a world gone mad, wracked by wantonness and destruction, there were also set aside a few cities of refuge.

Jewish Vilna and Soviet Minsk, I knew from an early age, occupied two opposite poles, the one representing loyalty and the other—betrayal. So when Max Erik packed up his library and boarded the train to Minsk with his wife and infant daughter, this could in no way be read as a smart, even courageous, career move. He had turned his back on Vilna. Never mind that in Vilna the best that this brilliant scholar could hope for was an untenured job teaching literature at the Jewish *Realgymnasium,* a junior college with a scientific and Yiddish curriculum, which the Polish Ministry of Education refused to accredit, while in Minsk, at the Belorussian Academy of Sciences, he would occupy a full professorship, sponsor academic research, and publish prodigiously. (Today his scholarly editions and critical essays are my bread and butter.) Erik had abandoned Vilna, his adopted Mother of Cities, and crossed to the Other Side. When thanks in no small measure to Erik's formidable talent, Minsk became the hotbed of Yiddish radical culture in the Soviet Union, it was the first to be purged, in 1937, Stalin serving as the rod of God's wrath.

All this, as usual, I was expected to piece together on my own. Mother's mind was still locked onto the scene at the Vilna train station, more for Ben's benefit than for mine, for how often was it that her firstborn deigned to pay a visit, his marriage to Louise having caused the onset of Mother's menopause, not to speak of the silliness of giving each of his three children names that started with the letter "J" instead of naming them after dead relatives, and more recently still, moving to the new Jewish suburb of Côte St Luc in order to become a member of Rabbi Hartman's synagogue, Tifereth Jerusalem, since when did a child of hers become so God-fearing that he needed to follow a rabbi? This wayward son clearly was in need of being reminded of his origins, and to seduce him the only way a mother could, she offered to sit down at the piano and play the Russian ballad that he so loved to hear her sing, but Ben had only stopped by to bring her the photographs, and could not stay even to eat a portion of compote, so she settled for my company instead, and sitting opposite me at the white enamel kitchen table began to describe how five months later, the same group of friends came to see her and my father head in the opposite direction, to the factory town of Krosno, known for its glass works, in the southeastern part of Poland.

It had been a long day, that fourteenth day of February, 1930, and Masha had done her own share of crying, especially when Leybl stood up defiantly at Grisha's house and said, "I drink a toast to the children of Fradl Matz!" The cords that had bound her tight were snapping one by one, and now, for the last time, she was surrounded by her best friends, Rivele, Pinkhes, Shmuel and Rivtshe Dreyer, Yoysef, Shloyme, Fima, and Sasha, and it was their turn to sing for her, the latest hit by Moyshe Broderzon, whose exuberant use of rhyme had made him the songwriter of choice for the Ararat, which had superseded Di Bande as her favorite Yiddish cabaret ensemble, to sing loudly, without fear, in the Polish city of Vilna—

> Cast your care away, keep your hope at bay—
> so long as there's still today.

It was a perfect choice, this song, part lyric, part anthem, a celebration of love, of the present moment, of the enduring power of song, and of that which bound them together:

> Do not grieve, brothers and sisters, each of you alone,
> Do not grieve, for longing is our common lot.
> Do not grieve, brothers and sisters, each of you alone,
> Do not grieve or yearn or worry for naught.

Was not the purpose of rehearsing this song, over a main course of sweet and sour meatballs on a bed of mashed potatoes, not merely to conjure up her so-called Circle of Friends, the envy of my friendless childhood, but also to conjure away her own guilt? Had she not transgressed in just the same way as Max Erik, by trading in Jewish Vilna for Krosno, with its dreary factory compound, a good forty-five-minute walk from the center of town, where there was no one to visit anyway and nothing much to do? Because that "desert of assimilation" generated no new songs, Masha would have to build on the existing repertoire. No time for singing duets. Leybl was rushing around in his lab coat all day long and was about to carry out a daring act of industrial espionage. Simply by watching the chief chemist mix the formula for the production of rubber, he was able to steal the trade secret, at which point the three silent partners from Sweden were sent packing and Leybl became part-owner and director of the whole Wudeta plant.

Krosno is where Mother, for her part, wasted no time trying to become Mother of the World. Then, in her seventh month of pregnancy, she contracted an inner-ear infection so severe the only thing that could save her was a trepanation, which could be performed only in Warsaw. "Everything would be great," Enoch reported to Rivele Amsterdam back in Vilna, "if Leybl didn't have such a sickly wife." Mother would never forgive him for that letter, either, poor Enoch.

It was touch and go. Before the operation they had to shave her head, traumatic in its own right, because it recalled her typhus and the loss of her beautiful braids. For two weeks her fever had raged, under the watchful eye of Vilna's leading GPs, Drs. Szabad and Yashpan. It was Yashpan who insisted on shaving her head, to alleviate the fever and to guard against lice. Masha cried bitterly. When Fradl noticed that her own hair was beginning to fall out, she called for Dr. Szabad, who replied, with his typical bedside manner, "Madame Welczer, you managed to preserve your own hair thus far in life. It won't hurt you to wear a wig"—a reference to her late husband, who, for all his much vaunted piety, had drawn the line when it came to his young wife's gorgeous locks. After Masha recovered and was rewarded with a green silk hat that covered her whole head, she still felt guilty about her mother's permanently thinned hair. So, lying in her hospital bed in Warsaw, Masha asked herself, "*Vi blaybt men lebn?* How will I survive this terrible ordeal?" And her answer was to instruct the small group of friends gathered at her bedside—among them Enoch and his current girl friend—to sing the one song that would give her courage—

> Do not grieve, brothers and sisters, each of you alone,
> Do not grieve, for longing is our common lot.
> Do not grieve, brothers and sisters, each of you alone,
> Do not grieve or yearn or worry for naught.

The birth was no less traumatic. Flitting in and out of consciousness, Mother remembers the Polish midwife shouting at the top of her lungs, "Come back, Pani Roskiesowa, come back!" And she did, unlike her good friend Krystyna, who died in childbirth a week later. It was a beautiful First of May when my brother was finally born, and all the workers of the Wudeta factory were gathered outside the window bearing spring flowers and singing Polish songs.

Tradition dictated that he be named Yisroel, after the late Yisroel Welczer, but the feelings toward her father were still conflicted, even though on his deathbed he had placed his hands upon her head and recited the priestly blessing. Rather than accept this love once and for all, Masha wished to make good the loss of her beloved brother Nyonya, Fradl's favorite, and so named her firstborn Binyomin. As Mother of the World, she refused to hire a wet nurse, and her milk was plentiful despite the operation and traumatic labor. If only Krystyna hadn't died, who as the eldest in a huge Catholic family would have shown her how to burp the baby so that little Benjamin would not throw up after every feeding, which made his parents that much more invested in his future—expectations that he made every effort to vindicate, calling out *Nartsizn!* Daffodils! from his perambulator at the age of three months (short for his favorite song, "Children, Buy My Daffodils"), and to anyone who asked, proudly proclaim, "*Jestem polskim Żydem,* I am a Polish Jew." He was a child of the new age aborning, my brother.

13

The Wooden Box

The journey to Moscow and Baku whetted my brother's appetite for more, and one day he returned from a solo trip to Paris with a whole set of photographs of Peppi. Who was Peppi? Peppi had been Ruth's governess in Czernowitz, hired to protect Mother's third child from the fate of the second, to free up evenings for Mother to perform her songs at the Masada Club, and late mornings to resume her clandestine correspondence with Seidman. Peppi had done such a splendid job raising a German-speaking *Frauline*— speaking German was de rigeur in a place like Czernowitz—that family folklore still preserved an aphorism from my sister, age three.

"Tante Elke," she is reputed to have instructed Elke Kieses (whoever she was), "women in front of other women have no need to feel embarrassed."

Somehow Ben discovered that Peppi was still alive, having survived the war in Paris, and had never married. Mother put on her reading glasses to take a closer look at the photograph and decided to bring Peppi over to be governess to Ruthie's younger son, thus freeing Ruth up to pursue her academic career, and Peppi was about to immigrate to French-speaking Quebec and rejoin our family when she was run over by a car and severely crippled.

Though I never set eyes on Peppi nor heard her speak German-accented French, an important relic was unearthed thanks to Ben's adventure. That night after Ben went home and Father had left for one of his interminable meetings at the Jewish People's School, Mother went upstairs, located her huge bundle of keys, opened the cedar closet, and took out a carved wooden box. Inside I could see packets of envelopes, the older ones wrapped in red ribbon, the newer ones in red rubber bands. Carefully untying a red ribbon, in a matter of seconds she found the envelope she was looking for and extracted from there lockets of delicate blond hair, which she placed in the palm of her right hand, a propitious moment, since she was now seated in the Library, formerly Ruthie's room, for me to sit down on the floor in front of her, a signal of my willingness to listen.

I knew without Mother telling me that the hair had belonged to Odele, her firstborn daughter, not to blond-haired Ruthie, her replacement. But did I know that Czernowitz was Father's big break? In 1934 he was invited to build the first rubber factory in northern Romania, and within a year Caurom (short for Cauchook Romania) was up and running. They lived on Urban Jarnik 4a, in the upper town, with the aforementioned Peppi as governess and a private chauffeur named Stefan, who drove the director to and from the factory compound. So smooth was the ride in the Packard, so luxurious the leather upholstered seats with their mahogany finish, that Leybl did not feel the cobblestones below. These creature comforts he did not take for granted, both because he still held fast to his democratic principles, and because his regimen of constant pain had already begun, the result of colitis that probably worsened in the wake of his mother's death. Leybl had been called to Odl's bedside to nurse her back to health and contracted diphtheria himself. Odele, then, was named after my paternal grandmother.

Whereas Krosno had been a sojourn in the desert, Czernowitz was for Mother a kind of homecoming. The huge neoclassical torsos on the façade of the Jewish Community Building reminded her of the two *bulvanes,* the half-naked torsos that stood guard at the entrance to her courtyard on Zawalna 28/30. Once again, the actors of Ararat could come to town, because Czernowitz boasted its own Yiddish theater, just down the block from the opera house. Now they could gather not around Grisha's table but around her own, with Father taking the pictures instead of Grisha, and with Zosia the Maid in full servant's attire standing at an appropriate remove from the foreign guests. Whereas in Krosno, the only showpiece was their dinner table made of inlaid wood, here they could patronize the arts, like Leon

Kopleman's painting of a war veteran on crutches, which Masha, however, found so revolting that she insisted on hiding it under the couch. Henceforth, all artistic initiatives were to be hers alone. Leybl put his foot down only once, when the writer Ber Horowitz came to town. He refused to allow this infamous womanizer to be their house guest, for fear he would seduce the chambermaid, cook, and Peppi, all on the same night. So Father insisted on putting him up in a hotel. Even so, Horowitz corralled Stefan into taking Masha and him for a drive into the Carpathian mountains, to locate the hut where, during the war, he had spent three deliriously happy months with a Ruthenian peasant girl. That six-hour trip cost Masha's newborn her morning feeding.

Ruth, as I said, was born to compensate for the loss of Odele, her sweetness and light a match for Benjamin's intensity. Six weeks after they arrived in Czernowitz—they had barely unpacked and bought new furniture—Odele got meningitis and "burned up" in five days' time. On the last day, she kept calling, Mama, Mama! from the nursery, but Mother refused to go in, for to do so would have meant to face her utter helplessness, not only a mother's inability to save her child but her own desperate insecurity since the day her own mother died, and under no circumstances was anyone to see how frightened she was. So Odele died alone in her nursery, and three months later Mother made her public debut (not counting the intimate gatherings at Grisha's house) as a singer of Yiddish songs at the yearly Hanukkah concert of the Masada Club.

Turns out, this carved wooden box was the lone survivor of a whole collection of such boxes that Mother started buying while still single and living in Poland, hers being the first generation of Jews that staked a claim to their country by touring the countryside, members of *Landkentenish*, modeled on the Know-the-Land-Movement of Poland, which placed a quota on Jewish membership and ignored historical sites of Jewish import. Not that Mother evinced much interest in local Jewish history. Why sign up for day trips to any of the surrounding shtetls, those quaint Yiddish-speaking market towns so redolent of Jewish folk life, when she could align herself instead with that branch of the movement championed by her brother Grisha who, in 1935, produced *Health Resorts and Tourism in Poland*, a landmark publication in the modern Yiddish orthography endorsed by sixteen of Poland's leading medical doctors and health specialists, and with Grisha in the lead,

Mother perfected the art of turning a hiking, skiing, or kayaking trip into a shopping expedition.

The finest boxes were made, of course, in the mountains of Zakopáne, 1898 meters above sea level, carved by local craftsmen in native dress, each box with its distinctive little key, and as her collection grew so too did the bunch of keys, which she kept on a ring made of fine silver, now linked to a sizeable bunch of utilitarian keys to her many closets and to the luggage locks for travel abroad, to Israel, France, Belgium, and Switzerland, but never back to Vilna, or to Krosno, or to Czernowitz, renamed Chernóvsti and implausibly annexed to Ukraine, where in 1999, on my own fact-finding mission, I saw the huge rubber factory that was built on the ruins of Caurom, found Ruth's birth certificate in the Kafkaesque Registry of Births and Deaths, walked by the Moorish-style synagogue (now a movie theater) that my parents never attended, and had myself photographed in front of Eliezer Steinbarg's brightly painted tomb, striking exactly the same pose as my parents had in the black-and-white photograph from 1936. But when I asked Mother over the phone where she had performed her songs, whether in the Yiddish theater or in the hall of the Jewish Community Building, she could no longer remember such an obscure detail, and this being our very last conversation, since she died three days later, "peacefully," as the death notice in the *Montreal Gazette* put it, I'll have to make an educated guess.

A Zionist club of male doctors, lawyers, engineers and their spouses (for women, under Romanian law, were forbidden from practicing a white-collar profession, so Mother once explained), probably met on the second floor of the Community Building, in an auditorium that could easily seat three hundred people. At Mother's shivah, Aunt Mandy told us that only two women performed at these holiday concerts: an overweight folksinger, who sang too loudly, and Masha, who accompanied herself at the piano. Of all the songs she had amassed in Vilna—her dowry, as it were—she could only perform the so-called *tishlider*, table-songs, and perhaps a "Bundist" song or two, for the lyric songs did not lend themselves to public performance in front of strangers. The whole point was to escape the pain, to overcome the fear, not to court despair.

Nor did she limit herself to recycling old songs. A new voice had been heard from Kraków, the voice of Mordecai Gebirtig, and his songs, brought to Czernowitz by Yoysef Kamien and Nadia Kareni of the Ararat, "spoke to her mood," for unlike the irreverent and sometimes raunchy repertoire of the Vilna years, these new songs spoke of child rearing, like the lullaby to "Yankele"; of young love, like the ever-popular "Reyzele"; of marrying off one's "Three Daughters"; of "The Golden Land" somewhere across the ocean; and, most apt, of Leybke dancing the Charleston. This jazzy song that celebrated the power of the Charleston to bridge the ideological divide between Zionists, Bundists, and members of the ultra-Orthodox Agudah, and which the singer addressed to her boyfriend named Leybke, became Mother's *cri de guerre.* What added to the thrill of performing it in public was her mother-in-law Odl's shocked reaction upon first hearing her sing the words,

> Embrace me, Leybke my dear,
> This you've learned, I know for sure.

How could anyone ascribe such immodest behavior to her youngest and most beloved son?

When Kamien and Kareni brought word to Gebirtig that there was a woman named Masha Roskes in Czernowitz who performed his songs like no one else, he sent her an autographed copy of *Mayne lider* (My Songs) and enclosed a manuscript of some unpublished songs. Singing from this songbook, all of whose lyrics she learned by heart, was for Masha "like praying from my mother's siddur."

So in Czernowitz, the place of her "second migration," she came to believe that she had reclaimed the songs that she never fully owned while still in Vilna, "the songs that we hadn't finished singing to the very end," and used the stage as her most inclusive forum, proclaiming, *"vu ikh gehér, zenen ale,* where I belong is where everyone belongs." Annushka, her sister, was also engaged in a rescue operation of sorts, recording Yiddish folk songs in faraway Kovno and even performing them on the Lithuanian airwaves. By sheer chance, Masha picked up a recorded concert of Annushka's singing on the radio during a brief visit to Krosno. But behind the scenes, other kinds of rescue operations were in the air, and on the morning of June 22, 1940 (according to my sister Ruth), when Masha and her two children caught the last train out of Czernowitz, to join Leybl who was in Bucharest desperately trying to secure exit visits for the family, there were three most precious things that in her haste she left behind on the table: a portrait of her father; her high school diploma made of parchment with her favorite photo of herself imprinted upon it, and Gebirtig's *Mayne lider*.

Can this be the final tableau? Having seen my mother in times of crisis, having witnessed how personal tragedy and the threat of danger confirmed her deepest conviction, that life is a battlefield, I can attest that the worse things were, the more calmly she behaved. So with everything else going on around her at Urban Jarnik 4a, Mother had the presence of mind to empty out all her carved wooden boxes and to lock each one of them. Whoever inherited the spoils, she said with a weary smile after replacing the lockets of delicate blond hair in the designated envelope and pulling herself out of the upholstered gray chair in Ruthie's room, would have to break open the locks. Of what use is a beautiful wooden box if its lock is broken?

14

The Last Seder Night

With so many stories, you'd think that the one that really mattered, the story of our exodus from Europe, would surely have been fished out of the sea of Mother's memory, an episode here, an insult there, especially as it happened over Passover, and our own seders in Montreal were so fraught with anxiety. Not for the reasons you would expect—not because of the need to clean the house top to bottom, removing all signs of leaven, every last incriminating crumb; not because of the special foods, though the timing of Xenia's *kneyd-lekh*, the traditional matzoh balls, generated plenty of tension between Mother, who ran the kitchen, and Father, who ran the seder—but on account of the guest list. It started with the poet Melekh Ravitch and his common-law wife, Rokhl Eisenberg, whom Mother detested, on account of her being a Communist. Mother must have intuited that the hatred was mutual. (In Ravitch's diary, now housed at the National and University Library in Jerusalem, the entries for 1952–66—the year of Mother's terrible falling out with Ravitch over something he let slip from his otherwise carefully guarded tongue— amply document the fierce arguments between Rokhl and Ravitch over whether or not to attend the Roskies family seder.) Not to mention Ravitch's vegetarian option, which added an unwanted burden to the menu of well-done roast beef and soggy asparagus, capped by Mrs. Gaon's chocolate hazelnut cake, so rich that no one could believe it was really *peysekhdik,* kosher for Passover. Add to this the presence of the Steiners, my brother's in-laws. Misha Steiner, of course, everyone loved, for if the seder went without a glitch, Mother would retire to the living room where she would accompany him in those sentimental Russian ballads that ended with Misha whistling like a Cossack. No, it was his wife, Ganuchka, a character out of Dickens, with her veils and tinted glasses and heavy eye makeup, whom Mother could not abide. But most of all, Mother resented the presence of gentiles at our seder, actually the one, Professor Harry Bracken, who could hardly be considered your average goy, since he taught philosophy at McGill. But even Harry was one goy too many. He was invited by my sister Ruthie, a token of her "revolt," her spitefulness. Bringing a gentile to the family seder was a warm-up act, so far as Mother was concerned, to the provocative things that Ruthie would say at the seder. When we got to the part about the five rabbis in Bnai Brak who retold the story of the Exodus all night long and my sister Eva revealed in the name of her home room teacher, Lerer Dunsky, that they were actually planning the Bar Kochba revolt against Rome, Ruthie countered this heroic reading of the passage with a contemporary fairy tale by Edmund Wilson, who imagined Elijah the Prophet showing up at a seder of Jewish intellectuals on the Upper West Side of Manhattan accompanied by the Messiah. Mightily irritated by such romantic garbage, my brother Ben burst out laughing. Thank God Ravitch succeeded in smoothing things over by proposing that the name Israel was an acronym for Isaac, Sarah, Rachel, Abraham, and Leah. I chimed in with the story about King David's ring with its all-purpose inscription, *gam zeh ya'avor,* "this too will pass," which I gladly repeated from one year to the next in the hope that Father would forget to call upon me when it came time to ask, *matzoh zo, 'al shum mah,* this matzoh, what does it signify? Father wanted an explanation in our own words and we never knew what object on the seder plate would be ours to expound upon or even what language we would have to do it in, because Harry Bracken, for all his knowledge of Judaism, did not speak a word of Yiddish. When we came to the Hebrew phrase *khayav odom,* each and every person must think of himself as if he personally had gone out of Egypt, Father would look up from the Haggadah to see if this year there was something new to offer. If we came up short or were getting signals from Mother to speed things up, the explosive singing of *"day-dayynenu"* not only proclaimed that God's manifold miracles would have been enough but also that by then we too had had enough and were anxious to move on to the *kneydlekh.*

At that critical mid-point in the seder, as Mother ladled out the steaming broth, which Ruthie and Eva distributed to everyone but Ravitch, Mother might have been reminded of how much she had hated schlepping all the way from Czernowitz to Bialystok for the Roskies Family seders, to Polna Street 20, where her eldest brother-in-law, Shiye, who was always busy opening and closing windows, inspecting his throat in the mirror, and taking his pulse at regular intervals, would arrive every year from Budapest with his feisty wife, Malcia, who made a bee-line to inspect the pantry and who so much wanted a girl that after Arthur was born she cut his hair in bangs until he was nine years old. Then there was Itshe, the one who rebelled against becoming a rabbi, who brought his haughty wife, Ida, to show off their beautiful daughters Hela and Sonia from Tarnow—Sonia, with the intellect and Judaic training worthy of a man, playing the favorite grandchild. Enoch finally settled down and married the Viennese-bred Mandy, whose shapely legs were the envy of all the other sisters-in-law. Only Perele, my father's sister, was out of the running. No one had a bad word to say about her. It was Perele, after all, who cared for Grandfather in the huge house with the floors painted a dark red where she too lived along with her family. It was they alone of all my uncles and aunts on the Roskies side who perished.

Picking up on Mother's story, Father might have reminded us that by then Grandfather Dovid was widowed and completely blind; still, he presided over the seder wearing a high white *yarmulke* and a white, silk-embroidered *kitl,* the huge dining room table set with fine china, crystal, and silver, all aglitter in the light of the chandelier. Had Benjamin and Ruthie not come down with scarlet fever, forcing our branch of the family to pull out, eight-year-old Benjamin would have stood up to recite the Four Questions at the last family seder in Bialystok. Instead, it was probably my cousin Rokhele, Perele's eldest daughter, who was given the honor. The only person who still remembers at this point in time is my Aunt Mandy, thanks to whom, and to my cousin Sonia's unpublished autobiography, I have pieced together the speech that my blind grandfather delivered, the very words that changed our life. Mother, had she been present, would have told the story differently, or might have found additional reasons not to tell it at all.

He had only to raise his hand to call for complete silence. "What would you say," he began, "about our getting out of Europe while there is still time?" He then proceeded to lay out a plan as fantastical as it was simple. The destination was Canada, "a good country in which to live and to build a textile factory." He believed that such a free country must have a liberal immigration policy as well, at least toward immigrants who came with the requisite skills and capital. For there was about to be a war in Europe, and Hitler was sure to attack Poland, as surely as he had just swallowed up the Sudetenland. Hungary and Romania would be next. There was no time to lose. Grandfather then tapped his hand on the table to restore order among his murmuring sons, the more so when he announced the precise order in which they were to set out: Itshe first, as the expert in textiles, along with the eldest grandson, Henry, who for all that he had eloped with his younger brother's governess knew a thing or two about the business and spoke some English. With that, the seder resumed, and later, to dispel the gloom, Dovid urged the assembled to bring their aged father over once they were settled and safe.

This happened in April 1939. By June, Itshe had left for Canada, promising to return for his wife and daughters within eight weeks. Shiye, calculating that wars broke out mainly in the fall, after the harvest, took his family vacationing in France and England, whereupon they boarded the *Queen Mary* bound for the New York World's Fair, which was Enoch and Mandy's destination, too. That left only Leybl of all Dovid's sons still on European soil when Hitler invaded Poland.

If Dovid had sent Itshe and Henry on ahead and two of the other brothers hadn't followed suit—*dayyenu.*

If two of the other brothers had followed suit and had failed to bring their wives and family across—*dayyenu.*

If they had brought their wives and family across and Itshe hadn't turned heaven and earth and spent every last penny of the family fortune to ransom *his* wife and two daughters—*dayyenu.*

If Itshe had turned heaven and earth and spent every last penny of the family fortune to ransom his wife and two daughters but no one succeeded in getting Dovid and Perele out of Bialystok—*dayyenu.*

No one succeeded in getting Dovid and Perele out of Bialystok and Leybl, my father, blamed himself for this failure.

Leybl, my father, blamed himself for this failure and Masha, my mother, blamed him for favoring his family at the expense of hers.

Compounding this failure, Leybl, my father, failed to reestablish himself in business in Canada and was forced to join up with his brothers.

But if Leybl, my father, hadn't been forced to join up with his brothers in Canada, we would not have moved to Outremont, where at least on Pesach we could invite whomsoever we wanted, deliberate over the Haggadah in our own way, and avoid retelling the story of the last family seder in Bialystok.

15

Lisbon

Who can forget the opening sequence of *Casablanca,* the greatest movie of all time, when a sonorous voiceover leads the viewer, whose knowledge of geography cannot be trusted, through the preferred escape route from Europe? Remember the point of embarkation to freedom? It was Lisbon, the same port city where my parents and two siblings ended up in the fateful summer of 1940.

Taken together, Mother's European photo albums, numbered 1–4, provide much more scope than Warner Bros. Wouldn't you want to see Ingrid Bergman as a brooding eleven-year-old? Her huge family circle? Her first outings with friends, her late-night parties? Ingrid Bergman in a flapper gown and a string of pearls, or better yet, in drag? Especially if you can't just order the video and replay that scene on the rainy tarmac where the lovers part forever, but you have to wait and wait for your mother to be in just the right frame of mind to remove the coveted albums from her main linen closet and offer to take you through them.

Any one of these photos can suddenly lift her spirits for the rest of the day, like the one of the impromptu concert staged by Grisha and her friends dressed in makeshift costumes. Erik, she laughs, tore up a copy of this very photo when he recognized the man with his arm draped around her shoulders as Pinkhes Kon, *mit di pukhke levoves,* that bleeding-heart Democrat.

But watch out for the family portrait in the Czernowitz album that Ben refused to pose for, in punishment wherefor Mother left for Vilna without him on her last trip home, in 1939. I know exactly what my brother must have felt, because she pulled the same trick on me after my son Aryeh was born and I made the mistake of displaying photos of the delivery at the dining room table. Shocked by the impropriety, Mother boycotted my lecture at the Jewish Public Library that evening.

Mother is happiest when holding an infant, this in stark contrast to the one and only icon of *her* mother, Fradl Matz, a miniature of the life-size portrait that hangs over our parents' bed. She wears a high lace collar, slightly open at the neck, with a tiara of her own light brown braids, and take a look, Fradl still has the high, tightly laced bosom of a bride, because she hired nursemaids for every one of her ten children, half of whom by that time had already been born.

When Father finally makes an appearance, near the end of Album 2, he is hard to recognize without his glasses, which he still took off when being photographed, or when he's wearing that black revolutionary-style shirt, or surrounded by other students, whether holding hands in a circle dance or in the chemistry lab in Stefan Batory, and also on account of the brooding, almost surly look in his eyes. Only after his engagement at the beginning of Album 3 does he start looking like himself, with black-rimmed glasses and the smile we know so well, equivocal, almost apologetic, as if to say: How does a boy like me come to hob-nob with these writers, artists, lawyers, and doctors? He stares at Grisha's camera with a weary smile, even on their official wedding day, when I expect to see some glint of triumph over the Black Canopy, the secret nuptials that he staged the day before (if there's any truth to that). Halfway into the Krosno Album there's another manly shot of him standing at the entrance to the Wudeta plant dressed in a white lab coat, and one more, in a tweed suit, as director of the Caurom rubber factory in Czernowitz. If only there were pictures taken when King Carol awarded him a medal for his services to the country.

How soon, I wonder, after posing in that tweed suit did Father say *"Ikh ken nit leyfn,* I'm incapable of running, *ikh ken nor forn,* I can only travel,"* which prompted him to set out for Bucharest alone, to secure the exit visas, issued on the condition of no return? Earlier that year, there had been talk of mother flying with the children to Annushka in Kovno. If I leave now, she said to Father, we'll never see each other again. And if only there were a photo of Boncescu, who was in love with Feygele, Aunt Malcia's married sister, the gentile who landed a job in the Romanian border patrol just in time to warn Mother of the Soviet advance so that when the phone call came, on the morning of June 22, 1940, Mother had exactly two hours to finish packing and make the last train out, but upon arrival in Bucharest twelve hours later, she began to hemorrhage from her illegal abortion at the hands of a quack doctor ("One false move, Madame Roskies, and you're dead"), and four-year-old Rutale came down with a stomach virus and despite news of the impending pogrom of which they were warned by a friendly Greek consul and despite something like a nervous breakdown Father made it across town to the market to get her an apple.

Each one of these episodes is a screenplay. Do I own the rights, I wonder, once this book is published?

The next episode belongs to my sister Ruth. Though Ruthie couldn't replace Odele in Mother's grieving heart, Ruthie, with her blond Aryan braids, palpably blond even in black-and-white, and with her impeccable German, became the family's greatest asset, as proven by the knitting basket given to her by the consul's wife that Ruth kept for thirty years; but what she remembers best, thanks to this photograph of the four of them posing in front of the Acropolis "in brilliant sunshine with our backs to the glory of Greece," quoting Ruthie now, are the smiling British soldiers in short khakis, who forced a few refugees to disembark at Gibraltar, and of course, the fateful last days in Lisbon.

There the visas are waiting, all right, as are four trans-Atlantic berths on the *New Hellas,* but when the ship lands in New York harbor they would need transit visas even for the few hours it would take for them and their luggage to be put on a train to Canada, and like something out of Sholem Aleichem, the American consul insists on an eye examination, in this case for Father, who was terribly near-sighted, and they are given the name of a local ophthalmologist who, it turns out, is away on vacation and won't return until after the ship has sailed. So the four of them trek back to the consulate where Father pleads his case in rudimentary English asking for the name of another specialist. The consul shakes his head. Then something snaps inside of Father, like that time he faced off the Polish Legionnaire on Great Pogulanka Street in Vilna, and he grabs the consul's hand and shouts:

"You are a crazy man! Will you throw away the lives of these children? Give me the name of another doctor or I will kill you!"

This is chronologically the first sentence in my story actually uttered in English.

Mother is sure that all is lost. Whatever else flashes through the consul's head at that moment, there is a spark of recognition, for after extricating himself from Father's grasp the American points to a photo of a blond-haired girl on his desk and says,

"Your daughter, Mr. Roskies, reminds me of my own. I'll issue the visas."

According to family lore, the *New Hellas* had lifted anchor on the second day of Rosh Hashanah, and according to *Strangers in Paradise,* the same boat also transported Franz Werfel and Heinrich Mann to safety. It would pull into New York harbor on the eve of Yom Kippur, and the trip would generate many happy tales, some with Greek words thrown in, and for dramatic closure, a German U-boat would sink the ship during its return voyage. But with the few days left to them on European soil my brother Ben seized the occasion to take a few pictures, one candid shot in particular, of my parents strolling in the middle of a cobblestone Lisbon street, with a brick building and other pedestrians in the background. And because Father is walking a half-step ahead of Mother, he looks exactly her height, and they are both smartly dressed, like a couple on their second honeymoon, and are wearing big smiles. But while Mother's head is tilted slightly to the left, as if bemused by some inner voice, Father looks straight ahead, as if eager to step right out of the photograph.

II

TALKING BACK

5

6

7

8

5

Studio photo of my uncle Grisha (Hirsh) Matz, Vilna 1920, soon after his return from Kharkov.

6

The official wedding day of Masha and Leybl Roskes, Vilna, February 14, 1930. Seated left to right are Grandmother Odl, the bride, and Aunt Perele, so short her legs don't touch the floor. My father completes the portrait, taken by Uncle Grisha. They are flanked by Aunt Nadianka's porcelain dolls.

7

Mother and her friends reenacting The Troki Concert in Grisha's house. Vilna, ca. 1925. Max Erik tore up a copy of this photo because Pinkhes Kon, "the bleeding-heart democrat" (on the far right), has his arm around Mother, who in turn has a cigarette dangling from her lips. Immediately to her right, wearing a party hat, is her half-brother Grisha (Hirsh) Matz.

8

Photo of the Yiddish cabaret actress Malvina Rappel, playing the role of a dervish, Poland, the 1920s.

16

Playing Solitaire

Just because I hated Field Day, Color War, team sports, and anything overtly competitive unless the game was already rigged, like Making Mommy Happy, didn't mean I couldn't compete against myself. All the boys in my class, for example, collected cards, and I learned how to trade and flip with the best of them. But the trading cards that really mattered to me were never in the running to begin with. Wild West, featuring the portraits and biographies of Jesse James, Wyatt Earp, Wild Bill Hickok, and Annie Oakley, were so life-like you could smell the sweat and horse shit, while most Jewish boys in Canada were enamored only of the Lone Ranger, Roy Rogers, and Dale Evans. My real favorites anyway were tiny-type reproductions from *The World,* the *New York Times,* and other period newspapers. There were three good reasons why I would never let on that I collected Front Pages: (1) at a quarter a pack, they were costlier than baseball cards and the fact that my parents spoiled me wasn't something to brag about; (2) square-shaped and not rectangular, they were very hard to flip; and (3) who but a brainy type was interested in yesterday's news? Front Pages reinforced my long-held belief that everything of importance happened before I was born.

After almost a year of collecting, I was only two shy of making up the whole 125-card set. Lately, however, I was finding a lot of doubles, as if the card manufacturer were deliberately testing my mettle. So one Saturday morning I decided, enough was enough. This was to be my last try, and to raise the stakes, I put only a quarter in my pocket. As I approached Kaplansky's on the corner of Bernard and McEachran, just up the block from the Adath Israel Congregation, which, if I didn't hurry, would soon be disgorging the Sternthals and other families I knew, an inner voice spoke to me and said: David, this time you will beat the odds. Since then I've heard this voice only once. But that's another story.

Mr. Kaplansky, with his thinning reddish hair and freckled face, greeted me as he always did, suspecting nothing. "One pack of Front Pages, please," I said, putting down the charmed quarter. Then, to hide the trembling of my hand, I turned my back to him and tore open the blue-and-yellow wrapper. Here's what I found inside, along with the square sheet of flour-coated bubble gum: STANLEY MEETS LIVINGSTON, STOCK MARKET CRASHES, AMELIA EARHART LOST AT SEA, ARCHDUKE FERDINAND ASSASSINATED, and HILLARY CLIMBS MT. EVEREST—mostly bad news by the world's standards but, for me, a winning hand. The first and fourth were my missing cards.

My passion for collecting had been long since spent when a boxed set of Yiddish cards arrived in the mail, from the "Wilner Farlag," c/o L. Ran, Jackson Heights, N.Y. Not cowboys, but a different Yiddish writer appeared on the face of each card, complete with his dates and major works. I did not know this L. Ran at the time, but one thing was certain: a card player he was not. He divided the deck into ten groups of ten, each representing another period of Yiddish literary history. There were Founders, Pathbreakers, Fighters and Rebels, Thinkers and Historians, categories that struck me as irredeemably unplayful. Trying my own game, I started to build a deck from those writers I had met in person.

It was easy to pick out the prophetic-looking H. Leivick (a "Pathbreaker"), but to include him would be cheating, because unlike my best friend, Khaskl, I missed seeing Leivick during his last visit to the Jewish Public Library, which left as the oldest candidate Avrom Reisen (born in 1876), one of the "Fighters and Rebels." Brief as his visit to our home had been, which Mother dominated with her stories about Zalmen, his brother (card 87, "Scholars of Yiddish"), I adopted Reisen to be my *zaydee,* the one I never had, and he returned the compliment by telling a Workmen's Circle audience back in New York that there was still hope for *mame-loshn* so long as there were Yiddish-speaking boys in the world like Dovidl Roskes.

Added to Reisen were Ravitch and Sutzkever ("The Generation of the Holocaust"), and Isaac Bashevis Singer, whom I had met just once, at my sister's. Four out of a hundred—a losing hand, I reckoned.

If you sorted the Front Pages by decade you could tell right away when it was most exciting to be alive: the Roaring Twenties; Ran's deck gave you nothing to go by but the writer's lifespan, which seemed to have begun for most of them in the 1880s, and maybe for a dozen in the 1890s. As for the rest, I stared in disbelief at what was left for me to sort on my green desk blotter. Counting Singer (born 1904) and Sutzkever (born 1913), there were only seven writers born in the twentieth century, and of that trifling number, three had already been murdered: Emanuel Ringelblum (born 1900) and Hirsh Glik (born 1922) by the Germans, and Itsik Feffer (born 1900) by the Soviets. That left four. Just four, another measly four in a deck of one hundred cards. Do the arithmetic. By the time I was fifty or sixty, there would be no cards left for me to play. Unless. Unless . . . the way to prolong the game was to become a Yiddish writer myself. Born in 1948, I alone could keep Yiddish alive into the next century. Maybe Reisen had been right after all.

If only I knew how to inflect the definite article! Despite fairly good grades and ten years of exemplary schooling, I still had no idea when to use *der, di, dos,* or *dem.* In my parents' huge library, which Eva and I had just finished reshelving the year before, there was, I now remembered, a copy of Weinreich's *College Yiddish,* where, on page 48, I found what I was looking for, the simplest and most revelatory sentence I had ever read: "In Yiddish every preposition requires the dative."

This straightforward rule, my eleventh commandment, had never been passed down, and no sooner did I resolve to obey it than I realized why. It meant relearning everything from scratch, memorizing the gender of every single Yiddish noun. There were easy ones to start with, like *di gas* and *di shul,* that somehow sounded feminine, but would anyone ever guess that *vayb,* the word for "wife," was neuter? Not the son of Litvak parents, who rarely used the neuter in the first place. Meanwhile, I made myself a set of flashcards to practice on and figured out a shortcut: When in doubt, use the diminutive. Can't remember the gender of *tish*? Just say: *dos tishl.* Similarly, *dos shteyndl, dos beymele, dos heyfl,* or *heyfele.* My spoken Yiddish suddenly turned very folksy and intimate.

That left the matter of spelling. Our school, founded way back when, had never adopted the Yiddish spelling championed by the YIVO and endorsed by Weinreich. I loved the modern look of these properly spelled words, especially the diacritical marks above and below certain letters, which not only distinguished an *ey* from an *ay,* a *beys* from a *veys* and a *pey* from a *fey,* but also, more important, distinguished Yiddish from Hebrew. Because our school had always insisted on the unbroken bond between them, in the zealousness of youth I was determined to fight for the liberation of Yiddish.

Armed with correct grammar and the modern orthography, I wrote my first full-length Yiddish story. Called "The International," it was about how, to break a deadlock, the United Nations voted to adopt Yiddish as the international language. Then I typed it up on my Hermes portable Hebrew typewriter, adding the diacritical marks by hand.

Where to submit this story in order to secure a place as a Yiddish writer? To Melekh Ravitch, of course, the memory bank of Yiddish culture. Ravitch could have won Ran's card game hands down, and then have played another two decks with all the writers he had known, whose correspondence he kept in meticulously ordered files, and whose biographies he was churning out, in volume after volume of his personal literary encyclopedia. I knew about these books because I had served as secretary of the Melekh Ravitch Book Committee, logging in the checks and helping to organize the celebration in his honor.

At that celebration I was chosen to read "My First Day in the Twentieth Century," a story about his public school in Galicia and how, at a New Year's assembly, he became so panic-stricken at the sight of so many priests that he blanked out on the number of years in a century, and all that stuck in his seven-year-old mind was the ominous Polish phrase, "*Swiat sie koncie, swiat sie koncie,* the world is coming to an end," which brought the house down.

So I dedicated "The International" to Melekh Ravitch, in honor of his seventieth birthday, and put it in the mail. To get a second opinion, I mailed another copy to Isaac Bashevis Singer. Perhaps he still remembered me from the ceremony at my sister's house where Singer, a Kohen, performed the ceremony of redeeming her firstborn son. Then I waited for my first reviews.

I didn't hear from Ravitch until he and Rokhl Eisenberg came for Friday night dinner, as per usual. He liked the story a lot, and asked me when this UN meeting took place and how I happened to be there. As for the dedication, he was very touched, but his birthday wasn't for another seven weeks. From Singer I received a short note, written in the antiquated spelling of the

New York Yiddish dailies. "I have read your essay 'The International,'" he wrote, "and have no doubt whatsoever that you possess the talent of a journalist, perhaps even of a creative writer." If Canada, he concluded, had produced a fifteen-year-old with such command of Yiddish, there was surely great hope for the language.

With a few tips from some of the major players, who seemed eager enough to help out, one could learn the rules. But to actually win this game of Yiddish solitaire would require an inner voice, stronger than the preachings of those who claimed to believe in the future of Yiddish without really believing in us; a voice mad enough to beat the odds, to go against History, against the armies of death, against God Himself, it seemed at times, so that Yiddish be put back on the table, into the cultural betting game, as a living contender.

As captain of my own team, and without signing up other players, this is what I ultimately scored: a nineteen-line bio (written by myself) in the last volume of the *Biographical Dictionary of Modern Yiddish Literature* (letters *kuf* to *taf*), a few pages after Melekh Ravitch and Leyzer Ran and not too far from Avrom Reisen.

17

The Soirée

Many were the professional writers who urged her to do it. *"Masha, far vos shraybt ir nit,"* they would ask, "Masha, why on earth don't you record your memoirs?"

Not just Melekh Ravitch (pen name of Zekharye Bergner), who showed the way by publishing *On Long Winter Nights,* the autobiography of his mother, Hinde Bergner, with generous financial support from *my* mother, money he then declined to use in full, but even Chaim Grade. You should have seen Grade's reaction when, in the course of innocent conversation— as if anything she said could be innocent—Mother fed him the following aphorism:

"Before she died, Fradl, my saintly mother said, *'Ale érevs zenen sheyn,* all the eves in life are beautiful: the eve of the Sabbath, of the festivals, the eve of an engagement. *Nor der erev toyt iz biter,* the eve of one's death—that alone is dreadful.'"

Grade, Mother must have known, was partial to maternal wisdom, for he jumped up from the living room couch and proclaimed: "Masha, if you don't commit this to writing, I will—in my very next novel!"

Well, he never did.

And neither did my mother, whose answer to these and other exhortations was always the same: I'm too busy.

Busy with what? With becoming a patroness of the Yiddish arts such as Montreal had never seen. According to legend, it was I. J. Segal, our most venerated poet, who put her up to it.

"*Ver, oyb nit Masha?*" she quoted him as saying. "Who else but Masha could mobilize the troops?"

When Ravitch went around collecting money to buy Yiddish typewriters for the Holocaust survivors overseas, Mother gave the first donation. Thanks to Chayele Grober, the Montreal Yiddish theater came back to life, and Mother lent a helping hand. No one sold more tickets to the opening production of Peretz's *Between Two Mountains* than she did, and through YITÉG, the Yiddish Theater Society, Mother befriended David Ellen and other young hopefuls beginning their careers on the stage, and met the painter Alexander Bercovitch, whom she commissioned to do an oil painting of my late grandfather, the one that now hangs to the left of my computer. Through Bercovitch she met the other painters, and bought from Gitta Caiserman a huge portrait of Chayele Grober to hang above the grand piano. By the time she rescued us from snobbish, self-hating, English-speaking, Westmount and relocated the family to an attached duplex on Pratt Avenue where we were surrounded by *ámkho*, our kind of Jews, who spoke Yiddish, everything was in place—poets, musicians, actors, painters—and Mother was ready to heed the call: *Ver, oyb nit Masha*?

My brother Ben's homemade records bear scratchy witness to some of those early gatherings, with Avrom Reisen and Vladimir Grossman, and my sister Ruth distinctly remembers sitting in the kitchen on Pratt Avenue with the poet Itzik Manger. This I find hard to believe, because already back in Czernowitz Manger had become a persona non grata to my parents. Manger, the native son who made good and was all the rage in Warsaw, was supposed to be feted at my parents' home in Czernowitz when Dr. Wischnitzer came running to tell Mother what had happened the night before in Manger's hotel room where Wischnitzer had spent an hour bandaging the head wounds of Rokhl Auerbach, Manger's common-law wife, whom he had beaten black and blue. Such a monster could not be received in civilized society. And in Montreal, hadn't Segal, who adored Manger, severed all ties with him on account of his crazy behavior? One thing I know for sure because I was there when it happened; Manger called Mother a *fete yidene*, a fat cow, over the telephone, and that cost him the last literary evening he might have had in our home. I met him at the Jewish Public Library instead, at a special meeting with Dora Wasserman's Montreal Yiddish Youth Theater, where he made fun of my anglicized accent in Yiddish.

I bet it wasn't until we moved to our thirteen-room house on Pagnuelo Avenue that Mother's soirées really took off. Remember her saying, "*Yidish muz geyn sheyn ongeton,* Yiddish must be properly attired"? Well, our new home on the hill was elegant by any standard. Just after you walked in, another set of French doors opened onto our carpeted living room that adjoined our dining room with the parquet floors, but counting the green swivel chair and the piano bench there was permanent seating for only ten adults, so it was my job to bring the folding chairs up from the finished basement where I kept my electric train. And although we were allowed to taste the party sandwiches, no one could go near Mrs. Gaon's apple strudel and chocolate hazelnut cake, which cost a fortune, and under no condition were we to reveal Mrs. Gaon's name to anyone, lest Dora Rosenfeld, who had pretensions to being a patroness of the arts on par with Mother, order the same cakes for her affairs. Dora might have spies everywhere.

Those who didn't arrive by carpool had to walk up the hill from the 29 trolley, later the 129 bus stop, on Côte Ste. Catherine. Rokhl and Ravitch always walked, probably on principle, because he was so mild-mannered and she was a Communist. But I felt bad if Lerer Dunsky didn't get a lift, seeing as how Lerer Wiseman, who might have picked him up, always managed to get one. ("Lerer" denotes a teacher in a Yiddish secular school. It is a term of honor.) One day, Lerer Chosid arrived by car, after he married that blonde *klavte* (bitch) who insisted on speaking only Hebrew. What did he see in her? What did she see in him? Mother said she just wanted a man in her bed, which was probably true, because when he got old, she dumped him in the Hospital of Hope and cut out of town.

How many Yiddish soirées did I sit through in the course of my life? Probably no more than a dozen. How many times since have I tried to replicate them? I've lost count. Yet they all coalesce into one in which I am fifteen years old, because I am always fifteen in my mind's eye, just starting to set my own course and knowing that I will never measure up.

From my regular spot underneath the piano I had no trouble identifying the speaker, even if I closed my eyes. Father, speaking from notes, gave the opening remarks.

"*Khósheve un libe fraynd,*" he said, "this evening is a very special one for Masha and me. As you all know, we came to this country twenty-three years ago in the very midst of the destruction of Jewish life in Eastern Europe, a life so full of spiritual richness and profundity, of physical charm and melodic harmony, yes, *melódisher zíngevdikeyt,* and above all, with so much warmth. The moment we arrived on these blessed shores we felt impelled not only to create a comfortable home for ourselves and our children but also an environment, *a svive,* in which to capture but a distant echo of that spiritual splendor. These literary gatherings are the modest fruit of our efforts. So today it gives me special pleasure to celebrate the publication of a book that tries, albeit not in Yiddish, to vivify our recent, severed, past, and to tell our story to the world at large. To be sure, Masha and I have a personal stake in this new work, yet we urge you, by all means, to speak your mind. The author is still young and has much to learn. And thank you for joining us on such a cold night."

It was Ravitch's turn to open the discussion, and Father's somewhat high-pitched Lithuanian Yiddish now gave way to Ravitch's Polish-Galician dialect, which still preserved something of its Viennese panache. As always, Ravitch had positive things to say, how much he appreciated the episodic quality of the book, which, he made so bold as to suggest, might have been inspired not only by Avrom Reisen's *Episodes from My Life* (Vilna, 1929) but also by his, Ravitch's, own *Storybook of My Life.*

"What a shame," said Ravitch with a smile in his voice, "that the novel was not written in Yiddish, because every chapter is just long enough for the Sunday supplement of the *Tog-morgn zhurnal.*" (Laughter.) "More likely," he continued, "with its heavy emphasis on sex, the *Forverts* would have picked it up."

"Ravitch!" Rokhl Eisenberg interrupted him. "He had no right to quote from your unpublished diary!"

"Rokhl, Rokhl, take it easy. Exhibitionism, like the sex scene in chapter 19, is an unfortunate debt to Yitskhok Bashevis, alias Warshawsky, alias I. B. Singer, who panders to the lowest instincts and is so much in vogue these days among readers of Yiddish literature in English translation. He wanted to get it published and thought there was no other way."

"Sex is the least of it," complained Rokhl Korn in her rasping voice, punctuated by her smoker's cough. "Where's the social landscape? The reader would hardly know that Jews were a minority in Vilna, less than thirty percent of the population. Granted, the courtyard on Zawalna 28/30 is a convenient, even necessary, novelistic lens, but why is there no mention, say, of Alexei, the hand operator who resided in the basement of the Matz Press and lived to be over a hundred? I have heard Masha tell of him on more than one occasion. He'd make a wonderful subject for a poem. Then to reduce the whole struggle between rich and poor to a few so-called Bundist songs! Jews did not exist in social isolation, even if Masha did, especially in Krosno, where there was a thriving Jewish community."

"Not only the social landscape!" cried Chava Rosenfarb, whose voice was easy to recognize as the only one from Lodz. "Rokhl, have you noticed that only two trees are mentioned in the whole book: chestnut trees in Vilna and a lone maple, the one standing outside on the front lawn?" (She forgot the linden trees in chapter 27.) "Where, I ask you, is the Vilíye River that courses through Vilna, or the mighty St. Lawrence that circles the island of Montreal? By listing street names, the author seems to think he's fulfilled his writerly obligation."

"I rather enjoyed the chapter about Jerusalem street names." This was the gentle voice of my teacher, Lerer Dunsky. "Someday I'd like to meet this Leyb Rochman, too. Sounds very charismatic."

Rosenfarb was not impressed. "A good talker, nothing more." I wondered if it wasn't Rochman's politics she really took issue with. "A writer, in my view, is duty-bound to transcend the solipsism of his characters."

"Solipsism," echoed Yehuda Elberg with his light Warsaw accent. "Solipsism is key to the character of Fradl Matz, an imperious, even vengeful, woman. See how seductive she is with her sons and cruel to her daughters, how she pits one child against the other, yet Fradl is depicted as all sweetness and light. If Fradl was such a saint, how could Masha have turned out the way she did?"

There was an awkward silence. I closed my eyes even tighter. Lerer Wiseman came to the rescue.

"*S'iz merkvirdik,*" he lectured the assembled guests in a Yiddish that betrayed no dialect, "how remarkable that although written in English, it reads like a work in translation. Is not the author trying to convey to an English reader the internal landscape of secular Yiddish culture? I faced the same problem when translating Dos Passos and Hemingway into Hebrew. It was a time when the spoken idiom had not yet penetrated into Hebrew

literary usage. The author, then, faced a daunting challenge: How to replicate a mosaic of languages—Yiddish, Hebrew, Russian, Polish, German—so
utterly foreign to the reader's ear? Look what Alfred Kazin does in *A Walker
in the City*. Of the two words in Hebrew and the one word in Yiddish that
Kazin throws in for local color, he manages to get all three of them wrong.
Bosher kosher, he reads the sign as saying! He doesn't know the difference between a *shin* and a *sin* in *boser*. He mixes up the nominative with the dative
and has his mother say *der heym* instead of *di heym*! Only the French dia-
logue with the druggist's wife, Mrs. Solovey, is rendered correctly, too correctly, if you ask me, for a fourteen-year-old from Brownsville. In the present work, I have to say that Masha comes out sounding more like a character
in Sholem Aleichem than in Tolstoy or Turgenev, where she rightly belongs."

"That's only in one chapter," said Lerer Dunsky, rushing to Sholem Aleichem's defense, "a rather clever device, if you ask me, to give the reader a
taste of what Masha's monologue really sounds like."

"Nothing new," said Sima Dawang, always the contrarian. "Mendele
does exactly the same thing in the fourteenth chapter of *Fishke der krumer*
(Fiskhe the Lame)."

"You're missing the whole point!" exclaimed Elberg. "For all the verbal
energy, verbal accuracy, Masha is not a representative type! How much Yiddish culture did she imbibe having lived with and through Yiddish for only
nine years of her life, from the death of her mother in 1921 until her move to
Krosno in 1930? How unfortunate that the author failed to flesh out his father, for Leybl came from the Yiddish heartland, even if his Jewish education was cut short by the war. What's more, Leybl is a character who lives in
the *real* world. History for him did not end in 1940."

"If my student will not take offense," said Lerer Dunsky, "rabbinic culture too is given short shrift. Judah Leib Matz, for all his merits, did not hail
from the Gaon's family."

"Masha's insecurity," said Rokhl Korn, picking up on her earlier line of
thought, "is the insecurity of a whole generation. Between her eighth and
sixteenth birthdays, Vilna changed hands seven times. From her cloistered
life one gets but a dim sense of these political upheavals."

"*Puste reyd*, what a pointless discussion, you'll forgive me." (Who's voice
was that?) "It is time for us to admit that the memoir is flawed at its core, no
matter who stands at the center of consciousness." (Could it be the voice of

Lerer Chosid? I never heard him speak at Mother's soirée before. Is this what happens to a man when a bleach-blonde woman jumps into his bed?) "The author is sadly deluded. Writing, he believes, is a redemptive act. How absurd to think that he can catalogue our lives, even going so far as to provide a genealogy, that through the death of a mother he can effectively mourn the end of a civilization. Don't get me wrong; the Kaddish is heartfelt, no doubt about it. But we don't need his Kaddish. And they, his English readers, they're not looking for dirges to recite while sitting on the floor. Yiddish for them is a laughing matter."

Mother clapped her hands, signaling the end of the formal program. On the way to the collation Lerer Wiseman took me aside and made me promise never to use the word *klavte* again. It made me sound like Philip Roth.

18

Cape Cod

Didn't we see? Rushing her like that almost made her forget to hide the jewelry in the cedar closet! *Sheyn voltn mir oysgezen,* think if we hadn't brought along the wet face cloth, it's already so hot and we have such a long road ahead, a good thing we're already past the Canadian-U.S. border, she worries that something might be wrong with our passports. When the border patrol looked at our luggage he refused to believe we were only going for two weeks. Are we comfortable back there? There's plenty of room at her feet for the extra pillow.

Too bad, I say to myself, we didn't take the Mercier Bridge to cross the border at Malone, catching a glimpse along the way of the giant teepee outside of Caughanauwake, but then it would have meant stopping at Huntingdon, tempting Father to drop by the factory for a bit, not just another delay, but another chance to be reminded of how Mother put her foot down when they came to Canada: Never again would she live in a factory town, that was something for Nat and Sally to do to save money, but four years in Krosno were enough, when the day's entertainment was a walk into town and back, every mother pushing her own perambulator, you had to prove to the other mothers how dedicated you were, and after Krystyna died in childbirth she hardly had anyone to talk to, and if we lived in Huntingdon, Dovidl might have fallen off the roof just like cousin David did and had a limp for the rest of his life, God forbid. So let's sing a Chastúshka, shall we?

> Po úlitsa khodíla
>
> bolsháya krokodíla
>
> aná, ana, golódnaya bilá!

What a relief to be singing so soon the song that never fails to raise our spirits, "A great big crocodile went walking on the street and she was ever-so-hungry." Guess what she read in the *Tog-morgn zhurnal* yesterday? That this was David Bergelson's favorite Russian song and he sang it to his granddaughter just before the Soviet secret police came to take him away.

The subject of Krosno comes up anyway, after we safely cross the border at Champlain, because Father compliments her on her new summer hat. What a laugh! It reminds her of Shmuel Dreyer's visit when he came to Krosno to check up on her after they were married. He comes in, Dreyer does, looks around, then compliments her on their dining room table made of inlaid wood. *Vos vúnderstu zikh?* Papale said after Dreyer went back to Vilna. "What else was there in our apartment to single out for praise?" Just so, her summer hat.

Who, indeed, were we the envy of? Certainly not of the other Roskies. See how Papale bends over backward not to provoke his brothers, or any of her sisters-in-law, may they live and be well. So as not "to tear their eyes open" he refuses to buy a new Oldsmobile, will drive this one into the ground. See if we don't have a flat tire as we had last summer. Why, we should have seen the Packard they had in Czernowitz! King Carol didn't own a finer car. Papale begrudged himself a chauffeured sedan, but as director of Caurom he had no choice, until they arrived in Lisbon and were waiting for a ship. There was a ship at anchor that could have taken them to Uruguay. Papele said no. If they were to quit Europe, it had to be for a country where all citizens were equal. Uruguay, he maintained, was like Romania, with a corrupt government, a tiny elite, and a peasantry still enslaved to the land. Papale was always such a democrat. Not like his brothers who walk all over him. That brother of his, a gangster without a revolver, took everything they had to ransom his wife and daughters, wouldn't let Binyomin in as a partner, had him banished to Lindsay instead, to get him out of the way, and cheated Papale and Ben out of their shares in Lion Rubber.

If only Daar hadn't died on the eve of their arrival to Canada, they could have gone into business with him and let the Roskies stew in their own juices. Time for a Bundist song. Papale, you sing the chorus.

> I am a little tailor of the best.
> *Chorus:* The best!
> I sew for the Rebbe a fur vest.
> *Chorus:* Fur vest!
> I take out all the cotton and pads
> and stuff it up with a bunch of old rags.
> *Yam-ba-ba-bam, yam-ba-ba-bam*
> *Yam-ba-ba-ba, yam ba-ba ba-a-m* . . .

Hearing Father sing is always a good sign. And Eva, in tenth grade already, tries to draw Father into a conversation with her knowledge of Canadian history. Isn't the Quebec peasantry, she asks, enslaved to the Church? A tiny English-speaking elite runs the banks and heavy industry, just as the Germans did in Romania. The Jews are stuck in the middle. Canada doesn't even have its own constitution. We're still subjects of the Queen! How can you compare them? comes Father's reply. The queen is but a figurehead. The government, industry, the universities, are open to all. You can grow up to be whatever you want, Evale, an historian, a novelist, even a politician. Only she can't become queen! I pipe in, giving Mother the opening she needs. Once, on Queen Elena's birthday, she tells us, it was decreed that all of Romania had to hang out purple banners. But there was a poor Jewish cobbler in Bucharest who couldn't afford to buy a swatch of purple, so he took his wife's purple bloomers and hung them out the window. Look! screamed the Iron Guards, the Zhids are making fun of us, and they started a terrible pogrom against all the Jews.

Their hatred of us, says Mother, was nothing compared to our own self-hatred. Now that she's onto her favorite subject, we know what's coming next, the song of the Jew-girls, the "Zhidúvkes":

> Those Jew-skirts are damn perverse,
> Gabbing all in Polish like Yiddish was a curse,
> So's nobody should ever tell
> They're a gaggle of Jew-gals.

They think Polish is the real parlez-vous,
Yiddish just a dumb cluck's howdy-do.
Peylish iz bay zey a shprakh
Yidish iz a miyese zakh.

These self-haters get what they deserve in the last stanza when their noses, the one thing they cannot camouflage, give them away, and that awful word *camouflage* is worse than any swear word. It reeks of rot, like that slimy phrase, *malheur de richesse,* which she reserves for the people she hates the most: the all rightniks in her midst, the nouveaux riches, by which she means the Jews of Westmount, the exclusive neighborhood to which they moved upon arrival in 1940, in order to be close to the other Roskies brothers. It was the last thing *she* wanted, but what choice did she have? Until the day she attended a wedding at the Shaar Hashomayim, a "temple" these Westmount Jews built themselves. It was the middle of the war and the news from Europe was very bad. Who even thought of making a fancy wedding in those days? As the bride starts walking down the aisle, the musicians strike up Mendelssohn's "Song Without Words," and Mother is shocked. Why that very melody? It had been set to words by Avrom Reisen after the playwright A. Vayter was killed in the pogrom of 1919, dragged out into the street by Polish Legionnaires and shot at point blank, right through his girlfriend who was trying to shield him with her body, and at the funeral all the youth of Vilna and all the leaders of the community walked behind the bier and sang:

The loveliest songs, the loveliest melody,
Do not sing them when fortune's rising,
Sing them during decline.
Ring out, sounds of glory,
Though the spring has passed us by,
Though the sun has long since set
Though the poet is dead.

How could they pollute this sacred hymn by using it for a mere wedding procession? Then and there Mother decided she had had enough. She was moving us to a Jewish neighborhood, away from all this hypocrisy. So on account of Mendelssohn's song we moved to Outremont, where she enrolled us in the Folkshule, and our Yiddish teachers raised us to be the proud Jews that we are.

She was right. Just outside of Lake George we have a flat tire, in the very spot where we were stopped for speeding the year before. What is it about Lake George? When will they ever finish building Interstate 87 so that we can pass it by? I bet it's our Quebec license plates that tip them off. It takes forever to get the tire changed, and from the sheepish way that Father takes out his wallet we know he must be paying through the nose. Either because her worst fears have already come true or because she always calms down when the going gets rough, Mother now abandons the *tishlider*, the Bundist songs, and the hymns. It is time for Aleksandr Vertinsky, the most popular song writer of their youth, and these songs she will sing in both Russian and Yiddish, in the translations nonpareil of that Vunderkind, Leyb Stotsky, who did them just for her, for Masha, the Nightingale, and to prove to all those assimilationists that the youth of Vilna sang in Yiddish not because they couldn't sing Russian but because Yiddish was their special pride, their world.

> Drink my girl, *Trink-zhe mayn meydele*, my sweet young thing, *tsartinke,*
>   *eydele,* This lousy wine, *ot dem farzoyertn vayn.*
> Both of us are destitute, both depressed,
> *Mir, fil gelitene, beyde farbiterte*
> Happiness is not given to us, *mir kenen gliklekh nit zayn.*

And what a world it was, full of lovers drinking their bitter wine, doomed to eternal unhappiness and scorn but always in such perfect rhyme.

Mother has worked her magic, just as she did on that March night in the Zakret forest, when she bewitched Father with another one of Stotsky's translations, from Polish, that time, not from Russian, because it is getting late and we must stop for the night at a motel, which father laughingly pronounces "motl," like the Yiddish name, and everything will have to come out of the trunk. And tomorrow, after a huge breakfast, we will set out again, Eva and I glued to opposite windows, locked in fierce competition after we hit the Mass Pike, over who can spot the most exotic license plates, she calling out Oklahoma, and I coming back at her with Mississippi. And this will keep us busy until we exit at Route 3 and begin our approach to the Cape. Here we will be met by the caravans of soldiers from some secret army base nearby, those handsome GIs who once liberated Paul Trepman from Bergen-Belsen, and to one of whom, with an amputated leg, cousin Sonia joyously gave up her virginity on the ship that brought her to America, the only civilian in a POW exchange, just before the end of the war. They wave to us from the back of their U.S. army trucks, yelling Quebec! Hey, Quebec! We are almost safe now, and for two weeks we will live in a wooden cottage with a shingled roof, and Mother will sit for hours in her forest of pine trees reading the Yiddish papers, the pines that must remind her of some other place, Druskienniki, perhaps, or the dacha in Ritro, the place where Father asked her to sew a button onto his coat because he had to visit his sick mother, and Beyliss, seeing them walking together, said, *Fun aykh vet zayn a sheyn porl,* you will make a beautiful couple someday, even though they weren't even going out yet and she was still involved with Seidman.

19

Double Feature

Montreal, like Vilna, was a Catholic city, full of churches, monasteries, nunneries, Jesuit schools built like Lukishki Prison, only on much greener grounds, with herds of black-robed nuns roaming the streets and a huge crucifix lighting up the sky atop Mount Royal. The most forbidden act was having an abortion. The second was going to the movies. Drive-ins were banned to protect Catholic youth from making out in the back seat of their jalopies and no one under the age of sixteen was admitted even to a regular movie theater, this to prevent another fire like the terrible fire of 1927 at the Palace Theatre, where untold numbers of children stampeded and perished in the flames. Exceptions were made only for *Snow White*, *Dumbo*, and Cecil B. DeMille's *The Ten Commandments*, provided you were chaperoned by an adult.

For all that, the hand of the Church did not reach to Huntingdon, a mostly English-speaking and Protestant town that lay very close to the U.S. border, or as far as Cape Cod where we vacationed. The Provincetown Art Cinema changed its foreign bill every other day, which meant that if we didn't go out for dinner with the Hoffmans we could see as many as three or four subtitled movies, in addition to the double bill at the Wellfleet Drive-In, a long and difficult Eugene O'Neill play at the Provincetown Playhouse and summer stock in Hyannis. The subtitled movies in Italian, French, Spanish, and Greek were especially important because from them I learned that the Church was not very popular in Europe, and some courageous film directors like Luis Buñuel had even made fun of the Last Supper. In *He Who Must Die,* the people of a Greek village crucified their local Jesus all over again. The love scenes in these movies were extremely forthright, which may explain why my parents shipped me off to Camp Massad, where I discovered to my horror that morning prayers were mandatory, a regime, as Mother would say, as bad as going to Catholic school. That summer I scribbled something really vulgar on the wall of our bunk. The shame of it was so great that my bunkmates were sworn to secrecy and have never to this day revealed the nature of my transgression and a year later God took pity on me and allowed the First Montreal International Film Festival to open at the Loew's where for one glorious week in June I could see five forbidden films every single day. It was worth blowing a whole year's allowance for the thrill of being the only high school kid among all those French speakers who looked as if they never went to church.

It was lonely, though, not having anyone to talk to about why the British working class had such a hard time falling and staying in love as compared to the French whom nothing, not even marriage, could stop, or why it was that only the Poles and Russians still made movies about the Second World War, until I was befriended by Henry Farkas, film reviewer for the Outremont High School *Rostrum.* On a Friday night in October, a few days after Simchas Torah, Henry invited me to join him for a screening of Leni Riefenstahl's *Olympiad Part I* at the McGill Film Society. No one checked our student IDs and the price of admission was only fifty cents. On the way home, Henry carried on about the dreamlike quality of the lighting, the split-second editing, the close-ups and strategic use of slow motion. I tried to discuss the glorification of the Nazis and how the Negro Jesse Owens stole the show. Mother explained to me that Henry was a self-hating Jew, like all the Communists who got kicked out of Hungary. After that, I went alone.

The Society ran three series: International Films, Silent Movies, and Cinema d'Essai. We swore by the same bible, the organizers and I, because by the time I went off to college they had screened almost half of the sixty-eight titles in Parker Tyler's *Classics of the Foreign Film* and we worshipped the same directors: Eisenstein, Lang, Renoir, and Bergman. I lived for those Friday nights. Going there alone, I never had to admit that the experimental films were completely beyond my comprehension. At first, watching

silent movies with live piano accompaniment made me laugh, until I understood how perfect they would be for seducing Esther.

Esther kept the largest file of my stories. These were neither the Yiddish
and English stories my second grade teachers had asked me to improvise in
class nor the action-adventures that I made up at Camp Massad, cousin
David and I vying for the bedtime slot, but rather the lascivious tales I produced in Mitlshul, Yiddish-Hebrew high school, each Tuesday and Thurs-
day afternoon, each one fitting on two sides of a sheet of lined paper folded
over in fours, with an illustrated title page and colophon. They were read by
all the girls before class was over, then given to Esther for safekeeping.

Stories I knew from listening to Mother were a powerful means of seduction, almost as potent as singing, but sitting in a darkened movie theater
was like going all the way. When Esther sat behind me in class, the only girl
not wearing tights underneath her short tunic, I could slide my right hand
up her legs, and after months of effort, when Lerer Chosid had his back
turned and there was no one else looking, she let me do it, touch her, there,
if only for the briefest instant, and I knew that everything now depended on
my finding the proper setting, not at her house, where her grandmother always shuffled into the living room just when I broke into a sweat.

I wouldn't waste a date on the International Series where the subtitles
demanded all my attention. The silent movies were easier to watch and had
the added advantage of bypassing the Quebec Board of Censors, who I
guess couldn't be bothered by one hundred students crammed into a science auditorium somewhere on the McGill campus. There were other sur-
prises. It turned out that the silent era lasted longer in the USSR than it did
elsewhere because Alexander Dovzhenko's *Earth,* the mimeographed fact
sheet confirmed, was made in 1930. In this movie I saw an Eastern Orthodox priest, the same kind of priest who refused to let Tevye see his daughter
Chava until after she was married, after which Tevye rebuffed her, spark-
ing a ferocious argument between Esther and Lerer Chosid in which he de-
fended Tevye's behavior, and the rest of the class sided with Tevye and Lerer
Chosid against Esther, who later got back at us by marrying a non-Jew
whose father was said to have been an officer in the Luftwaffe. The movie
also showed a horrific scene of a woman giving birth, and then something
even more amazing happened. Vassily's fiancée, learning of his death, tore
off all her clothes and ran about the hut completely naked, and although
this was the first time in my life I had seen a naked woman on screen, the

hysterical fiancée with her big breasts and black hairy triangle between her legs was the spitting image of Mother, who routinely walked around naked upstairs on Pagnuelo. So this is where Mother learned to do it. It was her Russian blood.

A month later the Society was showing *The Birth of a Nation,* the two-hour-and-forty-five-minute version. It was now or never. I sat in the aisle seat, Esther to my left. The place was packed. Either because the battle scenes were so riveting or because I was trying with my left hand that was draped over her shoulder, I made very little progress during the first hour and a half. Then I realized how much easier it would be with my right hand, with which indeed I was able to unbutton the top two buttons of her blouse. And at the precise moment when Elsie Stoneman, played to innocent perfection by Lillian Gish, was about to be raped by the venal Negro slave—as much as this sounds as though I were making it up, and my feminist friends will have my head for this—at the very moment before Elsie was rescued from a fate worse than death by the valiant Ku Klux Klan I slid my hand into Esther's bra and she whispered to me, "Don't be so gentle."

Late though it was when we got out, Esther insisted that I see her home, and when we got off the bus at Westbury I found out why. She wanted me to kiss her goodnight passionately the way it was done in the movies and I didn't have the wherewithal to say, Esther, I won't learn how to kiss a woman until I turn twenty, in Jerusalem, when Amit Rosenwasser will wait for her boyfriend to be off doing reserve duty in the Sinai to take me in hand.

On the number 129 bus going home I decided that the simplest way to get a woman to undress was to become a film director. So I wrote to Mother's friend in Warsaw, Regina Dreyer-Sfard, who taught at the Lodz Film Academy, asking about the course for directors. She wrote back in Yiddish that no one under the age of thirty was admitted, because you needed life experience before you could direct a film. How could I experience life if it was still so difficult getting into a regular movie theater?

20

Male Bonding

The Talmud says: Abba bar Kahana began his sermon with the passage, *You shall teach them to your children* (Deut. 11:19). If the father is insufficiently learned, he must hire a tutor for his son, as Joshua ben Peraḥyah said: Provide yourself with a teacher; get yourself a companion. How do we know this? Because it is written, *velimaddetem*, and you shall teach, which can also be read *ulemadetem*, and you shall study. The tutor must be the father's age; he may be older but no more than five years younger, as Rabban Gamliel said: Provide yourself with a teacher and avoid doubt. The tutor must be his pedagogue, guiding his ways and guarding him from sin, as Yose ben Yoḥanan of Jerusalem said: Whosoever gossips with women brings harm to himself, for he neglects the study of the Torah and will in the end inherit *Gehinnom*, as it is written (Num. 15:39), *Do not follow your own heart and your own eyes, by which you are seduced.*

Davar aḥer, here is something else: Abaye said in the name of Rabbi Hamnuna: A case concerning Montreal, the Jerusalem of Canada, with its many schools for Jewish children. In two schools the children studied without covering their heads, Heaven preserve us! boys and girls together, yet their teachers were very learned, having studied Torah across the seas. Such a teacher might study Torah with a child in private, as it is written: *You shall teach them to your children.*

Rabbi Simeon ben Lakish said: Let me bring a parable. To what may this [hiring of a private tutor] be likened? To a king who had four children, two boys and two girls. When the king was young, he fought many battles and was preoccupied with affairs of state. The schooling of his children he left to the queen. But in his old age, when he saw that the kingdom was secure, he remembered his parental duties. What did the king do? He resolved to instruct his youngest son in three things: swimming, self-defense, and books of wisdom. Swimming, because, as it is written of Pharaoh's daughter, *She named him Moses, explaining, "I drew him out of the water"* (Exod. 2:10). And the king appointed instructors to teach his son the sporting life. But the child was afraid of the water and outdoorsmanship made him sick. Self-defense, because once, while walking near a pagan temple, two *biryonim,* ruffians, had seized the prince, taken his wallet and given him a beating. But the son refused to learn the martial arts and kept his distance from pagan shrines. Books of wisdom: In the royal city there was an aged scribe who was also known as a philosopher. And the king said to his son: Let me hire this man to be your tutor and he will teach you self-defense, how to fight against ignorance and doubt, and how to swim in the Sea of Wisdom. And they studied together for five years, until the son went off to study on his own.

Rav Hunna and Rabbi Yirmiyah said in the name of Rabbi Simeon the son of Rabbi Yitshak: At the age of twelve a boy finds a *ben-gil,* a lifetime companion. At thirteen he finds himself a teacher. When Dovid-Hirsh was in school he had a classmate named Khaskl. Khaskl was fat and Dovid-Hirsh was skinny. Khaskl was poor and Dovid-Hirsh was rich. Khaskl lost his father at an early age and had no other siblings, and Dovid-Hirsh was the youngest of four. But whenever Khaskl was angry with his mother he locked himself in the toilet and read, and he read so much that he always knew when Dovid-Hirsh misquoted a source, which happened very often. And this is how they became the best of friends. They were riding together on a bus when Dovid-Hirsh turned to him and said, Will you be my friend? And Khaskl said yes.

Rabbi Ḥanina bar Pappa asked Rabbi Akiva: Why is it written (Deut. 11:14): *[The LORD] will grant the rain for your land in season, the early rain and the late,* and then (Deut. 11:16), *Take care not to be lured away to serve other gods and bow to them*? Because in the summer, a boy has many companions but few teachers. In the winter he has many teachers but fewer [real] companions. In the summer, a boy's observance is rather lax. In the winter it is monitored.

Rabbi Abbahu taught: It was said of Dovid-Hirsh that he once did a shameful thing during the summer. After assuming the age of mitzvot Dovid-Hirsh became rebellious and he refused to obey the commandment (Deut. 6:8) *And you shall bind them for a sign upon your hand and let them serve as a frontlet on your forehead.* The instructors were fearful of setting an example. If one young man were exempted from the *mitzvah* of *tefillin* [at morning prayers], what would stop the others from refusing as well? The Chief Instructor took serious counsel and found a solution, to rise before the whole encampment, say his prayers alone, then sit with Dovid-Hirsh and converse in the Holy Tongue six mornings a week while the rest of the encampment was at prayer. Only on the Sabbath, when *tefillin* are not worn, would Dovid-Hirsh join with the others, whether he prayed or not.

Rabbah bar Rav Hunna asked: What did the Chief Instructor discuss with him? One morning he expounded on the verse (Gen. 28:12) *Behold a ladder was set on the ground and its top reached to heaven.* On the top rung [he interpreted] stood the very pious, the lovers of the Land of Israel, and those who conversed freely in the Holy Tongue. On the next rung stood those less pious who were fluent in the Holy Tongue and were fervent in their love of Israel. Another rung down were those who had thrown off the yoke of the Torah, who spoke the Holy Tongue but haltingly yet never abandoned their love of the Land. And on the bottom rung stood the impious stammerers who yet loved the Land of Israel. Dovid-Hirsh considered the image of the ladder that the Chief Instructor had conjured up before him but could find no place for himself thereon, not even the bottom-most rung. And he lay down on his cot and cried all through the night.

How then did Dovid-Hirsh rouse himself from his despair?

He had a tutor named Reb Shimshen, whom the students called with great affection *Lerer* Dunsky. And Dovid-Hirsh wrote a missive full of anger and despair to his tutor and received back from him fifteen handwritten pages in beautiful script. And his teacher's words were as balm to his grieving soul, as it is written (Song of Songs 4:10–11), *Your ointments more fragrant than any spice! Sweetness drops from your lips.* There is no one ladder of perfection, he wrote in the letter, nor is there one fixed road. Jerusalem is the heart of the people Israel, but Sura and Pumbeditha, the great centers of Babylonian Jewry, are its mind, Seville and Granada are its torso, Vilna and

Lublin are its arms and legs. To climb from one rung to another demands fortitude, self-scrutiny, and intellectual rigor; not only in the summer of one's youth but all through life. When Dovid-Hirsh returned to the city he became Reb Shimshen's disciple.

Rabbi Ḥamma bar Ḥanina asked: How old was Reb Shimshen at the time? He was sixty-two years of age. And how old was the Chief Instructor? Eighteen or nineteen. As it is written (Ps. 126:5), *They who sow in tears shall reap with songs of joy.* See how the Chief Instructor sowed the seeds of doubt, while the tutor in the fullness of his years brought forth wisdom.

From whom did Reb Shimshen learn Talmud? From his grandfather, Hirshl the Miller. It is said that Hirshl built five mills in his lifetime, one more perfect than the next. Hirshl the Miller was very strict with his grandson. Once he caught him reading the First Book of Samuel. *Váyberishe zakhn,* he scoffed, reading fit only for women. At the age of eight, Hirshl hired a *gemore-melamed,* a Talmud teacher, for his grandson, a very gentle soul. When they completed the tractate the teacher gave little Reb Shimshen a kiss on his head. Seeing this, Hirshl protested: *Er hot im in gantsn avekgeharget,* he's killed the boy for good! The teacher later became a beggar. Downhill from the mill there was a shed where the peasants slept and, later, wandering madmen and beggars. Reb Shimshen also lived with two of his aunts and other relatives. He slept in his parents' bed.

When the Great War began, the Russians accused Hirshl of using the windmill to send messages to the Germans. They ordered the mill closed. But the mill was reopened whenever the wind was strong enough. When the Germans advanced, the Russians destroyed the mill and Hirshl began an illegal distillery. He was caught and fined by the Germans, but the Poles were even worse. They beat Reb Shimshen's brother within an inch of his life.

When Dovid-Hirsh sat next to Reb Shimshen, his tutor pointed out the place with his crooked forefinger, and Dovid-Hirsh imagined that the finger was misshapen not so much by age as by the amount of writing he must have done with it. When he repeated the lesson, Reb Shimshen walked around the study and corrected him from memory.

What was their order of study? Reb Shimshen followed the Lithuanian custom and began with the tractate Bava Metsia, the laws of lost and found objects, and he translated every phrase into Yiddish. But they did not follow the practice of Reb Tuvia, Reb Shimshen's teacher in the famous yeshiva of Eyshishok, of skipping all the lore and going straight to the law. What's more, Reb Shimshen consulted books like the Aramaic-English dictionary of Jastrow, for which one could be expelled from the yeshiva, let alone the other scholarly aids that he used as a matter of course, like Lieberman's *Tosefta kifshutah.* In Eyshishok the students read *Anna Karenina* while rocking back and forth and pretending to chant from the Talmud. Once Reb Shimshen had the privilege of meeting the world-renowned rabbi, the Ḥafetz Ḥayyim, the Light of our Exile, when he paid a visit to Eyshishok.

In the School of Rabbi Ishmael they asked: Was it not sinful of Reb Shimshen to tutor his disciple on Sabbath mornings? And did we not learn that he even tutored Talmud to a nun?

The Rabbis say: Reb Shimshen followed the Litvak method in all things. He rejected the display of extreme piety and scoffed at those who flaunted their sidecurls and fur-rimmed hats. Reb Shimshen did not attend synagogue with regularity and joined a congregation of Reconstructionists. What is that? A Jewish sect that does not pray to a supernatural God and does not require of men to put on *tefillin.* As for the nun, it is true. Dovid-Hirsh encountered her one Sabbath morning as he came for his lesson. But she studied no more than six weeks, some say because her Mother Superior forbade further lessons, and others say because she was confounded by the intricacies of the Talmud.

Until the age of seventy, Reb Shimshen taught children, youngsters, and adults every day of the week.

Until the age of seventy-five he taught *geshikhte* (Jewish history), Aggadah (rabbinic lore), and Tanakh (the Hebrew Bible).

By the age of eighty he finished publishing a critical edition of Midrash Rabbah on all the Five Scrolls (Song of Songs, Ruth, Lamentations, Ecclesiastes, Esther) with a parallel translation into Yiddish.

He educated thousands of students, as it is written, *You shall teach them to your children.* They were all his children. But he raised only one disciple, as it is written (Deut. 6:2), *So that you, your son, and your son's son may revere the LORD your God.*

In all the years they studied together, Dovid-Hirsh saw his teacher become angry only once. A new edition of the stories of I. L. Peretz was about to appear with Reb Shimshen's glossary of the learned phrases. One day a letter came from the publisher in Buenos Aires. The five volumes were to appear as *Khamisho khumshey Perets,* the Peretz Pentateuch. Woe is me! cried Reb Shimshen. Such sacrilege! I forbid them to use my glossary!

And another time, he berated Dovid-Hirsh for touching a female student in class, citing the verse (Num. 15:39) *Do not follow your own heart and your own eyes, by which you are seduced,* and he quoted Yose ben Yoḥanan of Jerusalem, who said: Whosoever gossips with women brings harm to himself, for he neglects the study of the Torah and will in the end inherit *Gehinnom.* Hell.

21

Études

Never again would I see Mother laugh so hard. The Montreal Yiddish Youth Theater under the direction of Dora Wasserman was putting on an evening of improvisations, billed as "Études," and the first act was in pantomime. Each young actor had to invent a role and stick with it, playing alongside but separate from four other members of the troupe. I chose Trotsky, as I imagined him haranguing the crowd in Red Square. Using a crate as my soap box, I began my "speech" deep in thought, haltingly, then gradually worked myself up to a frenzy. I knew it wasn't fair of me to upstage the other four actors, but I couldn't help it. The part Mother loved best was when I threw off my glasses and started waving them in the air, something, in fact, I had seen Rabbi Hartman do from the pulpit just two weeks before. As it happened, my hair was appropriately long for the role of Trotsky, because for a whole month already, we had been rehearsing *The Importance of Being Earnest* at Outremont High, which not only won me parole from Miss Cowper's Latin class and from chemistry with Mr. Gordon but also gave me a special dispensation to let my hair grow. I knew that Rona Altrows as Aunt Augusta would steal the show again, as she had the year before with her performance of Lady Macbeth—my wiry and always disheveled friend Rona, who alone could project our adolescent rage in iambic pentameter without even raising her voice. Talk about adolescent rage! At Northmount High, they were rehearsing *The Crucible,* with Esther playing Rebecca Nurse and the electrifying Anna Fuerstenberg in the role of Elizabeth Proctor. Directed by Marion André, these buxom girls in Puritan dresses really went berserk. The last time a woman on stage made me want to die was when Bryna Cytrynbaum played Hannah Senesh awaiting her execution at the hands of the Gestapo, and here in *The Crucible* there were so many of them about to be burned at the stake. But I hated this Marion André. At a screening of the 1937 *Dybbuk* at the YMHA, he made fun of the sets. So what if the tomb-stones were fake? The rest of the film was made on location, in the heart of prewar Poland, and the actors then perished in the war, or at least some of them did, and after I finished college I would make Yiddish films, maybe even before then, because Jules Dassin, who was married to Melina Mer-couri, had just bought up the screen rights to *The Last of the Just,* which he was planning to make entirely in Yiddish.

That's what I really wanted, to strike out on my own, to stop being graded for learning someone else's repertoire, to make things up as I went along; to play Trotsky, and get away with it. Didn't Mother's hysterical laughter prove that I could? The time had come to act.

"I am sixteen years old," the letter began, "and have been attending the pub-lic tribute in honour of the Jewish martyrs for the past five years. I must say that I found this year's memorial programme quite disappointing and in-comprehensible."

For the first time, the complainant went on, two keynote speakers were invited, the poet Jacob Glatstein to deliver the standard address in Yiddish and another to address the crowd in English, this, ostensibly, to attract a younger audience. As the youngest member of that audience could testify, however, the strategy had failed. The vast majority of those in attendance needed no English exhortation to remember their murdered kinsfolk.

"Dear David," came the swift reply from Leon Kronitz, chairman of the Eastern Region of the Canadian Jewish Congress, "You are probably right . . . that we were not successful in bringing out the non-Yiddish-speaking crowd to the tribute. But would you please tell us . . . what would *you* do to get them to attend?"

What would I do? I'll tell you what I would do! I would scrap the whole deadly format and start from scratch. What young person in his right mind would show up to hear not one lecture, but two? Who cared if some cantor turned the Memorial Prayer into an aria? That six fidgety schoolchildren were called upon to light six symbolic candles? The only real moment was when everyone stood up to sing the "Partisans' Hymn," but for that you didn't need to organize a mass rally, mimicking what the Nazis used to do. The way to get young people to attend was to have young people tell the story, act it out, shake things up. This was our story, after all. Who wrote the "Partisans' Hymn" if not Hirsh Glik? Born 1922. That made him all of twenty-one when he wrote it. How old was Mordecai Anielewicz, leader of the Warsaw ghetto uprising? Twenty-four. What I would do? Make Yiddish young again. Put Yiddish back where it belonged, in the mouths of people who could stand up and fight.

And I already knew who my partners-in-glory would be, for unbeknownst to Leon Kronitz, there was a movement afoot to bring Yiddish back, without a congress, without compromises. Unbeknownst to him, another letter had gone out, my first letter in Yiddish to someone my own age. His name was Gabby Trunk, from New York, and we had spent a Sunday afternoon together playing with my electric train, a large-gauge American Flyer with a double transformer, to which he, an ardent Bundist, was indifferent, and which I, truth be told, had also outgrown, but what made the afternoon so much fun was that we had decided to speak to each other in Yiddish. There was an awkward moment when the subject of his *lager* experience came up. If he was fifteen, how could he have been in a concentration camp? A DP camp, maybe? Other Bundists my age, like Khaskl, were also born on the Other Side. It turned out that Gabby meant Camp Hemshekh, the Bundist summer camp in New York state where Mother decided not to send me because Arthur Lermer's kids went there, but her word for camp was *zumer-kolonye*, a summer colony. When I got to know Gabby better we settled on the neutral-sounding *kemp*.

The night Gabby went back to New York I wrote him a letter. I suggested that we start our own Yiddish magazine. Gabby read my letter aloud to his Yiddish class at the Jewish Teacher's Seminary, and the teacher, Dr. Mordkhe Schaechter, urged them to take up the challenge. Twenty years before, he reminded them, Uriel Weinreich had founded and published *Yugntruf,* the Call of Youth, the perfect name for a magazine. And why stop there? *Yugntruf* could mobilize Yiddish-speaking youth all over the world. So the Yiddish class drafted a call to action, which was published by every Yiddish newspaper in the free world, and through the Camp Hemshekh network we organized branches in New York, Philadelphia, Montreal, and Toronto. An international Yiddish youth movement.

No sooner was *Yugntruf* called into being than we became a constituent member of the Montreal Jewish Youth Conference (MJYC, pronounced "Mike"), along with B'nai B'rith Youth (from assimilated homes), Pirchei Agudat Israel (from the yeshiva world), three branches of United Synagogue Youth (from Conservative synagogues), and, most important, the Zionist youth movements Betar, B'nai Akiva, D'ror, Habonim, Young Judea, and Hashomer Hatsa'ir. Anna Fuerstenberg belonged to Hashomer Hatsa'ir and in line with Marxist doctrine refrained from wearing make-up or a bra, and I was happy to be labeled a lackey of bourgeois capitalism so long as Anna took part in the first-ever commemoration of the Warsaw ghetto uprising organized, written, and performed by Jewish youth. (Montreal, like Vilna, was a hyper-organized community. Even when you rebelled, you ended up somewhere else on the political spectrum. And what a spectrum it was, if you could run away from the Lubavitch yeshiva and end up scrubbing floors on Friday nights in the *ken,* the "nest," of Hashomer Hatsa'ir.)

It proved a whole lot easier to improvise on stage than to work in committee. The script for our commemoration took an extra month to edit, because everyone's position had to be respected and we couldn't agree on how to balance Yiddish, Hebrew, and English. The Bundists and I insisted that as the language of the martyred, Yiddish deserved a special place. Anna countered that too much Yiddish would alienate the youth we were trying so hard to attract.

Running our local branch of Yugntruf was no less trying. What else was there to do besides send out letters? Fortunately, our founding conference was about to take place, on Sunday, August 30 in New York, and there were many important tasks to divvy up. The New York branch, inspired by Dr. Schaechter, made everyone a responsible Something, with an official title, a practice that Anna, when I bragged about it, mercilessly ridiculed. So I didn't tell her that as Chief Initiator I was appointed to chair the opening session and deliver the opening address.

We went down by train, the whole committee, Reyzl Fishman leading us in song. The way the other passengers looked at us reminded me of Mother's story about the summer colony outside of Kraków where she and the Vilna contingent won over the polonized students by singing in Yiddish. Now it was my turn.

We met in the main hall of the YIVO Institute on Fifth Avenue and 86th Street, seeing as it was Sunday, when the YIVO was normally closed. The Decorating Committee had put up a huge banner over the dais that read THE FIRST COMMANDMENT—TO SPEAK YIDDISH and another over the Founder's Gallery, which included portraits of Sigmund Freud and Albert Einstein, with a quotation from the poet Mani Leyb, AND JEWS SPEAK YIDDISH, AND YIDDISH IS SO BEAUTIFUL. I had just met Dr. Schaechter for the first time on Saturday and was shocked by the discrepancy between the fiery rhetoric of his articles and letters and his actual demeanor. He was short, balding and very East European–looking. Only the youth, however, would be permitted to speak or to vote and this time, for once, there were many more of us in the hall than bald heads and gray beards. We were all dressed up for the occasion, even Gabby.

Youth the vanguard of change was the theme of my opening address, delivered with great conviction, without consulting my 3×5 index cards, and without forgetting the elocution lessons drummed into me by the Yiddish word master, Hertz Grossbard, in private lessons, mind you, arranged by Mother as a way of supporting Grossbard who couldn't live off of performing one-man recitals of a high-literary repertoire. If I hadn't been embarrassed, I would have pulled off my glasses. This was followed by the reading of many reports, ending with fifteen-year-old Berl Pinchuk reporting on publications. Berl recommended that for lack of funds we publish the magazine in mimeographed form, at which point Mordecai (Matvey) Bernshteyn, representing the Jewish Socialist Alliance, jumped up and asked my permission to speak. Stepping up to the dais, Bernshteyn pledged before all the assembled, in the name of the older generation and the *milyonendike masn,* the millions of Jews, of Greater New York, to raise five hundred dollars on our behalf, so that *Yugntruf* could appear as a real, printed journal. He was great. It felt like a May Day rally back in Warsaw.

Just before we broke for lunch, Leybl Zilbershtrom, who was a good five years older than the rest of us, declaimed the "Yugntruf Call to Action," and whosoever was prepared to sign on, he explained, was entitled to vote in the afternoon's deliberations. The whole point of the conference was to ratify our constitution, which would make us a bona fide movement.

Never had I heard a Yiddish meeting conducted this way before. Armed with procedural terms that Dr. Schaechter had prepared beforehand on a typed sheet, the Constitution Committee presented the delegates with our

Ten Principles, each as a separate voting item, and even if I knew the Yiddish terms I couldn't have played a part, because unlike most of the delegates, I had never been a member of a student council and had never learned Robert's Rules of Order, so I had no idea what a friendly amendment was or when you were allowed to call a question, and I could see from the way that Matvey Bernshteyn was whispering into the ear of the historian Isaiah Trunk, Gabby's father, that the older European-born generation didn't have a clue either, and it was thanks to the logic and rigor of these rules that a fight didn't break out over Principle Number Nine, which called for barring any member "whose everyday behavior belied the basic principles of the movement," and only with great tact and perseverance did Tamar Miller, who chaired the afternoon session, get us to agree on a less punitive phrasing. Yugntruf was a school for civil obedience.

Two other things happened at the end of the day. First, Leybl Zilbershtrom came up to me and said, using the polite form of address, "*Fraynd Roskes,* it isn't becoming for you, as the founder of the movement, to speak Yiddish with an English accent. You should try practicing your *reysh* in front of a mirror." Second, Dr. Schaechter introduced me to the legendary Max Weinreich, a founder of the YIVO, who complimented me on my speech and then looked sternly at me with his one good eye and said, "*Fraynd Roskes, di yidish-forshung darf aykh hobn,* the field of Yiddish needs you." No matter that I was planning to become the youngest Yiddish film director in history, either by apprenticing under Jules Dassin or by going off to study cinematography in Łodz.

JEWSPEAK

9

10

11

12

9

Mother and son. Montreal, 1956. Photo by Hertz Grossbard taken in the sun porch of our "Dream House" on Pagnuelo Avenue.

10

The four siblings. Montreal, 1957. Eva and Ben on top, David and Ruth below. Photographed one Sunday morning by Benjamin Roskies with a self-timer in our parents' bedroom.

11

My parents, Leo and Masha Roskies, relaxing in Chequessett Village, Well-fleet, Massachusetts, ca. 1958. Photo by Benjamin Roskies.

12

Mother and son. From the last set of photographs taken at her grandson's wedding, Montreal, June 8, 1998. Omega Photographers.

22

Sutzkever's Address

In late May 1967, my mother picked up the phone in our home in Montreal to call the Yiddish poet Avrom Sutzkever in Tel Aviv. From the screaming headlines in the three Yiddish dailies to which we subscribed, she knew that UN Secretary General U Thant had capitulated to the demand of Egypt's president, Gamal Abdel Nasser, to pull the UN Emergency Force out of Sinai. The Egyptians and Syrians were now massing their troops for war on the borders of Israel, which for all intents and purposes had been abandoned to its fate by the rest of the world. Mother offered to wire funds so that Sutzkever, his wife, Freydke, and their daughter, Mirele, could fly to Canada for safety.

What Sutzkever said to her in reply I never learned. They had not been personally acquainted for very long; when my parents left Vilna in 1930, Sutzkever, born in 1913, was an adolescent, and their paths never crossed. But Mother's Montreal salon was a fixture of the Yiddish-speaking world, as well known as her financial benefactions to Yiddish poets and artists, and in the late 1950s they had at last met. My guess is that he now laughed at her offer to help him leave Israel.

By this time, in any case, I was in Boston, in my sophomore year at Brandeis, and I was a confirmed "exilic" Jew, a disciple of George Steiner and theoretically loyal to no land, beholden to no living place. For me, at the cosmopolitan age of nineteen, no one could carry the mantle of Jewish moral authority, teach the authentic traditions, or speak for the sacred dead unless born and trained in the Old World, as theologians like A. J. Heschel and Joseph Dov Soloveitchik, writers like Elie Wiesel and I. B. Singer, and scholars like Brandeis's Nahum Glatzer had been. Or, by way of radical contrast, Herbert Marcuse, another European teaching at Brandeis and then at the height of his influence.

Along with millions of my generation, I had joined in singing hymns of protest led by one of our own, Bob Dylan (né Zimmerman). When it came to seducing girls, however, I would resort to the Yiddish I learned at my mother's knee. My most effective song by far was "Beneath the Whiteness of Your Stars," written by Sutzkever and set to music in the Vilna ghetto during World War II. "Beneath the whiteness of your stars," I sang, "Stretch out toward me your white hand; / All my words are turned to tears—/ They long to rest within your hand." From Mother's stories, I knew that Yiddish songs invariably worked magic, though what happened next she never taught me.

But in May 1967, aspiring cosmopolitan or no, it was for the Jewish state that I felt most deeply. I was thus doubly disappointed by my parents' response when, in the first week of June, with war in the Middle East a certainty, I asked their permission to volunteer for the Israeli home front. I lacked all practical knowledge, they counseled. Furthermore, should the war end in Israel's favor, I was already scheduled to leave in two months' time to spend my junior year abroad in Jerusalem. They were right; I stayed put. Indeed, by the time I arrived in Israel in late summer, as part of the largest group of students—some three hundred strong—that the American Friends of the Hebrew University had ever flown over, a real army of kids exactly my age had routed the Arab foe and liberated the Old City of Jerusalem.

Besides taking university courses in Yiddish literature, I planned to tour the Yiddish landscape of Israel. I soon found everyone who was still alive. In the Tel Aviv phonebook alone, there were more Yiddish novelists, poets, essayists, journalists, actors, directors, thinkers, scholars, and communal leaders than I could possibly hope to meet in my ten months in the land. With telephone tokens in hand, I called up the whole Yiddish world, using the identical words of introduction: *"Kh'heys Dovid Roskes. A studént fun Kanáde. Kh'volt zeyer veln zikh bakenen mit aykh.* My name is David Roskies. I'm a student from Canada. I'd so much like to meet you."

At the top of my list were the living legends from Vilna who had known my parents during their student years. I started with Izye Rosenshein and moved on to Dr. Alexander Libo, the dashing captain of Vilna's Maccabi rowing team who had hidden out in an underground bunker and, alone among my parents' inner circle, survived the war and who was still, in his late seventies, practicing medicine in Tel Aviv. The patients I saw in his waiting room were as old as he, and spoke every European language, not Hebrew. Over a glass of Israeli grapefruit juice, a drink I was already hooked on, Izye Rosenshein told me that on the day in 1944 when the Red Army liberated Vilna, what was on Mrs. Libo's mind was whether her dress would still be considered stylish by the women above ground.

I had invested more, however, in meeting Mark Dvorzhetski, another famous physician from Vilna now living on Tel Aviv's Dizengoff Square. A heavy-set man with enormous black eyebrows, completely bald, he greeted me at the door of what looked to be a fancy apartment. Younger than Dr. Libo by about two decades, he spoke the same Vilna Yiddish as the Palevskys of New York and Tevke (Ted) Sheres of Montreal—former partisans, all—with a crisp, spicy diction.

I had brought him a copy of my play, "Hineni," which we had performed at Brandeis, both the English original and a Yiddish translation. In this drama about the failed 1943 uprising in the Vilna ghetto, the narrator's lines, I told Dr. Dvorzhetski, were taken verbatim from "Apologia of a Physician," an essay he had written in Paris soon after the end of the war. "Thoughts are disquieting and memories astir," he read, knitting his huge eyebrows. "Like my grandfathers before me, I rise at midnight to weep for the destruction of the Temple. It is the ancient ceremony of nocturnal reveries in a new form and with a new content." He was curious to know how I had portrayed Jacob Gens, the head of the *Judenrat,* and did I know that Zelig Kalmanovitsh's son, Shalom Luria, was living on a kibbutz? He asked nothing about me or about how a young, Canadian-born Jew had come to speak fluent Yiddish. I had sought him out to commune with his sorrow, and that was enough.

My secret goal while in Israel was to publish the tenth issue of our Yiddish student journal, *Yugntruf,* by drawing solely on local talent. For sharing such literary ambitions, there was only one address that mattered in the upscale northern part of Tel Aviv.

Rising slowly to the top floor, in an elevator car just big enough for three passengers, I pictured myself as a young provincial writer, Hebrew manuscript in hand, having made my way to Warsaw to appear at the doorstep of the great I. L. Peretz. Greeting me in a satin waistcoat, smoking a pipe or cigar, Peretz would determine whether my forte was lyric poetry or realistic sketches, and explain to me why it was necessary that I switch from Hebrew, read merely by thousands, to Yiddish, spoken by millions.

The voice I had heard on the intercom below could only have been Freydke's. This was the "F. Levitan" to whom the young Avrom Sutzkever had dedicated his poem "On My Wander Flute," when they first fell in love. "What is left to do in such an hour," he had written, "O, my world of a thousand colors,/ except/ to gather into the knapsack of the wind/ the red beauty/ and bring it home for evening bread." Never was a poet's wife more aptly named—Freydke, meaning joy. God, how youthful she still looked, with her jet-black hair!

The inside of the apartment was cool and calm, even in the midday heat, with Chagalls and other priceless paintings on every wall. Some were portraits of Sutzkever himself at various stations of his life, here with dark-rimmed glasses, there with a shock of brown hair atop a bohemian-blue turtleneck sweater. The coffee table was cluttered with books in Yiddish, Hebrew, Russian, Polish, French, and German. Sutzkever's desk faced us as we sat on the couch, offset by a wall of books and files crammed with manuscripts and literary correspondence. This was the desk, I imagined, where he had put the finishing touches on his great epic poem, *Geheymshtot*, "Secret City," about the last ten Jews living in the sewers beneath Vilna.

Sutzkever was dressed in a plaid short-sleeved shirt, open at the collar. His hair had thinned since I had seen him last, at an unforgettable Hanukkah gathering in Montreal in 1963. His forehead was now like adamant, harder than flint.

Why had I walked all the way in such heat?

"Vayl ver es kumt tsu aykh iz oyle-regl," I wanted to say, because coming here signifies an ascent. Instead I replied, referring to him in the honorific third person, "Does he not live on the top floor? If not higher?" Returning at that moment with a tall glass of grapefruit juice, Freydke laughed with pleasure at my allusion to Peretz's famous story about a saintly Hasidic rabbi.

140

"Ach," she said, "here, we live in an elevator building, but how sorely Abrasha misses his mailman!" When they had lived in a third-floor apartment elsewhere in Tel Aviv, said Sutzkever, taking her cue, the mailman would yell up to him from the street, in Yiddish: "Sutzkever! Leivick just sent you a manuscript!" "Sutzkever! Here's a large envelope from Opatoshu!"

It was my turn to laugh. I laughed at the invasion of a writer's privacy. I laughed at the chutzpah of a simple Jew hawking the great names of Yiddish literature for all the world to hear. I laughed at the subversiveness of an Israeli mailman yelling in Yiddish in the Hebrew city of Tel Aviv. In fact, Yiddish writers routinely used to provide their readers with their home address. But now that Peretz no longer lived at Jerozolimskie 83 and Hillel Zeitlin no longer held forth at Szliska 60 in Warsaw, Sutzkever's apartment was the one place where every Yiddish manuscript could still find a home. Someday too—God willing—a manuscript of mine.

Like the mailman, you never came to Sutzkever empty-handed. You had to bring news of the world, preferably news about the Yiddish world. But any Jewish or literary news would do as well. So I reported to Sutzkever about Professor Khone Shmeruk, his relative by marriage with whom I was studying in Jerusalem, and about what I was hearing from home. Yes, it was true that Mother and the poet Melekh Ravitch had had a falling-out. How did I know it was for real this time? Because she ordered the bronze bust of Ravitch removed from our living room and brought down to the basement. Had I attended the funeral in New York of Uriel Weinreich, whose brilliant career as a scholar of Yiddish linguistics had been cut short by leukemia? No, I had not. Nor had I even met this man, who was to have trained me in the field.

Surrounded by all these books and works of art, protected from the midday heat and the unbearable humidity, seated on the couch with Sutzkever to my left and Freydke to my right, I knew that to begin talking shop, to discuss the feasibility of publishing our student magazine in Israel, would be tantamount to sacrilege. The purpose of this exchange was to create a mood, to start things rolling, to set the stage for memories, while, lurking just beneath the surface of our words, hiding just beyond our circle of intimacy, were the forces of evil that only yesterday had destroyed Vilna, destroyed Yiddish, destroyed our people. Our mundane anecdotes—like Sutzkever's poetry—were holding the demons at bay.

Vilna, 1928. It was raining cats and dogs, and fifteen-year-old Abrasha Sutzkever was completely broke. What to do? The latest movie was playing at the Piccadilly across the street, and he was determined not to leave the spot until he had found money for a ticket. So he looked around and looked around, and there, swimming in the gutter, lay a whole zloty. With the change he bought himself an ice cream.

Vilna, 1943. Sutzkever and thirty-nine other captive Jews were working in the building of the Yiddish Scientific Institute—YIVO—outside the ghetto as part of the Paper Brigade, charged with locating cultural treasures for the Germans to loot. (The real treasures they hid from German eyes. But that's a story I learned much later.) He and Rokhl Krinsky were working as a team when he suddenly turned to her and said, "Rokhl, go over to that shelf and pull out the seventh volume of the *shas*"—the Talmud—"and I promise that you'll find American dollars hidden inside." Rokhl, a woman long under Sutzkever's spell, knew better than to ask questions. She went over to the shelf, pulled out the seventh volume—*Gittin* ("Divorce"), I think it was—flipped through the huge folio pages, and found . . . $125 in cash.

Skeptics will say that Sutzkever had hid the money there himself. I ask you: Where would a Yiddish poet in Nazi-occupied Poland procure such an unimaginable sum of foreign currency? So the only rational explanation is Sutzkever's clairvoyance. I neglected to ask, however, what they did with the money, whether they used it to buy food or arms. But did it matter?

In other stories, told against the backdrop of the ghetto, or of the partisan brigades, or of Moscow at the height of the postwar Stalinist terror, the figure of Sutzkever once again prevailed over certain death by his ability to read the hieroglyphics of history. In the shadow of the Kremlin, he had said to his wife: "Freydke, you'll see. Some day there won't be enough wagons in Moscow to cart all these statues of the Little Father [Stalin] into the dump." Freydke, with a big smile, nodded.

After the war, Sutzkever labored mightily to rescue the *sheymes*, the sacred fragments written by the dead. Back in Vilna, a young man named Avreml Golub ran up to him and whispered in his ear, "*Gebn tsi nit gebn?*" (That is, do I relinquish the archive of the Kovno ghetto to the NKVD, or not?) "*Nit gebn!*" proclaimed the oracle.

As I had not come to that first visit empty-handed, I did not leave empty-handed. In addition to the latest issue of *Di goldene keyt* (The Golden Chain), the Yiddish literary journal that Sutzkever had been editing since 1949, he presented me with the latest exquisitely published volume of his verse, inscribed with a doodled self-portrait suitable for framing. Could this be in return for Mother's financial largesse? Why *did* she—and not she alone—support him so lavishly? Was the glory of a poet not to be measured by his poetry alone? Ach, I had much to learn.

Six weeks later, on a mild September afternoon, Sutzkever had business to attend to downtown, at the Peretz publishing house on Allenby Street, and I was happy to tag along. What better opportunity to ask him whether he knew of anyone who could typeset our student journal, with all the requisite diacritical marks? To use his own typesetter, he explained as we boarded the bus, was out of the question; the press that published him was a co-operative, affiliated with Israel's labor federation, the Histadrut. Suddenly I heard the driver calling us to the front. Sutzkever had let me board ahead of him as—so I thought—an act of *noblesse oblige.* Actually, he had meant for me to pay his fare. Making light of my embarrassment, he promptly deposited the coins.

After all those years hobnobbing with writers and artists in my parents' home, I felt horribly inept. Far worse, I had failed the test of religious imagination, I who fancied myself exquisitely alive to manifestations of the sacred in the realm of the everyday. Sutzkever was no mere poet or raconteur. His poetry was scripture, his home a sanctuary, his person a priestly oracle. Pilgrims bring offerings, however modest, to a shrine. Was I any different?

But the afternoon was not yet over. His meeting was with the director of the publishing house, Shloyme Shvaytser, and Sutzkever's rage at this poor man, occasioned by two misprints in the latest book that had appeared under their joint imprimatur, was terrifying to behold. God help me if I were ever to be on the receiving end. But then, as if to make amends, both for the scene I had just witnessed and for my shameful performance on the bus, Sutzkever insisted that I come home with him for a light supper.

We ate in the living room, seated on the couch, and after drinking a *lekhayim,* he and Freydke proceeded to tell me the story I most wanted to hear.

It was the story of their miraculous 1944 airlift to freedom on the strength of his epic wartime poem "Kol Nidrei." The manuscript had been carried on foot all the way to Moscow by a partisan named Yurgis. After it was read aloud at a public gathering organized by the Jewish Anti-Fascist

143

Committee, the committee's two chairmen, the writer Peretz Markish and the actor-director Shlomo Mikhoels, arranged through Justas Paleckis, the prime-minister-in-exile of Soviet Lithuania, for a Red Army plane to be sent into the forests to rescue the great partisan-poet. By the skin of their teeth, Abrasha and Freydke made it to the landing strip on a frozen lake. In the cockpit of the tiny two-propeller machine there was room for only the pilot and the Yiddish poet; with Freydke strapped down in the fuselage, they made their narrow escape. Speaking of bodies—Freydke interrupted Sutzkever's recitation—I should know that the male partisans in the Narocz forest were utterly indifferent to the filth and lice; but every other day, in lieu of bathing, she alone would roll naked in the snow.

With his austere forehead and sorrowful eyes, I thought this was how the prophet Ezekiel must have appeared to the exiles in Babylonia: Ezekiel who, if this was what it took to save the word of God, would swallow a scroll inscribed with lamentations, dirges, and woes; Ezekiel, who, for the benefit of a remaining few believers, would rehearse and rehearse his transfiguring visions of punishment and salvation. How blessed I was to be numbered among them—and to have gained the confidence of Mrs. Ezekiel, too.

As Sutzkever ushered me out, I noticed hidden among the oil paintings a small tin plaque covered with rust. It read "Wilkomirski 14."

"Oh," I said, "that was your address in Shnípeshik, where you lived with your mother in an attic. There, on Hanukkah, as you were laboring over your first poem, she presented you with a fountain pen in a box of gopher wood."

"You know about that?" asked Sutzkever with evident delight.

"I heard you read a poem about it—in Montreal."

"Yes," he said after but a moment's pause. "That was a splendid evening."

Sitting on the crosstown bus on my way back to the Tel Aviv bus terminal, I relived the evening in my mind, and suddenly everything snapped into place.

In 1963 Sutzkever had been on an extended lecture tour in the United States and Canada, with several appearances in my hometown. One was a black-tie affair at the Ritz Carlton sponsored by the Histadrut, from which I had been spared. Now it was the first night of Hanukkah, and the Vilna compatriots had invited the Sutzkevers to an intimate gathering at Montreal's Jewish Public Library. My parents were out of town, and for some reason my sister Ruth, who had arranged his first visit to Montreal a few years earlier, was also unable to attend. So I represented the family.

Except for the fact that the tea and cake were served before the program instead of afterward—which enabled me to approach Sutzkever, hand him a copy of my first Yiddish story, "The International," and tell him about my literary plans—the evening proceeded as always. The usual suspects got up to speak: Mr. Grossman, high-pitched like a schoolmarm, and our elder statesman Melekh Ravitch, who praised the honored guest for having assumed moral responsibility for all of Yiddish literature. And then it was the turn of Mr. Rywusz.

Rywusz was no public speaker. In a heavy Russian accent, he began to reminisce about the ghetto, the round-ups, the killing field of Ponary where thirty-five thousand were murdered, the Night of the Yellow Passes, the work brigades, the capture of Itzik Wittenberg, commander of the ghetto's fighting forces, the failed uprising, the flight to the forest, the encirclement, the betrayals, the miraculous airlift of Abrasha and Freydke. When he finished, Freydke got up. She was supposed to thank the assembled guests; only she couldn't, because she started to cry. Whereupon a Mr. Mandelbaum jumped up from the audience and insisted on saying a few words, insisted on reliving a Hanukkah celebration in the forest twenty years earlier with Abrasha, Freydke, and Shmerke Kaczerginski, recalling exactly how they lit the candles—in memory of the ancient miracle in the Temple, or to honor the murdered millions? And what words were spoken, and how later, when they smelled the German bodies burning on all the highways, it was the smell of vengeance, the vengeance they had sworn to take when they formed the brigade named *Nekome*, revenge. Then he, too, burst out crying and his wife had to lead him out of the auditorium.

Sutzkever had the last word. Speaking as if in a trance, he went around the room, calling out the names of his old Vilna friends: Czuzhoj, the buddy he had gone swimming with on the far side of the Vilíye river; Tevke Sheres, "with a gaze so steadfast and purposeful that it could make the enemy wither away." Sutzkever looked suddenly younger. He had been summoned back, to a time before the slaughter, and now, heeding the summons, he proceeded to celebrate yet another first night of Hanukkah.

It was 1928, he said, he was fifteen (my age exactly), and his mother, wearing a rose-colored kerchief, walked into the freezing attic where they lived at Wilkomirski 14 in the Vilna suburb of Shnípeshik and found him writing a poem. The poem he would read to us now had been written in memory of that "first poem."

As the bus turned left onto Ibn Gabirol Street toward the terminal, I remembered how very disappointed I had been with Sutzkever that night for choosing this particular poem about his childhood, with its invocation of the gift of the pen in its gopher-wood box.

"What did you expect?" asked my friend Khaskl, an aspiring Yiddish poet himself, when I complained to him the next day, "that he would trot out 'The Teacher Mira' that we memorized as schoolchildren?" Gopher wood, Khaskl reminded me, was the wood that arks are built of, to survive the mounting floodwaters.

"He should have read one of the poems that he wrote while fighting with the partisans," I protested, "with the purple juice of berries instead of ink."

But Khaskl, I now understood, had been right. What rescued Sutzkever from death was not the military airlift but the muse, the muse who paid him visit after visit after visit, whether in the luminescent frost of a Vilna suburb or in the enervating heat of Tel Aviv. And to ensure that this heavenly letter-carrier would not get lost along the way, Sutzkever, perhaps on the day the Jews of Vilna were rounded up and marched into the ghetto, or perhaps afterward when there remained of them nothing but their ashes, had managed to salvage the tin plaque bearing his Shnípeshik address, so that decades later the muse might be led to meet her anointed poet in fiery embrace on the uppermost floor.

23

Leybl's Ark

Finding his street, Yordei Hasiráh, Those-Who-Landed-in-a-Lifeboat, was not easy—a narrow U-shaped street tucked away in the Katamon section of Jerusalem, where massive Arab villas stood out amidst overgrown gardens and gnarled trees. Jerusalem was no planned city, like Tel Aviv. Nor did I expect to be greeted at the gate by a barking dog, since most Yiddish writers I knew hated dogs.

"*Sheket, sheket!*" a voice called out from inside. Although it was just after five, Mr. Leybl Rochman appeared at the door in a maroon-colored bathrobe, his shock of black hair disheveled, as if I had caught him napping. Before I could invoke our phone conversation, he waved a handwritten manuscript in my face, another in a series of articles about the Six Day War, he explained, that had to be mailed out the next morning to the Yiddish daily *Forverts* in New York. Could I imagine such a thing? In the days before the outbreak of war, the Burial Society of Greater Tel Aviv had mobilized its gravediggers to be prepared to bury the thirty thousand corpses expected to be sent back from the front or to perish in their homes. Were it not for the miracle of Jewish arms, we would have been slaughtered all over again, our cemeteries filled to overflowing.

By now he had led me through the narrow kitchen—the main entrance to their subdivided part of the villa—and into the dining room, where, on the ceiling and on every wall, I saw them: a sea of torsos, naked arms, legs, buttocks, breasts, and multitudinous eyes, drawn in black charcoal, a few in red, orange, and yellow, writhing, birthing, dancing, beseeching, some with their faces hidden in their black tresses, others with huge skulls and penetrating stares, anatomically askew yet emphatically alive, erotic yet innocent, and into the next room as well, the salon, where a few goats insinuated themselves among the human figures, at once sacrificial and beneficent. Only figures underwater defied gravity like that, or swimmers in some celestial ether.

A story accompanied these murals, the work of his daughter Rivka, drawn when she was twelve, in the course of a few weeks. "I need a wall!" she had cried, as if possessed, so they moved heavy furniture at her command and let her transform the walls.

"In Zion," Mr. Rochman concluded with a flourish, "will the cadavers take on flesh and blood. Exactly as prophesied."

His name was Leybl, just like my father's, only unlike Father, unlike anyone I had ever met, Rochman didn't speak; he made oracular pronouncements.

They lacked all sense of pride, his people, Israel. The gentile nations spat in their face and the Jews called it rain. Centuries of self-deception had so dulled their senses that, even now, when friend and foe alike acknowledged the miracle of Israel reborn, precious few would hearken to the call. He didn't mean me, God forbid; he meant the others of my generation, who once again were willing to spill their blood for every conceivable cause save their own. Hadn't the young Jews of Poland, so smartly dressed in their blouses and neckerchiefs, marched through the streets with red banners on the First of May? Did their selflessness avail them any? When the enemy descended, they were the first to be sacrificed on the altar. Like all true prophets, I thought, Leybl's wrath was directed most fiercely against his own people.

My phone call had taken him by surprise, first because our mutual friend, the writer Yehuda Elberg from Montreal, had not informed him of my coming, and second because no one in those days ever heralded his arrival by calling. People just dropped in, anytime from 5:00 PM to midnight, for tea, compote, and homemade nut cake, baked by Esther, petite and black-haired, who would soon return from her expedition into town to buy Rivka a special set of pastels and later, at a time when most Jerusalemites were getting ready for bed, dinner would be served, the tiny kitchen dispensing food enough for all who found refuge there; and Morwa's barking would announce each new guest, who, depending on his place of origin, would move the conversation from Yiddish to Hebrew, occasionally to French, but never Polish, which language Esther read late into the night. She read Hemingway and Faulkner, Balzac and Proust, but deferred to Leybl on matters literary and metaphysical, as ultimately did everyone who sat down at the table, either the octagonal wooden table in the dining room or the glass-covered table in the salon that doubled as the master bedroom.

Different from the Sutzkevers, where the only young people I met were the children of other Yiddish poets—like Kaczerginski's daughter, who spoke a richly idiomatic Vilna Yiddish with a slight Spanish accent—the Rochman home was open to the young, especially since the break-up of Leybl's informal seminar in Yiddish poetry, attended by poets, professors and translators like Chana Faerstein and Robert Friend. Rochman missed the years spent one-on-one discussing Kafka and reading the tales of Reb Nahman of Bratslav with his disciple Aharon Appelfeld, now a married man trying hard to break into Hebrew literature.

They came from everywhere: the journalist Lenemann and the translator Litvin, Leybl's former buddies from Paris; any of his present colleagues from the New York *Forverts* who happened to be touring the country; the writers Yekhiel Hoffer, Moyshe Gross-Tsimerman, and the gnome-like artist Meyshele Bernstein who, four months later, would get up on the table and play his fiddle in honor of Shiye Rochman's bar mitzvah; in short, the whole Yiddish diaspora, from Melbourne and Johannesburg to Mexico City and Winnipeg, including, what surprised me, such figures of the Hebrew pantheon as Avraham Yaari and Shlomo Zemach. They sought out Rochman's company for the sole purpose of speaking in the mother tongue, as if, I imagined, Yiddish itself were a source of refuge, their surrogate home. These conversations, however, tended to focus on the past, on Minsk Mazowieck, once a city of six thousand Jews, from which Leybl and Esther were among a handful of survivors, about the Porisover Rebbe and his court in Warsaw, and about the Paris years, while what Rochman loved most were the streets of Jerusalem and the turbulent present.

So my appearance in the Rochman home came to be regarded as a portentous event, for indeed I eventually brought the others of my generation into Rochman's orbit, a veritable troop of young English-, Hebrew- and

Yiddish-speaking intellectuals, the whole of our Shomrei Ha'umah group from Montreal; various of my comrades-in-arms from *Yugntruf*; my classmate David Shulman from Iowa; each of my female friends in turn: Leah (formerly Lindsay) from Highland Park, Illinois, Tami from Kiryat Hayyim, Ilana from outside Philadelphia, and Dassi (short for Hadassah) from Brooklyn, for whose sake I shaved off my beard, the beard I had grown at Brandeis in order to play the role of a Vilna partisan.

Among them all, young and old, I occupied a privileged position.

I alone lived with the Rochmans for five days during the freak blizzard in February when the heating in our dorms broke down.

I alone sang solo at Shiye's bar mitzvah party.

I alone helped Leybl proofread the galleys of his novel *With Blind Steps Over the Earth,* about survivors who journey in several simultaneous time frames, a huge work that would have changed the face of Holocaust literature if only enough people had survived in the world who still read Yiddish.

To me alone, one midnight, Leybl read aloud the whole of Moyshe-Leyb Halpern's apocalyptic poem, "A Night," from the 1927 Warsaw edition of Halpern's *In New York,* which is how we discovered a textual variant that even Professor Shmeruk was unaware of. In that edition, Halpern's travesty of the Sermon on the Mount was severely censored—not the first time, Rochman assured me, that Jewish rage against the goyim was expunged, and not the last.

I alone kept Esther company while Leybl was busy editing the news for the Yiddish broadcasts at Kol Yisrael radio.

I alone routinely went walking with Leybl at all hours through Jerusalem Old and New.

I alone was in love with his daughter.

More accurately, perhaps, I was in love with the idea of being in love with her. Ever since I learned from Mother that Hannah Miransky, who had played the seventh Hanukkah candle to my sixth at the Hanukkah pageant of the Jewish People's School (then still located in the old part of Montreal), was the daughter of the Yiddish poet Peretz Miransky, from Vilna—information that availed me little, since the Miranskys moved to Toronto at the end of third grade—I was on the lookout for another literary match. Meeting Kaczerginski's daughter at the Sutzkevers was nothing but a wicked tease, for what were the odds that someone currently living with an Arab lover would ever be inspired to help me get to know Jerusalem?

Besides, the Rochman family itself was partially to blame. Esther took a keen interest in my on-again, off-again relations with the opposite sex, taking the opportunity one afternoon to remind me of other talented young men who had had domineering mothers, like Marcel Proust. If only, she laughed, Proust had gone slumming with the Yiddish writers and refugees in Paris after the war—that would have liberated him! Oh, the stories she could tell!

Likewise, Leybl's discourse was replete with pairing and procreation.

"*Shnayim shnayim,*" he once said to me in jest, describing his own household, "*zókhor unekeyve,* just as God commanded Noah, 'two of each, male and female.' " This he said in reference to his pets Morwa and Losza; the former named for the bitch with white spotted fur that had stood guard outside Szube's granary in the very last months of the war, after persistent rumors of hidden Jews and the sexual tensions between them and their saviors made hiding behind a partition and then in a deep pit at Auntie and Felek's farm no longer tenable; and the latter a tomcat comically named after Felek's cow; the two pets somehow coexisting at the Rochmans, just like the two parakeets that Esther kept in a cage, and—not to mention them in the same breath—like Rivka and her kid brother, Shiye, a budding violinist.

Entering a courtyard through a narrow, winding street in the Old City reminded Leybl of a birth canal, as drinking our afternoon tea together once prompted him to say, "Making love is like pouring boiling water over tea leaves. Just watch them open up."

"Leybl," I had the presence of mind to reply, "I'm still waiting for someone to *read* me the tea leaves."

And Rivka was to blame, for being so inaccessible.

On the one hand, of all the young people, to me alone she spoke in Yiddish, christening me, from the start, *Duvid-ersh,* as if the two of us had met on a commuter train between Minsk Mazowieck and Warsaw. Lacking Esther's dark sensuality, Rivkele's fifteen-year-old face was still childlike, almost cherubic, her curly hair almost as short as a boy's, yet the naked torsos that swam overhead were amply supplied with nipples, breasts, and wombs. The only anatomical detail lacking was male genitalia.

At the table, on the other hand, Rivka spoke little, limiting her role to that of Leybl's Hebrew articulator. Occasionally, she would draw out my female friends in conversation. That winter, a small sink was installed in her bedroom at considerable expense; thenceforth she would only have to emerge to attend to crass bodily functions.

One Friday afternoon in April, only Rivka was free to walk the dog, and I offered to accompany her. Morwa was delighted. Yet instead of heading for the park, Morwa led us in the opposite direction, first up Bilu and right on Mishmar Ha'am, National Guard Street, where, twenty years later, David Shulman would buy the house on the corner of Negba and raise a family, and on to Halamed-Heh, Street of the Thirty-Five, where the very next summer, that heady summer of '69, Abby miraculously appeared on the scene, as carefree and unselfconscious as her floppy blue hat and ultra-short yellow shift, and after the Friday night meal, which I cooked with too much garlic, as aphrodisiac, sometime after midnight, when Bernie and his current girlfriend, Sharona, had fallen asleep on the floor, I suddenly felt Abby's naked body next to mine. My memories of all these places were yet to happen. Meanwhile Morwa dragged us on to the Misgav Ladakh Lying-In Hospital at the corner of the Conquerors of Katamon, where Leah aka Lindsay, my first love, would almost hemorrhage to death during the last of her nine pregnancies, and continue to the end of the Street of the Thirty-Five where new apartment buildings were going up, that part of the street to be renamed in memory of Eli Cohen who would be hanged as a spy in Damascus in 1971. Morwa's destination was the rock-strewn and bramble-covered forest at the end of Hagedud Ha'ivri, The Jewish Legion, where our very own Rabbi Hartman would someday erect a temple of learning, named after his father, bringing Jews, Christians, and Muslims together to study the word of God, but because that day had not yet come, Morwa was finally allowed to run loose and I had the courage to say:

"Speak to me, Rivkele, speak to me about those figures you drew on the wall."

"What do you want to know, Duvid-ersh?"

"Are they alive or dead?"

"What do *you* think?"

"I think they're the dead."

She shook her head so quickly, it looked like an Israeli yes.

"What else?"

"Speak to me," I said, "and tell me who they are."

"Those whom God refused to admit into the ark."

"You can see them through the porthole?"

Again she shook her head.

"What are they saying?"

The question, I hoped, would prompt her to recite a Hebrew poem, one of her very intimate poems to God. Instead she turned to me and said:

"Sing me the song you sang at Shiye's bar mitzvah, you know, the one about the rivers running dry."

And so I did: my favorite Yiddish love song, the lament of a girl who misplayed her love and now feels like an empty ditch after the rivulets have run dry, like an empty jug that no one will come to replenish. This time, I sang on key.

Returning home, we took Emek Refa'im, Street of the Valley of the Ghosts.

24

Between Two Mountains

We were harrowing the soil at Packard Manse, an ecumenical retreat in Stoughton, Massachusetts. Joel was sweating profusely and there were grey rings under his eyes.

"Spiritual renewal," he said, "has always come from this neck of the woods. Walden Pond is not too far from here. And Brook Farm was located in West Roxbury."

"What was Brook Farm?" I asked, grateful to take a breather. I knew that Brandeis students would trek to Walden Pond with their marked-up copies of Thoreau.

"A socialist commune," Joel explained. "Hawthorne worked there for nine months and later alluded to it in *The Blithedale Romance*."

"So that's why we all ended up here," said Kathy, straightening her kerchief. "New England is the birthplace of utopian experiments."

I looked over at Shammai, the only one among us laboring in pleated trousers and a white shirt, his prominent nose and marvelously disheveled hair adding to the anomaly.

"Shammai," I spoke up, "reminds me of the first Zionist pioneers, the *halutzim*. Close your eyes, and we could be back on the banks of the Kinneret."

"May it be Thy will," pronounced Shammai with a flourish, "that the seeds we sow be blessed in equal measure."

"Amen," the three of us replied in unison.

The agricultural work we did in return for room and board. Rabbi Everett Gendler, who lived at Packard Manse and had just returned from a year in Mexico, cheerily offered hands-on instruction in the ancient art of tilling. There were forty of us now, two-and-a-half times larger than the founding group. In September we would move into our own quarters, a rambling three-story wooden house on College Avenue in Somerville, around the corner from Tufts. Our first task was to forge a community, so here we were spending five days together, tilling the New England soil, breaking bread, and trying to overcome our terrible self-consciousness.

George, from Gloversville, spent most of the time in bed, with a migraine. Evenings, Kenneth, who had stepped out of another world, played Baroque music on the piano accompanied by the serenely beautiful Elizabeth. The few bona fide couples—Art and Kathy, Barry and Janet, Ronny and Manya, Michael and Ruthie, Charles and Kathleen—appeared to have the easiest time of it. I sought out the single men who seemed most quiet, studious, and approachable. Both Joel and Mike later joined my circle when I offered to teach Yiddish songs.

The one person we had in common was Arthur Green. During my freshman year, Art had paid a visit to Brandeis, his alma mater, and we spoke to each other in Yiddish. He had been Professor Mikhl Astour's only Yiddish student. Once, Art had come late for class and found that the professor—a true Litvak—had already begun to lecture, in front of an empty classroom. So we had a good laugh, and I invited Art to attend the next Yugntruf conference in New York, where he was studying to become a Conservative rabbi. Five years later, the brightest and the best of his graduating class—including Art himself—were now the core faculty at Havurat Shalom Community Seminary, with official accreditation from the Commonwealth of Massachusetts. The Havurah was Art's soul-child, and the child had come of age.

My entry into the group came with none of the usual Sturm-und-Drang. I had no interest in Eastern religions and had never spent time in a monastery. I was not seeking a 4-D deferment from the U.S. Army. I had never taken mescaline. But I had returned from Israel with an overwhelming need to be part of something, something innovative and vital. Despite the wealth of new personal contacts, the romance of Yiddish was wearing off, even as the campaign to unify the Jews through a language was wearing me down. The search for a new language, equally threatened but destined to last, linked as it was to a time before time, had led me to Franklin Street in Cambridge, where a small group of young Jews were doing their own thing and where visitors were allowed to attend *Shabbes* morning services— it was during one of these visits that my father had joined in the circle dance, revealing a genetic link to Hasidic fervor that I had not known about. Nor did I take in that there was a two-track membership: those who were committed to study full-time at the Havurah, and those who were pursuing graduate studies elsewhere but whose presence in the Havurah was strongly desired. I belonged to the second group. Ironically, what made me so desirable was the world of Yiddish, my living connection to the East European Jewish past.

Hasidism was to be my main course of study, not the *Buber-mayses,* God forbid, those prepackaged fairy tales that Martin Buber had lifted out of the vast Hasidic library for the delectation of ultra-assimilated German Jews and their sympathizers, but the real thing. Because I could read Hebrew and had an undergraduate degree in Near Eastern and Judaic Studies, I was sent to the head of the class and, come September, I would be taking Art's advanced seminar. Meanwhile, July and August were free, so my first item of business upon returning to Jerusalem was to start building my own Hasidic library. Fortunately, I met Aharon Appelfeld during my first *Shabbes* meal at the Rochmans, and he offered to take me shopping in Meah Shearim. I was shocked by the squalor, by the bedraggled Hasidic figures defying the Mediterranean heat in their long black gabardines, difficult to reconcile with their festive, even regal, demeanor when we prayed and danced together at the Kotel, the Western Wall. Aharon and I were both bemused by the proclamations plastered on every filthy wall, which cried out against autopsies, the Israeli government, indecent attire, and television. He was equally bemused to see me emerge from Schreiber's Books carrying the heavy yoke of Hasidic Torah. This is what I bought: *Toldos Ya'akov Yosef,* the two-volume *Seyfer Baal Shem Tov, Degel Maḥane Efraim, No'am Elimeylekh,* and the *Kedushas Levi,* each sacred tome, Aharon explained to me, containing the Zaddik's name in its title. Then, just as we reached the corner of Meah Shearim and Strauss Streets, we bumped into Art and Kathy. I made a big display of my acquisitions and from the look in

Aharon's eye I could tell that I was behaving like an over-eager student kissing up to his professor. To save face, I invited them to the Rochman open house.

And that is how I brought the two mountains together.

Morwa barked happily as I ushered Art and Kathy in: Art—tall, rotund, and serious; Kathy—dark-eyed, small, wiry. Art was unperturbed by the hallucinatory murals. "Um, William Blake," he said, "they bear a powerful resemblance to Blake." He had a habit of pausing before each statement, and giving out a judicious "um," as though breathing in the idea, and now I heard him do the same thing in Hebrew, an amazingly fluent, learned yet modern Hebrew. Leybl, as usual, occupied the chair with armrests at the head of the octagonal table. Besides him and Esther, there was only one other guest, a certain Shimon, and from the maroon beret neatly folded into the shoulder flap of his khaki uniform you knew he belonged to an elite paratrooper unit. Leybl was drawing him out about a successful commando raid on the Isle of Green near the Suez Canal and Shimon answered him reluctantly, in monosyllables. Leybl was clearly buoyed by Shimon's presence.

"*U-va, vos ikh her!*" Leybl exclaimed, turning to me. "You would not believe what Shimon's been telling me! Your hair stands on end." Since my return, Leybl had begun to use the intimate form of *du,* as to a member of the family.

There was no need for preliminaries. Leybl knew very well who Art was, and I had done my best to prep the guests from America. The rest of us were soon left far behind, as Leybl and Art began to compare the two great schools of Hasidic thought: the Bratslaver and Elimeylekh of Lizhensk. I got more of what they were saying when the discussion turned to the proto-modernism of Nahman's style and the Bratslaver's affinity to Kafka. Leybl was in his element.

"Yes, we're living in miraculous times," he finally proclaimed. "And only here can the sparks of holiness be reunited."

"Um. The sparks can be rescued from their husks outside of the Land as well," Art demurred. "We have learned from Reb Nahman that the seeker's soul is born into a world of falsehood, and that is where the redemptive struggle must be waged."

"What are you talking about?" said Leybl, leaning forward in his chair. "Who was Reb Nahman, and how did he reveal himself? A direct descendant of the Baal Shem Tov, this spiritual giant did not assume the mantle of leadership until after he had trodden the soil of Israel."

"And returned immediately thereafter to the Ukraine," replied Art with a smile.

"The Land was desolate. It was during the Napoleonic Wars that he arrived here. Were Nahman alive today, he would be sitting on his wooden throne. Have you seen it? [Art nodded.] His chair in Uman was broken into fifty pieces and was painstakingly reassembled in Jerusalem by his disciples. It took them years, decades, to smuggle each piece out of Russia. Now the chair stands ready for its occupant, ready for the coming of the Messiah."

"As the supreme zaddik of his generation, Nahman believed that he was harbinger of the Messiah. His brief sojourn in the Land was but one small act in the messianic drama."

"And the rest of the drama?"

"Um. On his fateful voyage to the Land, there was a moment when everything seemed lost. Reb Nahman resolved that should he be sold as a slave and prevented from fulfilling the commandments, he would still be able to observe them in spirit. That is why so many of his heroes must live in disguise. His heroes, all of whom, as Yosef Weiss has taught, are aspects of himself, must join battle with idolatry. In order to do so they must even cut themselves off from their disciples, from prayer, from public observance."

"Ah, I know where all this is leading!" Leybl shouted. "To your so-called Havurah. You call yourselves the Fellowship, the Order of Holiness, and you, I suppose, are its Master of Prayer!"

"I am tone deaf, Mr. Rochman. When I *daven*, I sing off-key."

"This is true," I threw in, hoping to defuse Leybl's anger.

"You're like . . . ," Leybl continued, brushing my comment aside, "like grownups dressed in knickers. You've created an *alef-bet* movement for beginners, for children from assimilated homes, who have lived thus far in ignorance, knowing nothing about our culture, about the mighty flow of Jewish life. But you," he said, looking me straight in the eye, "you, Reb Avrom, and you, Duvid-ersh, you are Jews to the depths of your soul. You speak our languages. You cannot live other than as Jews. Why are you playing your childish games? You sit here, in Jerusalem, Jerusalem reunited, and talk of cutting yourselves off, about living in disguise. I'll tell you why. You're afraid to own up to your own Jewishness. Afraid to draw the necessary conclusions. Afraid to make the commitment at this historic juncture."

"Our *ḥavérim*, the members of our fellowship, are extremely diverse," replied Art, his voice much deeper than usual, "but together we seek to subordinate our personal needs—emotional, intellectual, professional—to the needs of the Spirit. Each of us is engaged in a search for holiness, each seeks his own unique path in the celebration of life's divinity. We have found—and founded—the Havurah in our search to realize the Kingdom of God in human affairs—"

"Holiness! The Kingdom of God!" Leybl cried. "Spiritual masturbation is more like it. Spilling your seed for naught. Total self-indulgence. Forgive me for speaking to you so harshly. We have shared words of Torah. I can see who you are. That is why I am in shock. You belong here with us. Where but in Israel can a Jew like yourself realize the Kingdom of God in human affairs?"

"Um. If the human spirit is to survive in our age, there will need to be many such attempts. The Havurah sees itself as part of a great effort to preserve human values and religious truths that are elsewhere being swept aside. Israel is another such effort."

"Are you out of your mind? How can you compare the two? Jerusalem and Somerville! You speak of holiness. Fancy yourselves heirs of the Essenes, I imagine, 'subordinating your personal needs to the needs of the Spirit.' *Lehavdil, lehavdil!* There's absolutely no comparison. The Essenes renounced everything—their families, their livelihoods, Jerusalem, the Temple. Walked around in animal skins. Lived for the moment when the Romans would quit this holy soil. Not in Boston did they sojourn but in the Judean desert. Holiness—holiness can be achieved when you are purified in suffering. Parents who, God forbid, lose their children, are put to the ultimate test, as it is written, '*bikerovay akadesh,* through those near to Me I show Myself holy,' and then it says, 'And Aaron was silent.'"

"Suffering can take many forms," said Art, and looked briefly, inexplicably, in Kathy's direction.

"Tell me something. Your subordination, your self-renunciation, is this not a matter of personal choice?"

"It is. Each *ḥavér* enters into a voluntary covenant."

"Oh, so very eloquent. So seductive. Shimon here, I bet he too would happily enter into a voluntary covenant, spend his days pouring over the *No'am Elimeylekh* and the *Kedushas Levi*. I bet Shimon's parents, survivors like me, orphans like me, would also love for their children to volunteer in the service of preserving universal human values. But Shimon has a country to defend, a people to defend, his parents to defend, and Shimon's parents cannot sleep at night, worrying about their son. They are not playing at voluntary covenant."

"We are not playing either."

"Compared to those around you, perhaps, who yearn for the fleshpots of Egypt. I do not doubt your idealism. But to what does it finally commit you? That is what I want to know. When does your 'covenant' become binding? When do you stop picking and choosing?"

"Um. We are committed, now and forever, to the spiritual renewal and meaningful religious survival of the Jewish people. To achieve this end, the particular path may change. The particular path *must* change. To remain potent and true, it must be subject to self-scrutiny and experimentation."

Shimon, who had remained silent throughout, stood up to take his leave, saying, "*Shalom, Mar Rochman*," then turned to Art and said, "I'll look you up some day, in Somerville. But where is that exactly? I've never heard of it before."

"Near a place called Walden Pond," said I.

"And Brook Farm," said Kathy.

25

Kotsk

After they had learned how to pray, Mother's generation learned to sing love songs, revolutionary hymns and satiric ditties. They were convinced that modernity was a one-way street. Then my generation came along. My generation decided to turn itself around. We apprenticed in the traditional arts.

If only—if only I could handle the silence.

To forswear the taste of meat was less of a problem at the Somerville Havurah, the kitchen having been strictly dedicated to a dairy and macrobiotic cuisine. Joel, the Californian, brought avocado into our lives and we, the grateful residents at "Uncle House," christened him Admiral Avocado. In due course, we learned the fine art of eating artichokes, most delectable in the dark, feasted on Portuguese wine and Irish bread, were guided by the perplexing recipes in *The Moosewood Cookbook*, and when the world was too much with us, found solace in homemade apple ice cream at Steve's or in pizza at Simeone's. The preparation and consumption of meals took up much of our time. To celebrate our first Sabbath, Ruthie taught the other women how to bake *ḥallah*, and in honor of Rosh Hashanah, Kathy resurrected her grandmother's gefilte fish recipe from Kansas City.

A separate staircase led from the communal kitchen up to my room on the second floor, a room with no door and one of the two naked windows broken. When he saw how greatly I feared for my privacy, Charles, Mender of the Sanctuary, fashioned me a new door, and Ruthie invited me over to sew my own purple burlap curtains on her sewing machine. Even with a strict rotation, however, and despite the words of Scripture that Danny posted in the bathroom, *Neki khapayim uvar-leyvav,* He who has clean hands and a pure heart (Psalms 24:4), the house was always filthy, and for months I went around like a madman turning off the lights to save on electricity. Finding reefers strewn about the classrooms, Shammai was convinced that we'd be busted, whereas I was on the lookout for the Health Department. Until the day I discovered notches on one of the door jambs, with the names Christopher, Penny, and Jamie written in different colored ink, identical to the notches attached to the names Eva and David in the pantry back home. A house, I decided, had a life of its own. And when the time came to paint the exterior, I cast my ballot for bright yellow, and volunteered for Section 7 ("includes the ceiling, posts, and railings of the porch, and the lattices under it, and the wall where the door is, but *not* the floors or the steps," which was Epi's assignment, Section 8). My handiwork was universally admired, as was the ceramic plaque from the Jerusalem Potter on Via Dolorosa that I had commissioned before leaving Israel, the Hebrew words "*Havurat Shalom*" executed and embellished with subtle craftsmanship as befitted a master whose father had fled Armenia during the massacre. The plaque greets all who enter the building from College Avenue to this very day. As for Krishna Cat, I barred him from entering my room on account of my allergies.

The silence. If only I could handle the silence. Silence at communal meals. Silence before, during, and after prayers.

The Havurah, I learned, had been conceived in silence. The founders had foundered on the shoals of the prayer book, its words and melodies rendered obsolete, if not obscene, through abuse and overuse, and oftentimes it happened that if no words of the liturgy held true, no words were offered up, for the cardinal rule was to respect where the leader of prayer was coming from. Providentially, there were some who by the second year had broken through the wall of silence to arrive at wondrous new modes of prayer even while the rest were still learning and stuttering. I who had studied the siddur with Lerer Dunsky for an hour every Friday morning in seventh grade, the only period we had to cover our heads, learned quickly how to *daven:* how to signal the place by chanting, what prayers could be set to song, how the psalms flowed into the blessings, flowed into the petitions, flowed into the angelic choir, flowed into the *Amidah*, the standing prayer, flowed into the reading of the Torah on a special pillow with a loose-fitting velvet coverlet. What the Hebrew—in part so obscure and in part so transparent—could possibly be saying to me I resolved to take on faith. If my betters had struggled and prevailed, then that was good enough.

My debut as the leader of prayer was to occur on Shmini Atzeres, the eighth day of Sukkos, and I asked Larry, who had been a year ahead of me at Brandeis and now sported a full beard, to give me a few pointers. But Larry, who loved to kibitz, failed to warn me that on the Three Pilgrimage Festivals—this being Sukkos—the liturgy was ordered differently from weekdays and the Sabbath and Art had to set me straight in mid-service, doing it in singsong, because we had learned from Reb Zalman Schachter that in order to "*Sing a new song to the Lord*" (Psalm 149), it was permissible, indeed, laudable, to chant the words in English whenever the spirit seized you, and although the translation in Philip Birnbaum's *Siddur Ha-Shalem* (according to the Sephardi Rite), hundreds of used copies of which we inherited from a defunct synagogue in Roxbury, was not designed for responsive readings, we chanted them nonetheless, substituting "You" for "Thee" and "Thou," so hearing Art interrupt me on page 333 by chanting the italicized words "*On festivals the Reader begins here*" did not cut me to the quick. I was by now so in love with the prayer book, enjoyed such intimacy with its every jot and tittle, that when my turn came again, on a regular *Shabbes* morning, I chanted Birnbaum's explanatory footnotes along with the recitation of the Psalms. Years later, I met Philip Birnbaum at a bus stop on Broadway in New York. An American-born Hebraist, he was very pleased to learn how much our Havurah enjoyed using his edition of the prayer book. I spared him the other details.

It was the silent meditation I could not abide.

We sat on cushions on the floor, Eastern style, men and women together, and those who needed to focus their spiritual energies—Steve Z., Janet, Art, Burt, Michael B., Noam, Richie—signaled as much by covering their heads in a *tallis* and rocking silently back and forth, but why were the rest of us required to sit in silence too, or feel that our movements or chanting disturbed the inner calm of those more mystically inclined? I resented their spiritual one-upmanship, the implication of a two-tiered devotion to God. Silence, I held, was not a Jewish form of self-expression.

Reb Zalman, of large and robust mien, our elder sage, the first to have been married and divorced, found ever-new ways to fill the silence. One *Shabbes* morning he dedicated to mime and movement. There was a body language to serve the Lord; different ways, he demonstrated, of *shockling*, of swaying back and forth for each Hasidic sect, one for Lubavitch, one for Ger, one for Karlin, and one for whomsoever; as there were different musical ways to serve the Lord, and seeing as today was also Bach's birthday, we listened to a Nonesuch recording of the Brandenburg Concertos for the remainder of the service.

Chief among Zalman's disciples was Richie. Unlike me, Richie waited until he was fully prepared, which coincided with the Havurah spending *Shabbes* at the Marist Retreat Center. "Please join me on the floor," he instructed us as we entered the large carpeted room from which the chairs had been removed. Then he led us in breathing exercises, with eyes closed, to relax our muscles that we might relax our mind. His was the only voice that spoke. Otherwise, you felt only the presence of the *ḥaver* to your right and to your left, the tips of whose fingers you were invited to touch. Together we escaped the regimen of secular clock-time and entered the temporal sphere of the Sabbath, a time beyond time, punctuated by the first allowable sounds: NE-NE-NE, SHA-SHA-SHA, MAH-MAH-MAH, NE-SHA-MAH, NE-SHA-MAH, the Hebrew word for "soul," and while we continued our mantra, still flat on our backs, Richie explained the *kavvanah*, the spiritual intention of the word, which grew so naturally, so inevitably, from our breathing, had its root in the word for breath, NE-SHI-MAH, so that with every breath that we drew we were singing the praises of the Lord, as we continued on to parse the psalm, KOL HA-NE-SHA-*MAH* TE-HAL-LEL *YAH*, every breath shall praise the lord, ha-le-lu-yah. One word, Richie taught us, if uttered with proper *kavvanah*, with every fiber of our inner being, was worth the whole liturgy, worth all of *Shabbes*.

There were those whose ability to handle silence was legendary. Steve Z. was invited to join the Havurah after he and Art had sat for half an hour staring at each other and smiling. That Cheshire Cat grin appeared whenever you looked back at Steve long enough. Steve Z. lived in the huge attic with Steve E., with whom he shared two other things: a capacity for marathon silences and a concubine, Rosie. I saw her once in the bathroom, and she did not look Jewish. Imagining what the three of them did together besides smoke dope would keep me up at night during those first six months when I awaited Abby's return from Israel. Steve Z. was a child of survivors and would have spoken Yiddish to me, if he had spoken at all. Steve E.'s story was very different. Estranged from his father, a free-wheeling, drug-using film producer who owned apartments in Greenwich Village, Tokyo, and Paris, Steve had more to do with his mother, voted one of America's five most successful businesswomen, but since joining the Havurah had moved closer to his grandfather, an Orthodox rabbi. Steve E. had been reborn as a Jew atop Cadillac Mountain in Maine. He had climbed the mountain in order to discover the still, small voice of God in the flowers and mosses. Alone up there and wearing nothing but his *tallis,* he observed the vegetation, studied the contrast between colors, between plant life and solid granite, earth and sky, until the *tallis* became the animal skin that primitive man had fashioned for self-protection, and Steve became Adam, whereupon he began to name the things he saw, and offered up a sacrifice of berries and herbs on a makeshift altar. Thenceforth Steve E. observed those commandments that had been passed down to him on his personal Sinai.

When we studied, we studied about the vagaries of speech, and these Hasidic teachings were anything but transparent. They could be learned only from a master, as Art had learned them from Abraham Joshua Heschel.

"All of your words each day are related to one another," Art translates from *Likkutei Yekarim,* the earliest known source on the teachings of the Besht, the Baal Shem Tov. "All of them are rooted in the first words that you speak." This means, according to Art, that special care must be taken to guard one's tongue in the morning, a time when *my* thoughts tend to stray in all the wrong directions, save for those mornings when I come downstairs to find our senior teachers engaged in kabbalistic study. The Besht warns next of the dire consequences of careless speech, of wasting words. "He who speaks without thinking," we read, "is likened to someone—Heaven forfend!—who spills his seed for naught, for amongst the human species, thought is the Whole Being, the human form, and the proof thereof is that when a man has an extraneous thought during the act of intercourse, he gives birth to an image, and even when he is not engrossed in thought during intercourse he cannot consummate the act. Thought is wisdom and speech can be likened to giving birth, for letters are being fashioned when one thinks, making thought a form of writing, so if a person does not think about what he is saying, he is wasting his seed, for speech is the essence of one's very being."

The Besht, it appeared, knew all about wet dreams, as he knew that extraneous thoughts could wreak havoc in bed. Art would gently prod us now to become a vessel for these words, to be vexed by their challenge, and the one who was most adept, who spoke personal words of truth without overstepping the bounds of intimacy, was Manya, Manya my study-partner, who was the first married woman I felt close to. Manya wouldn't laugh if I told her my problem. My problem wasn't the sexual explicitness of the imagery. My problem was making sense of the rambling, meandering style, the free associations from one arcane realm to another. Where had I heard this before? Why was it so strange and yet so familiar? Of course. The answer, I should have known, was obvious: the Baal Shem Tov's scribe was talking just like Mother! If you couldn't follow the logic, that was your problem. If you didn't know the shorthand, you obviously weren't yet initiated. Did I need to learn another secret language? Though Art made it seem well worth the effort, I never did.

At communal meals, which were supposed to be eaten in silence, there might have been an opening for Arnie and Larry, our inveterate kibitzers, or for Epi's joyous laughter, were it not that long ago our founders had attended summer camps where they came to hate, with a visceral hatred, the raucous singing and table-banging at meal time. No *tishlider* or Bundist songs at our table! The table was our altar, and any meal consumed by a holy fellowship demanded that one emulate the sanctity of the Temple. That is where Shammai came in. Shammai's family owned Goldenberger's Book Store on Eldridge Street on New York's Lower East Side, and Shammai himself had grown up listening to the original Hasidic LPs that carried warning labels not to play them on the Sabbath and Jewish holidays. Thanks to Shammai's intervention, the prolonged silences at meals were alleviated by the singing of *dveykes-niggúnim,* haunting melodies without words, repeated over and over again, or by other melancholy tunes set to the words of the liturgy.

And then there was the Joy of the Sabbath. While the meal following Kiddush was always eaten at home in small groups, the Third Sabbath Meal was eaten together, informally, late in the day. How better to get acquainted with all the new members than for them to share words of personal Torah. Kenneth spoke of his strong desire to take monastic vows after spending months in a Trappist monastery and of how he had taught himself Hebrew by translating the Book of Job. Joel described a mystical journey at the end of which he spoke in Hasidic Hebrew. It made no sense, but it was beautiful. After a prepared speech that I read aloud about my search for symbols in the East European Jewish past, Manya said, "I have the feeling that the person who presents us with his talk is actually offering us a feast, as we sit here at the table. A feast." And then we sang a *niggun*.

But where was the silence when we needed it most? When instead of silence we faced each other with hostility and resentment? Already by November, barely two months into the year, a breakaway group whom we called the Dortonians, because they mostly lived *dortn*, "over there," on the far side of Powderhouse Circle, were agitating for radical change. Some people, they protested, had their academic credentials while others did not; some would get them, others wouldn't. However their academic future played out, it did not depend on the success or failure of the Havurah. A high risk community is what the Dortonians demanded, meaning a place where people were willing to take chances, because their spiritual lives were at stake. It was impossible, Shammai admonished them, to "get into everyone's *kishkes*," which is to say, to achieve total openness and intimacy with every single member of the group. So every *haver* was invited to present a position paper and to meet for a solemn conclave.

No one would forget Jim's prophetic anger on that night. Precisely because he kept a low profile, dividing his time between chairing the Jewish Peace Fellowship, running an inner-city drop-in center for draft resisters, and studying Hebrew and basic Judaism at the Havurah; because he had made a clean break with his privileged past; because he was low-key and rarely smiled, Jim's every word carried moral suasion. "We're a sham community," he stated as a matter of fact, "a bunch of friends who started a seminary and invited other friends who wanted draft deferments so they could do their thing." Invoking the *brit*, the original Covenant that Art had drawn up in Year One of the Havurah, Jim argued that only a small but committed group could bind itself to the Divine Life, whether as individuals or as brothers and sisters in a community, a community that pooled its income and forswore materialism. Jim wanted to limit us to a core group of intense spiritualists. "The super-Jew life," he read from his prepared statement, "seems to me to be very difficult without a whole community of super-Jews. Particularly in the conflict between Jewish and other ambitions—and this for me is a real conflict, not a cliché—the support of a core community is probably a necessity if being a Jew is to win out."

The solution was to create a small group within the larger one, of people like Jim who wanted a total immersion program, staffed by the "credentialed" members, like Joel and Michael S. To foster the building of community, one evening a week was spent around the fireplace, just hanging out. Those who had studied for the rabbinate at the Jewish Theological Seminary of America told of its stultifying and emasculating regimen. It sounded pretty rough: how so-and-so routinely humiliated his students, how so-and-so slobbered all over himself in the cafeteria, how so-and-so stuttered. (When I got to the Seminary six years later, it wasn't hard to match the parody to the person.) Others told of their acid trips, taken, to be sure, far from communal property. Art's experiences with LSD, ascribed to one "Itzik Lodzer" in the pages of *Response Magazine,* were already an underground classic.

"Tell us about your Shavuos retreat!" someone called out to Ronny, who, with his wild dark hair and huge moustache, moved, after some hesitation, to the middle of the circle. The celebrants, he began with a nervous laugh, were himself and Manya, Kenneth and Lizzy, and Shammai. They were staying in a cabin right on the Massachusetts-Vermont border, the cabin in one state, the outhouse in the other. This, he explained, was important for the story. Shammai, preoccupied with the problem of evil, was in a very bad way, so his friends decided to enact his rebirth by forming a human womb, then swaddled him in a *tallis* when he emerged "reborn," from the birth canal. Once the acid really took effect they began to see the fiery, winged creatures described by the prophet Ezekiel. "All well and good," the same voice interrupted, "but where did the acid come from?" Ronny shook his head. Could it have come from Timothy Leary himself? Shammai wasn't around to ask.

In the midst of this heavenly epiphany, the travelogue continues, a neighbor knocks on the door, and Ronny remembers thinking, This is good, because who would discover our bodies if we were to die here? And the neighbor seems to be speed-talking, while all that Ronny can articulate are disjointed syllables, when suddenly he needs to pee something awful, and he heads for the outhouse across the border in Vermont, but there's someone in the outhouse. Who can it be? And Ronny is so distraught that he launches into an anguished soliloquy whether 'tis better to piss or to pray. Meanwhile, Kenneth, too, has left the cabin and has climbed up a tree and Lizzy in a panic is trying to get him down, at which point Larry, who simply couldn't resist, starts singing Carlebach's "I lift up mine eyes to the Lord, whence cometh my salvation."

"My salvation cometh from Vermont!" I shouted in ecstasy.

A fellowship we had at last become. It remained for us to enact the second half of our name, *Shalom*. On Friday, November 9, 1969, we drove to Washington, thirty-nine of us, in separate cars. Jim stayed behind. No human being, he argued, no inclusive community, and no parade of marchers ever stopped a war. I was with Charles and Kathleen, Ronny and Manya. It took twelve hours in the pouring rain. Bumper-to-bumper from Baltimore. An apocalyptic traffic jam. Indeed, the Sons of Light were arrayed against the Sons of Darkness, exactly as prophesied by the Dead Sea Sect, only the symbolism went slightly awry, because those who supported the evil in Viet Nam had their headlights on, while the carloads of smiling faces and fingers making the peace sign did not. Having come to protest as Jews, we were being fed and put up in the Union of American Hebrew Congregations Social Action Center, one block from the South Vietnamese embassy. Our songs and Sabbath meal were suddenly disrupted by the sound of four thousand kids, carrying red flags and chanting HO, HO, HO-CHI-MIN, led by the Weatherman in their white motorcycle helmets and black leather jackets (was my friend Khaskl among them, I wondered?), followed moments later by screams, the sound of something popping, and the smell of gas. "It eats into your eyes," I wrote to Abby, "and when you cry, the pain is only aggravated. It makes you cough uncontrollably, makes your nose run, and you can't stop sneezing between coughs. It makes you want to run away from yourself and hide. Dying that way," I concluded, "must be too horrible for words." On Saturday we marched, linking arms and singing, singing Carlebach songs and Sabbath tunes, lending our bodies to the ritual of protest, and on the drive home, we watched the long line of cars magically thin out over Delaware and New Jersey. In Massachusetts snow had fallen, and this peaceful blanket of early winter gave peace to the world from Sturbridge to Framingham. It was early morning and we sang "Here Comes the Sun."

Now that we were home again and reconstituted, I invited my *haverim* to visit me in Montreal over winter break. The house would be ours, and my parents, who were off visiting Ben, Louise, and the children in Israel, would never know. As much as I tried to convince my parents that the Havurah was a replay of their youthful idealism, Mother would have none of it. For one thing, she was angry that I read Abby's letters before I read hers. How could she possibly have known? Because the same thing happened to Sasha Gelibter when he went off to study in Vienna. He left behind a sickly mother and a girl friend, and whenever he received mail from home, from Vilna, he would read the letters from his girlfriend first. And Sasha, I should know, met a terrible end at the hands of the Germans. Then Mother was angry that I stopped calling them on Friday nights. The only telephone in the Havurah was located in the kitchen, adjacent to the chapel, and however much I tried to keep my voice down, those *davening* could hear me babbling away in Yiddish. And finally, she mistrusted our curriculum. It was all right to study the Bible, but not with Bible criticism, because criticism led to skepticism, and skepticism led to intermarriage.

In the end, only a few *haverim* took me up on my invitation, and only Joel was there for the big snowstorm. It was the second real winter of his life, the first being when he had flown in from California to interview for the Havurah. Three feet of snow had fallen and even Montreal, with its navy of snowplows, was paralyzed. In his pea coat, Joel, too, was unprepared. We were snowbound with nothing to do. So I telephoned Rokhl Korn, who lived up the hill, fifteen minutes by foot in normal weather, and asked if we could come over, Joel and I, ostensibly to get copies of her collected Yiddish prose, published privately in Montreal. In fact, I just wanted Joel, a fellow Yiddish-lover, to meet her. And the two of us headed off, making tracks in the pristine snow, which was still falling, Joel thrilled with "this strange, manna-like substance," and I, exhilarated to be climbing my own version of Mount Cadillac, when out of nowhere, I thought of a song, the most appropriate song, a song of pilgrimage, to the Polish town of Kotsk, wherein once lived the great master Rabbi Menakhem-Mendl, from whom I was descended on my father's side, and this was my song, by virtue of Jacob Zipper, the principal of the Peretz School, who had taught it to Ruth Rubin, who had recorded it on an LP, the contents of which I had memorized. And I sang this pilgrimage song to Joel to help direct our feet and uplift our spirits, and he learned the song so well that he translated it into English, thus:

> To Kotsk one does not ride, to Kotsk one goes on foot,
> For Kotsk is now in place of the Temple,
> Kotsk is now in place of the Temple,
> To Kotsk one must make a pilgrimage,
> Make a pilgrimage.

Joel knew as well as I did that in our spiritual lexicon, Kotsk was no longer in Poland; Kotsk was in Somerville; and if any place was "in place of the Temple," it was Havurat Shalom.

> "*Regel*," you know, is the word for "foot,"
> To Kotsk one must travel on foot!
> Singing out, and dancing about;
> And when Hasidim go forth to Kotsk,
> They go there with a dance,
> And when Hasidim go forth to Kotsk,
> They go there with a dance.

We were the new Hasidim. It wasn't at all clear why, of all the different paths, we had chosen Hasidism. Perhaps because Hasidism taught that God must be served *be-gashmiyut,* by reuniting the mind with the body, and too many of us had gone either to one extreme or the other, and there really was nowhere else to go, not back to the shtetl, not back to Israel, not back to suburbia, not back to a disembodied Judaism.

> "*Regel*," you know, is the word for "habit," One must make a habit of going to
>   Kotsk!
> Singing out, and dancing about;
> And when Hasidim go forth to Kotsk,
> They go there with a dance,
> And when Hasidim go forth to Kotsk,
> They go there with a dance.

And when Joel and I brought this song back to Somerville and taught it at the Third Sabbath Meal, it became our unofficial hymn, because Yiddish was the language that bound us to our Hasidic forbears, Yiddish embodying the wholeness that we longed for and could never fully achieve, and whenever we met, however many years had elapsed, I would link arms with Joel, and with George, who sang the harmony, my two *haverim,* as we led the others in the Kotsk Song, singing so loud that even Art's voice, hopelessly flat, became one with the choir, singing of the place where we had prayed and protested, feasted and fought, where silence, if properly directed, could be stronger than words.

CHAPTER TWENTY-FIVE

"Regel," you know, is the word for "Yontef" [festival],
Good yontef, good yontef, good yontef, good yontef!
Singing out, and dancing about;
And when Hasidim go forth to Kotsk,
They go there with a dance,
And when Hasidim go forth to Kotsk,
It is a major Yontef.

Looking for Krosno, for Czernowitz, for Vilna, for Vilna in Jerusalem, for Jerusalem itself, I had instead found Kotsk.

26

The Sale of Joseph

When they once asked I. B. Singer why he didn't write for the theater, he is reputed to have said: "Because every Yiddish play is essentially the same. It starts with a heartfelt Kaddish and ends with a raucous wedding."

Well, it's almost time for the wedding.

In the end, Abby would never do for the role of Havurah spouse. She drove a sports car and spent much too much time making up her eyes. Could you see her wrapped up for hours in radical self-confrontation? And other than her one word, *kókhlefl*—dipper, busybody—which she changed from a term of opprobrium to a term of endearment, Abby didn't speak Yiddish. Not that Miri spoke Yiddish either, but that didn't stop her from organizing the Brandeis Yiddish Theater, and when I, now a popular Yiddish teacher on campus, failed to audition, she offered me a walk-on role that required no memorization and was sure to steal the show. How could I refuse? The scene, a lively collage based on Uriel Weinreich's *Yiddish-English English-Yiddish Dictionary,* would have brought a grudging smile even to Singer's lips.

After the cast party I learned that Miri was housesitting for a retired rabbi and when he returned home she had nowhere to go, and staying the

night seemed a natural thing to do, and I was sick of communal living anyway because for $120/month Mrs. Fiorello would rent me a five-room split-
level apartment, plenty of room to share with Miri, all of whose worldly pos-
sessions easily fit into her used VW. So Miri unpacked her wardrobe of
peasant blouses and long skirts, her books by Abraham Maslow, her Reform prayer book, and her extra copy of Weinreich. We resolved to speak
Yiddish and to keep a kosher home.

With her long braid, small hips, and modest breasts, Miri fit right in to
Somerville. She didn't much like being called Pocahontas, on account of her
blouses being from Mexico and her skirts from Taos, but neither did the
haverim appreciate her calling them by their Yiddish names. Art became
Reb Avrom, Kathy—Kreyndl, Mike—Reb Mordkhe, and Joel—Reb Yoyl.
Otherwise, everyone acknowledged that this was a match made in heaven,
all except for Abby, who wondered why, despite her best efforts, I had suc-
cumbed to my prefabricated fantasies; and Ben, who was disappointed
with his kid brother for not marrying the girl who made him walk on air;
and Mother. Mother, I was the last of my siblings to learn, considered no one
good enough to marry any of her children.

A dutiful son until then—could anyone prove that I had read my girlfriend's letters before I read my mother's?—I was forced to take a stand
when Mother so utterly rejected my choice of bride. Miri and I moved up the
wedding date from September to early June.

It was to be a do-it-yourself wedding, at the farthest remove from my sister Eva's affair in Montreal at the Tifereth Jerusalem synagogue with hundreds of guests and a half-dozen rabbis. The Havurah had arranged to celebrate the joyous festival of Shavuos at a Lebanese Catholic monastery in
Methuen, Massachusetts, not too far from the Dannon Yogurt factory. Since
Shavuos marked the marriage of Israel to the Torah, throwing in a wedding
was only natural. An hour before the guests arrived, the *haverim* remembered to remove the crucifixes from the prefectory where the reception was
to be held over lox and Crown Royal whiskey brought down from Montreal.
Whoever could come, would come. Of my three siblings, only Ruth and her
family, and grudgingly, the parents. From Miri's side—no one.

The Havurah ethos was everywhere in evidence. The ceremony was held
out-of-doors, Hasidic style. With the help of the married women, the bride
had fashioned a beautiful *tallis* adorned with Navaho embroidery to be used

for a huppah, and the groom's best friend, Joel, stayed up the whole night doing the ketubah in a carefree Hebrew script in several colors of ink, modeled both on the one that Reb Zalman had made for Ruthie and Michael, and on Ben Shahn's *Alphabet of Creation*. Charles on the flute and George on the guitar accompanied the processional with the slow and haunting Modzitzer melody to "Shrine of the King" from the Friday Night Service, and finally, two rabbis officiated: Art on behalf of the Havurah, and Manny Goldsmith on behalf of Yiddish. After the breaking of the glass, one of the last remaining crystals that Mother had salvaged from Czernowitz, the klezmer musicians struck up a *freylekhs* and everyone danced.

"Some *purim-shpil* you staged," said Mother as I walked her back to the car. Father and Miri were pulling up the rear, out of earshot. "A fine parody of our huppah at Fradl's graveside. The groom is furious with his parents, so he moves up the date of the wedding: your father, all over again, only instead of *him* staying up the whole night crying, it's your friend who stays up, making the ketubah. The bride, for all intents and purposes, is an orphan—more orphaned than I was, if you consider that I still had my brother, Grisha, to lean on."

"*Purim-shpil*," she said. Indeed, from that moment, she seemed to me like Mother Rachel, crying out from her tomb as her son Joseph is led into captivity:

MOTHER RACHEL: Oh Joseph, my son, you are truly woebegone.
   Sitting at my table you learned all the lessons wrong.
   Wasn't it obvious that I married your father on the rebound?
   The very sight of Seidman walking on the street gave me chills up and
      down.
   Isn't that why you rushed into Miri's bed, like a forlorn clown,
   Because her need for you was so overblown,
   Because you alone—how ennobling!—could be her savior, you alone?
   You fool. Did I mean for you to repeat my life? And now?
   I had no choice. No prospects. No home.

JOSEPH: But I thought she was like you!
   Spunky, creative. So in love with Yiddish theater.
   We could do so much together.

CHAPTER TWENTY-SIX

She believed in the things I believed in more than I did.

Didn't we in fact put on Yiddish plays—an original play for children on the Warsaw ghetto, and a Purim play in traditional costume?

Professor Shmeruk was so taken with my performance of Jacob the Patriarch that he urged me to become a Yiddish actor.

Miri and I even wrote a book together, about the Jews of eastern Europe.

Ours was to be an ideological union, modeled on yours.

We inscribed each other's name, in Yiddish, on the inside of our wedding bands, just as you did.

We made aliyah to a foreign country, same as you.

We organized a reading circle in our home, to mimic your soirées.

We spoke only Yiddish, corresponded in Yiddish, dreamed in Yiddish.

(Bursting into tears, JOSEPH prostrates himself at MOTHER RACHEL's grave and cries):

I wasn't out to parody your life but to replay it—without disease, without war, without the landscape of loss.

I wanted to get it right, this time!

MOTHER RACHEL (in a ghostly voice from behind the cardboard grave): So, what happened?

JOSEPH (weeping bitterly): Doing theater became hateful to her.

Living in Israel became hateful to her.

Speaking Yiddish became hateful to her.

I became hateful to her.

(Before MOTHER RACHEL can offer him final words of comfort, the Midianites, dressed like Cossacks, drag poor JOSEPH off to Egypt.)

27

The Two *Bulvanes*

When Ida Erik was liberated from Soviet captivity, Mother refused to see her. This, despite my brother's pioneering trip to Moscow in 1967 (and mine in 1971); despite the Great Exodus from the Soviet Union that we had marched for, picketed for, petitioned for but never dreamed would happen; despite Ida's trip to New York upon the invitation of her brother-in-law, Dr. Leon Merkin; and most brutally, despite Ida's five-day visit to Montreal where she stayed at the home of Rokhl Korn, just a short walk from our house on the hill. They corresponded, they spoke on the telephone, but Mother refused to see her. "*Sheyne bilder,*" she said, quoting her favorite bon mot from the poet I. J. Segal, "*muz men kukn fun der vaytns,* beautiful pictures ought to be looked at from afar."

A defensible position, perhaps, when you carried the picture gallery in your head, but what if you had never seen the original, when you had been collecting card-size reproductions for twenty-three years? When I received a mysterious phone call in the summer of 1971, asking me and my new wife to appear at the office of the B'nai Akiva Zionist youth movement at Cooper Union in downtown Manhattan concerning a possible trip abroad, it seemed like a ticket to the Louvre.

Some Louvre. At the bare desk, flanked by portraits of two bearded men—Theodor Herzl and some rabbi—sat a trim, white-haired gentleman who introduced himself as Aryeh Kroll. He wore a white shirt with a wide-open collar and short sleeves neatly folded as high as they would go, kibbutz-style. Only his steel-blue eyes gave him away. These eyes had never known fear. To play our parts, one of us needed to speak Hebrew. That was me. The rest of the interview Aryeh conducted in a British-accented English, a throwback to the Mandate period; maybe—who knew?—to the Haganah and the good ship *Exodus*.

We got right down to business. In the wake of the Six Day War the Soviets had severed diplomatic ties with Israel. At the same time, however, they were beginning to allow a trickle of *aliyah*, immigration to Israel, and from this trickle, from this great and untapped reservoir of Jews, a veritable stream might someday flow. (Yes, a kibbutznik, all right.) The obstacles to immigration were many. To apply for an exit visa required a personal invitation from relatives in Israel, whether real or imagined.

"All Jews are responsible for one another," I showed off my knowledge of classical Hebrew.

The Dutch Embassy in Moscow, he continued without allowing a smile, was acting as go-between.

So where did we come in?

It was in the vital interest of the Israeli government to maintain close ties with Soviet Jewry, and now that Israelis were barred from entering, young American Jews with a knowledge of Israel were being recruited to go. We would travel as tourists, first class. Our assignment was to deliver a small parcel of Hebrew textbooks. Otherwise, we were to attend synagogue and answer questions.

Over there, our movements would be watched. Our hotel rooms, we could assume, would be bugged. We were to avoid visiting private homes and under no condition were we to smuggle anything out. Not even the tiniest scrap of paper. Addresses were getting through via other channels.

Nothing fancy, then. The more cautious we were, the less likely that the Soviet authorities would get wind of the operation. Young people, even younger than us, had been going over since 1968. Some had been harassed. A few had been expelled. Should we be thrown into prison, however, the Israeli government could do nothing to help. Just stick to our alibi and all would be well.

"We haven't lost anyone," he said, probing us with those steel-blue eyes, "yet."

As for the itinerary, it was up to us. We could choose between the Russian and Central Asian republics. What, I had a connection to Vilna? Good. In that case, they were sending us to Moscow, Leningrad, Riga, and Vilna. I had just enough time to apply for a new Canadian passport. Not to give the Soviets any sign of my travels to Israel.

Moscow was no Louvre either, just rainy and cold. The ubiquitous gray was alleviated only by huge red banners and billboards celebrating the 24th Party Congress held earlier that summer. Gray and red, nothing else. The pride of the latest Five-Year Plan was the new Intourist Hotel where we were staying, a huge eyesore around the corner from the Kremlin. For the first time, apparently, the tourist season would last through September, and our Intourist guide had her hands full. She was most pleased with us, a young married couple on their belated honeymoon, and we were happy, because according to my primitive map, the Arkhípova Street Synagogue was only a fifteen-minute walk away.

Even to our untrained eye it was obvious who they were. They were young, male, bearded, wore an Israeli flag in their lapel, greeted one another with the Jewish Defense League thumb shake, and spoke a modern Hebrew that put mine to shame. They were a species of the young "idealists" who peopled Mother's stories. The portrait gallery was already taking shape.

"*Yesh lakhém sefarim?*" he asked, before even saying *Shalom*. His name was Avigdor Levit, and he ran the largest of Moscow's five semilegal ulpanim, intensive Hebrew classes. Sadly, we apologized, the textbooks we were carrying were not slated for him.

"*Beseder.* Okay."

The shortage of Hebrew books, he allowed, was not as great in Moscow as in Leningrad, where hundreds of books had been confiscated and burned during the recent show trials. The bigger problem was money. Eight hundred *refuseniks*, we learned from Aaron Khesin, had been fired from their jobs on the eve of the 24th Party Congress.

"You know," said Leonyd Zolotúshko, the third member of the Troika, "were the Union of Moscow Bakers to go out on strike, the whole city would starve."

We didn't get the joke. Under Soviet law, he went on to explain, it was a crime not to be engaged in productive labor. So the Jewish intelligentsia found jobs—delivering bread. Aaron, an exception, had kept his job as a lighting technician at the famed Obrastsov Puppet Theater because Obrastsov himself stood up for him.

"May his name be for a blessing," said Leonyd.

"Amen," said Aaron.

Avigdor gladly accepted fifty rubles from us to subsidize the October rent.

All this happened during our first hour in front of the synagogue. We arranged to meet again with the Hebrew-speaking *refuseniks* and then we were approached by a well-dressed man in his early forties who addressed us in fluent English.

"My name is Lev Navrozov," he said. "Since the life of a Soviet Jew begins anew from the day he applies for an exit visa, I am but a babe in the woods, merely two months old."

Our two-month-old acquaintance was a self-employed translator, thus unaffected by the wave of firings, and he offered to introduce us to the most famous Jewish translator in Russia, who was standing just across the street.

In a city dominated by utilitarian dress in hues of gray, she stood out immediately in her stylish pants suit and silk scarf. Just as the mound of meticulously coiffured black hair accentuated the smoothness of her forehead, her oval-shaped designer glasses called attention to her laughing, utterly self-confident eyes. To complete the picture, she greeted us in French.

"Meet Esther Markish," said Navrozov.

"English?" she asked.

"Yiddish," I replied.

In our month-long tour of four Soviet cities, Esther Markish was the only woman we met who was an activist in her own right, not a helpmeet to her husband. Yet once we got to know each other—and every encounter, no matter how brief, had to count for a lifetime—I discovered that she *was* in fact her husband's helpmeet and therein lay the source of her defiance. Esther was the relatively young widow of Peretz Markish, the Yiddish Byron, the Yiddish Mayakovsky, first emissary of the October Revolution to the youth of Warsaw, and the most fearless Yiddish writer to be imprisoned, tortured, and executed by Stalin.

I knew all about him: from Melekh Ravitch, who together with Markish had launched the Expressionist revolution in Yiddish poetry; from Avrom Sutzkever, who met Markish in 1944, when he stood atop the Soviet-Yiddish pantheon; from Rokhl Korn, who knew the secrets of Markish's love life;

from Professor Shmeruk, who revealed the tragic push-and-pull between Markish the Jew and Markish the committed Communist; and from Professor Hrushovski, who reveled in Markish's exuberant prosody.

"This young man has studied Markish's work," Esther explained matter-of-factly to her coterie of admirers in Russian. "Markish is well known in the West." Then turning to me, she said in Yiddish, "I am inviting you to my home to deliver a lecture on a literary theme."

"Esther," someone whispered in her ear, "are you not afraid?"

"Afraid?" she replied. "They should be afraid of me."

The cream of the Soviet-Jewish intelligentsia came to hear me lecture on major trends in modern Hebrew literature, with Esther translating from Yiddish into Russian. She had been allowed to repossess only half of their prewar apartment on prestigious Gorky Street; the other half they shared with Russian hillbillies. Markish's writing table dominated the living room-dining room. On it were displayed photographs and many of his books, not the copies confiscated by the Secret Police on the night of his arrest, but replacement copies donated over the years by friends. Before I began, Esther's son David went over to the telephone, turned the dial to zero, and lodged it in place with a pencil. That way, he explained, the Three Letters (code name for the KGB) could not use their phone as a listening device. Afterward, the film director Moisei Kalik regaled us with his latest antics. He had requested a transfer of funds from the State Bank to the Israeli Association of Film Directors to pay his membership dues. Yesterday, the bank wrote back that it would look into the matter. By the time I left Moscow, I knew exactly what to give David Markish as collateral until we met again, on Israeli soil. I gave him my black-and-red knitted *yarmulke*, with the name DAVID embroidered in Hebrew.

"She's still waiting for the second knock on the door," Esther said of Ida Erik, a reference to Ida's extreme caution, her unwillingness to sever the bonds and join the resistance. How ironic! Max Erik had been the first in Poland to herald Peretz Markish and "the language of Yiddish Expressionism." What's more, in Mother's stories, Erik served as the mouthpiece of biting sarcasm aimed at Vilna's petty bourgeoisie. I never heard her quote a kind word from him. In class, he would routinely ridicule his students for not being sufficiently quick-witted, but apparently never picked on Mother. Somewhat reluctantly, then, on my third day in Moscow, with the phone number that Ben had given me, I made contact with Ida, whose Yiddish was a little rusty and who seemed reticent to speak it over the phone.

There were four of them living in the modest apartment: Ida, her sister-in-law Regina, Ida's daughter Nelly, and Sasha, her grandson, the apple of their eye. I already knew from my brother about Nelly's disastrous marriage to a Ukrainian that had long since ended in divorce. Regina was inscrutable and Nelly was silent, while Ida herself spoke very quietly, in half-sentences.

"It was only a matter of time," she said, as I sipped a hot glass of tea sweetened with cherry preserves. "The Institute had already been closed, and some of its leading academicians had already been arrested. They came late in the night on April 10, 1936. 'Where are your weapons?' they demanded to know. 'Here is my weapon,' replied Sala" (Ida's nickname for her husband). And he pointed to the pen lying on his desk.

"Yes," she allowed, "we have some of Sala's letters, written to Nelly and me from prison and from the camps. No, not here, not with me."

I knew she was lying. Then again, I was under strict orders from New York not to smuggle anything out.

"How did he perish? He was never beaten, never tortured. He got a light sentence. Only five years at hard labor. Thirty-eight at the time of his arrest. He could have survived, if he had wanted to. Lyuba Epstein, a former student—ask your mother about her—was a nurse in the camp. To her he confided what he was about to do. He slashed his wrists. Not out of fear. Out of protest. To live on would be to acquiesce to the great deception—the greatest deception of all times."

"Would you like a piece of cake?" asked Regina.

"I probably owe my life to Max Erik," I blurted out in reply, hoping to distract them from their sorrow. Then I told of the letter that Erik had sent from Minsk to my parents in Vilna. "The Soviet Union is truly wondrous," he had written, "but it's too rugged a place for Masha."

"Is that so?" Ida retorted sharply. "Then why wasn't it too rugged for me?"

When Mother heard this line in the story, she exploded with laughter. That laughter, I knew, signaled a moment of vindication—and sheer vindictiveness. Poor Ida. For some hilarious, inscrutable reason she had been meant to suffer, while Masha had been meant for a life of peace and security. To see Ida face to face after all these years would be to confront her lifelong rival.

"I drove right by your home," Ida later told me in her brother-in-law's New York apartment on West End Avenue. "It's a red-brick house with a big maple tree on the front lawn. And she wouldn't let me in the door."

Worse yet, to show Ida her amazing good fortune—this thirteen-room house with its capacious closets, its every wall adorned with original paintings, its shelves bursting with china, *chachkes,* and books—would mean to rewrite Mother's master narrative of orphanhood, abandonment, and betrayal. Why else did Stalin and Hitler come to power if not to render the past irrevocable?

Or maybe her refusal was simply a way of holding on to that precious moment at the Vilna train station, late in 1929, when Ida and her flamboyant husband went in one direction, Masha and her dependable Leybke in another?

Vilna was the other Soviet city where I had a personal contact. I was to look up Rokhl Gurdus, the sister of Lyuba Blum, whom I had met in Montreal. Either because the life of a spy was wearing me down or because Lyuba was the widow of the famed Abrasha Blum, a leader of the Bund and hero of the Warsaw ghetto uprising, I called the Gurduses directly from our hotel, without bothering to locate a phone booth. Rokhl's husband came right over, and even our Intourist guide was impressed: a bemedaled Red Army officer, the director of Vilna's leading *gymnasium,* high school for the humanities, Zalman Gurdus spoke Yiddish for all the world to hear.

I had already scouted out the famed courtyard on Zawalna 28/30 where Mother was born and knew that it housed a police academy. Nonetheless, Zalman thought he could pull some strings and get us inside.

"Just take a look," he said, after admitting defeat. "All the Jews of Vilna they murdered, and the two *bulvanes*—the half-naked torsos that held up the entrance—they left standing."

Zalman had not joined with three hundred other Vilna Jews back in March, when they assembled in Ponar to light *yortsayt* candles on the site where the bones of six children had recently been exhumed. His own children Lida and Vinya had attended, and personally, he had no quarrel with those, like Eitan Finkelstein, who were agitating to leave for Israel. But Zalman Gurdus, born in Vilna, would not be among them. He was as proud of his school as the teachers and students were proud of him. There, in the basement, they had installed the only museum in the USSR to commemorate the

Holocaust. Two extremely shy girls in school uniforms gave us the tour in textbook English.

In the portrait gallery as I saw it then, there was no place for someone like Zalman Gurdus. His name would not appear on the memorandum I sent to my "control" in New York City. Gurdus would die as he lived, a proud Soviet Jew.

Twenty-nine years later, I finally entered Mother's courtyard, and when I passed between the two freshly painted *bulvanes*—all of Vilnius seemed freshly painted that summer—the long and spacious yard was empty. The police academy was gone and Vilnius University (formerly Stefan Batory, Father's alma mater) had yet to take over the premises. All there was to see were scattered linden trees down the middle; on the right, three-story apartments with large old-fashioned windows, and two-story rows to complete the rectangle. Had I come alone, I would have just sat there, on one of the narrow benches beneath the lindens, until dark, with no need or desire to carve my name into one of the trees, poor substitutes, anyway, for the beloved chestnut trees chopped down for firewood during the Second World War. Seeing as there were five of us, however, I sat the others down on the cobblestone walkway and told them the Vilna stories that I was working on for my book. No one could contradict me now. Even Ilya, our young guide, had to bow to my superior knowledge. Here, I pronounced, was Kochanovsky's Kindergarten; here the press of Judah Leib and Fradl Matz, later of Fradl Matz and Yisroel Welczer; here the orphanage, and there, Badaness's Bakery. No other place in Vilna, no other place anywhere, for that matter, was so totally mine to people as I saw fit.

Though the wooden doors were unlocked, I couldn't bring myself to go inside. What were the rooms without the huge copper vat that the Kaiser never got his hands on, without the Royale, the grand piano at which Aunt Rosa was wooed by Jewish censors Erlich and Kornicker, without the miniature ark that housed the priceless Torah scroll and mantle?

28

Yom Kippur

For Lyutov, Isaac Babel's alter ego, the prototype of manhood was the Cossack. In the final, politically correct version of *Red Cavalry,* Lyutov rides off into the sunset, Cossack-style. I too have a manly persona in my head named *DAH-veed.* Ever since meeting Tami, my measure of manhood is to walk along the shores of the Mediterranean holding hands with a beautiful Sabra and speaking accentless Hebrew. As unseemly as it is to admit, I still keep trying.

Tami (short for Tamar) taught me the semiotics of names in spoken Hebrew. *Dah-VEED* is the standard Hebrew pronunciation of my name, with the accent on the second syllable. When Israelis get really close to someone, however, the accent shifts to the first syllable. Why? Because this mimics the way one's foreign-born parents, if they happen to come from Poland, would pronounce it. To the Sabra ear it sounds quaint, folksy, and adorable. When Tami started calling me *DAH-veed,* I took offense, thinking she was making fun of my Yiddish accent. What did I know?

Tami was what Mother called a "platonic lover." She took me under her wing, as women were wont to do, during my junior year abroad in Israel, for although her buddies—those who were still alive, that is—were all veterans of the Six Day War, she was enrolled in most of my Yiddish classes at the Hebrew University. Why was Tami Azzulai studying Yiddish? Because of the

Kiryat Hayyim connection. In Kiryat Hayyim, just north of Haifa, Yiddish was introduced as a foreign-language elective in high school. She took Beginner's Yiddish and liked it. So did her kid brother, Shmulik.

The Six Day War was very much on her mind when we hung out on the main lawn of the Givat Ram campus. Let me tell you, she said, what happened when I visited the boot camp where some of my friends were stationed during the tail end of the fighting. We were fooling around in one of the barracks. Then Yigal picked up a pair of sneakers and started playing Monkey-in-the-Middle. "*Hishtagata*? Have you gone mad?" I yelled at him. Those sneakers belonged to Gadi, who had been killed outside Kuneitra the day before. "*Mah yesh*?" said Yigal. "So what? If I had been killed, Gadi would have done the same thing." And he went on playing. And you know something, *DAH-veed*? Yigal was right.

Tami was fearlessly footloose, never more so than in the Old City of Jerusalem. What the Arab merchants made of her lithe body, short-shorts, and sandals I could scarcely imagine. The veiled women looked the other way. When the younger men came on to her she shrugged them off: a wildflower, seemingly indifferent to her own exotic scent. No way would she ever let on how much traipsing through the garbage-strewn alleyways of the Old City, so recently regained, meant to her, and even I, her trusted confidant, rarely glimpsed what was really going on. Once she took me to Mount Zion to show me the spot where, before the war, she would stand for hours on end, almost close enough to touch the Old City walls, certainly within the sight-line of the Jordanian Legion, and daydream. And once, as we were chatting away on the number 15 bus, she jumped up from her seat when a soldier got on. Tami stood bolt upright for two or three seconds, then collapsed next to me on the seat. "I could have sworn it was Boaz! He looked just like Boaz!" She closed her eyes to fight back the tears.

The Azzulais treated me like family. Mrs. Azzulai gave me Shmulik's bedroom and made him sleep at a friend's house. I borrowed Shmulik's bike when Tami and I went riding to the beach. That's where I first began to dream the implausible dream of walking along the Mediterranean arm-in-arm with someone as free-spirited as Tami and speaking Israeli Hebrew at an effortless pace. The next morning, at 5:15, I was awakened by Mr. Azzulai, who insisted that I join "the boys" at their daily exercise. Mr. Kagan, director of the aforementioned high school, was already waiting for us in the car. At the beach the two men did their thing. After taking a brisk swim in the ocean, Mr. Azzulai walked on his hands for ten minutes. "Ben Gurion can do it for half an hour," he informed me.

I visited the Azzulais one more time, in the summer of 1969. Then I lost touch.

When the siren went off at four in the afternoon, I thought to myself: Israel—what an amazing country! They remind people that it's almost time for *Neilah,* the Closing of the Gates of Prayer. But when Miri and I showed up at the synagogue, we were told to rush right home and turn on the radio. Egypt had launched a surprise attack all along the Suez Canal. This was the beginning of the Yom Kippur War.

Unlike the other "Anglo-Saxons" who had come on aliyah, who had bought a subsidized apartment and were using up their *zekhuyot,* their duty-free privileges, on cars, refrigerators, and TV sets, Miri and I were living on my graduate fellowship in an unheated rental. Let those who needed it—the flood of immigrants from the Soviet Union—receive government hand-outs. A monthly rent subsidy was all we would take.

So with no TV and no one to watch with, we never saw our Israeli friends break down and cry when POWs in Egypt were paraded in front of the camera. We didn't see Israeli jets being downed. We neither knew nor wanted to know how close we had come to being annihilated. Instead, Miri and I resolved to go about our normal routine. To be sure, I donated blood at the head office of Americans and Canadians in Israel, which happened to be next door, and managed to pass out. At night, we dutifully covered the windows with black paper.

Each day, people combed the newspapers for the names. I figured: why bother? I don't know anyone in uniform.

But I was wrong.

On my way to the National Library, Chava, a former classmate, stopped me and said, "Did you hear what happened to the Azzulais?" Shmulik's jet, she reported, had been shot down over Syria. I was more amazed to learn that little Shmulik was a pilot than that he was dead. And Tami's brother-in-law Shimon, a tank commander in the Golan Heights, was MIA. "You know," Chava said, almost in a whisper, "the Syrians treat prisoners very badly."

I thanked her for the news and continued on my way.

What should I have done?

I should have gotten on a bus and headed north, to Haifa, and from Haifa to Kiryat Hayyim. I knew the route. I knew the language. It might have taken a little longer than usual, because most of the buses had been commandeered, but I would have reached the Azzulai home.

I would have found the door open. After entering in silence, as one always enters a house of mourning, perhaps I would have found Tami sitting on a low stool, as tradition dictates, next to her parents and her sister. Most certainly they would be passing around a photo album—two photo albums, one of Shmulik, and one of the wedding, for Tami's sister was a newlywed, and was visibly with child. How stunning Tami looked, wearing nylons and a formal gown in those wedding pictures! And drinking *mitz eshkoliot*, grapefruit juice, I would still have been there when an officer arrived with the news, the terrible news about Shimon, that he had been captured by the Syrians, and tortured, and his body dismembered and his genitals stuffed into his mouth.

Does the Arab Code of War, I might have said to myself, require that one dismember the enemy after he is dead or beforehand? Does the Code require that the heart still be beating when the genitals are cut off? I needed to know this, for one hears so much these days about Arab honor. And how many POWs would they barter in exchange for his mutilated body? No one drives a harder bargain than the Syrians.

If I had come, my words would comfort no one. Mrs. Azzulai would never recover anyway from the death of her son and her son-in-law. But at least I would have been there, together with my friend Tami, instead of reading Yiddish chapbooks in the National University Library.

The one thing I'm proud of—and this was Miri's initiative, not mine—is that before leaving Israel, we returned our rent subsidy, every last penny of it. It took some doing, because the Ministry of Absorption was not set up to take refunds. This, in contrast to one of our American friends who made a killing on his apartment in French Hill, returned to the States, and then wrote a book denouncing Zionism. Whatever transgressions I was guilty of, which no Yom Kippur War or Yom Kippur prayer could ever expiate, I committed by omission.

We left Israel in early June 1975. Through the window of the El Al jet I could see a man, stripped to the waist, working in a manhole just off the tarmac. It was two in the afternoon and very hot. Doing whatever he's doing, I said to myself, he's more of a man than I. Now, as I relive that moment of closure, I want to say: and more of a Jew.

29

New York Jew

All right. So you dropped out of Havurat Shalom. So you gave up on your dream—and your brother's and your sister's—of living in Israel. Isn't teaching at a seminary the next best thing? Here it is 1985 and you're already an Associate Professor. And what's wrong, may I ask, with being a New York Jew? Ruth would give her right arm to live in Manhattan. Instead, your sister's stuck in Montreal, a big fish in a small pond.

"Be a tail to lions rather than a head to jackals," according to *Sayings of Our Sages,* 4:15.

Come off it. You're here anyway. Make the best of it. You said yourself there's a cultural revival going on.

When did I say that?

In chapter 9.

Not exactly. What I wrote was "a few refugees from the old Havurah . . . had formed their own congregation on the Upper West Side." I would hardly call that a renaissance.

What about the YIVO? The Atran House? The Forward Building? Ratner's? Gus's Pickles? If Yiddish lives anywhere, it lives in the Big Apple.

What lies will you tell me next, what falsehoods? That Maurice Schwartz is playing Hershele Dubrovner at the Yiddish Art Theater? That Jacob Glatstein is waiting for me at the Café Royale?

Look, Roskies, every other year you organize a pilgrimage to the Mount Carmel Cemetery in Glendale, Queens, charter a bus to visit the graves of Sholem Aleichem and Moyshe-Leyb Halpern. You still love Sholem Aleichem, don't you?

Leave me alone!

Wait, wait. I have a better idea. How about the widows? I've just come from Irving Howe. Now *there's* a New York Jew for you! D'you know what he's up to? Writing a whole *megillah*, he is, about Yiddish widows and all the hoops they've made him jump through. Why not beat him to it and check out a few widows? You they'll love. They'll ply you with tea and stories.

Say, who are you? Why are you bothering me? Can't you see I'm busy?

Busy beating your breast. Busy cupping a corpse.

Show me your feet!

What?

I'll believe you if you show me your feet!

And with that, he disappeared, for as everyone knows, from the smallest imp right up to the infamous Ketev Meriri of talmudic fame, devils have *gendzn-fislekh*, the claws of geese, which also means "quotation marks."

The Devil's banter gave me no peace. Not so much the business of becoming a New York Jew as the mention of widows, which reminded me of Evelyn. Undemanding Evelyn, who had been waiting many months now for me to call.

Where exactly did she fit in the roster of Yiddish widows? For sure not among the combative types, like Esther Markish, or the custodial widows, like Esther Rochman. Since Leybl's untimely death at the age of sixty, Esther was trying to maintain the open house. So far, I was told, people were still coming over for tea, compote, and homemade nut cake, despite the empty seat at the head of the table. One thing was certain: Evelyn was not on Howe's list or anyone else's.

Were it not for a conversation with Benjamin Hrushovski, my Vilna-born professor, who considered Mikhl Licht a great undiscovered talent; were it not for my lecture on "Three Yiddish Modernists: Glatstein, Leyeles, and Licht" at the Jewish Public Library in Montreal; and were it not for Mikhl's old friend Shiye Tanenbaum, whose job it was to monitor the Yiddish press for any mention of the name Licht, I would not have met her either.

The note I received, forwarded to me from Montreal, was handwritten in a flowing English script, and enclosed was an ad for my lecture with the name LICHT circled in blue ink. The note was from Evelyn, who invited me to pay her a visit, should I ever be in New York. The return address was 80 La Salle St., well known to me as the Morningside Gardens apartment complex, for it was located just one block up from the Seminary. "A person's joy," Mother had always taught me, "lies at the very threshold."

Evelyn was everything that Mother was not. Petite, for one thing. She greeted me at the door looking much like the young woman in the archival photos that I had found, except a little plumper, her hair no longer in a pageboy. She spoke in a high-pitched voice and with a matronly demeanor, which seemed to go with the regulation-size apartment. Her palette was different from Mother's—she hated the muted "menopausal colors"—and at our first encounter wore a simple maroon-colored jumper over a bright yellow blouse. Her walls, like Mother's, were covered with oil paintings and pastels, only these landscapes and still-lifes were all her own, the landscapes painted during her annual summer retreat in Sorento, Italy. Most astonishing was her menu. For the next ten years she plied me with stories accompanied by tea, jam, and toast, toast made out of plain white bread from the local Coop. Americans, even artists, actually ate this stuff.

A life-sized sketch she had drawn of Mikhl in the early twenties was the only visible icon to his memory. But was there anything of which Mikhl Licht was not a connoisseur? Gregorian chants (learned from Eastern Orthodox priests), classical music, opera, jazz, painting, sculpture, aesthetics, philosophy, literary history, and, of course, poetry—he studied them all. The equestrian arts he had mastered while growing up on the Countess Poniatowski's estate, a "little prince" raised there by an aunt and mentored by Yakob Berri, a dentist and legal advocate, who sent Mikhl's essay on Gogol's "The Nose" to Lev Tolstoy; the Count wrote back that this nine-year-old had great literary talent. New York may have been too small a place for him.

Was there a famous writer with whom Mikhl did not hobnob? No sooner had he arrived in America at the age of twenty than he made contact with Ezra Pound, T. S. Eliot, Gertrude Stein, William Carlos Williams (a great friend of the Jews), and Marianne Moore. Writing under various pen names, he published verse in *The Pagan,* (the original) *Playboy, Smart Set,* and *The Little Review,* complete sets of which Evelyn still owned.

So Mikhl was to Evelyn's stories as Vilna was to Mother's. What their repertoire had in common, as retold for the benefit of the impressionable young man who took mental notes while eating bread at their kitchen table, was the theme of promiscuity.

Many were the affairs of the heart that bedeviled the New York Yiddish literati! Never ask a Yiddish writer "How's the wife?" or "How's your husband?" To be safe, you asked, "How's the family?"

The ménages à trois? Don't ask. And don't ever write them down.

Do I remember Regina Fershter? Her husband was killed during the Revolution. So one fine day she walks into the office of *Der tog* on East Broadway and asks to use the john. A few minutes later she calls loudly to Lev Landau, who comes running and finds her standing in the john, stark naked. (I can ask Landau. He's still alive.)

Whereas of Mikhl, Chava Minkov would proclaim: "You're the only man I can kiss on East Broadway and no one will suspect me of sleeping with him." Chava stayed with them, in fact, when she ran away from her husband. And whom did Evelyn's uncle, the philanderer Dr. Isser Ginzburg, finally marry at the age of eighty? That's right. Chavele Minkov!

Uncle Isser had his own reserved table at the Café Royale on Second Avenue, where the older, establishment poets, Avrom Lyessin and H. Leivick, would sit, because he treated them all to drinks. This earned him the right to call Leivick *Binder-blinder-der-goylem,* meaning something like "binder-blind man-clay monster," after his famous play "The Golem."

When Glatstein needed three hundred dollars for an abortion—one of his students at the Workmen's Circle School was with child—he turned, quite naturally, to Mikhl, who raised the not insubstantial sum by selling a small Chagall. (The world's ingratitude was another theme. Glatstein never paid him back, and the Chagall would now be worth a fortune.)

Not for naught did Mikhl wear suits of white linen. That's how he first appeared, at a lecture by the anthropologist Alexander Goldenweiser, held at the Anarchist colony in Stelton, New Jersey, where most of the bungalows were rented out to Yiddish writers. Evelyn was all of eighteen years old at the time, studying at Rutgers. Mikhl happened to be on the same train going home, and at Newark station, where they had to switch, he ran after her and asked, "Where will you go to atone for your sins?" And she replied, "I haven't any sins."

That purity of spirit carried over to his work. Mikhl worked for the Jews but wrote for himself. He never earned a cent from his poetry, that's for sure. All his books he published at his own expense, and Evelyn designed the covers. Her favorite was the cover to *Vazon,* where the letters doubled as a bouquet of roses. He worked nights at *Der tog* preparing the ads, and sometimes he translated popular hits for Molly Picon to sing in Yiddish over the Jewish radio station WEVD. The editor of *Der tog* pleaded with Mikhl to write theater reviews, but he refused. Journalism, he maintained, polluted the pen. But when the staff at *Der tog* went out on strike, and Glatstein and Leyeles both crossed the picket line, Mikhl severed all ties with them, forever.

"Thank you," I said to Evelyn. "These lessons are most valuable. They really worked, I can see, to make Mikhl what he was, a uniquely free spirit throughout the twenties and thirties. Can they work for me, too, do you think?"

"David," she replied, "what you need is to meet some gentiles. New York is full of gentiles. All you have to do is venture forth from the Upper West Side." And as if she were my fairy godmother, a flyer arrived in my mailbox not ten days later announcing a "Humanities Seminar for Visiting Scholars" to be held at NYU on "The Theory and Practice of Biography." True, in order to qualify, I had to be engaged in writing a biography, which was not currently the case. Would it matter if I made one up? With Evelyn's blessing and a little nudge from my private, Yiddish-speaking devil, I sent in an application.

NYU was a schlep. Normally I didn't go anywhere that wasn't within reach by bicycle, and here I had to switch trains at Times Square and wait for an irregular letter-train to take me to 23rd Street. But judging from the list of participants, it looked as if I were in luck. With the exception of the eminent biographer Kenneth Silverman, who was to conduct the seminar, only four of the thirteen other scholars had recognizably Jewish names. One, Brenda Wineapple, had graduated from Brandeis a year behind me. What most impressed me about my fellow Jews on the list was their total and unselfconscious embrace of the majority culture. Edwin Gittleman was writing about Robert Gould Shaw, the sculptor of the famous Civil War monument. Herb Leibowitz was doing a biography of William Carlos Williams. Gail

Levin was completing a catalogue raisonné of the painter Edward Hopper, and Brenda was starting work on Janet Flanner. Most stunning of all was Ken Silverman himself, who had won a Pulitzer Prize for his biography of Cotton Mather. Cotton Mather! It was like writing about Jesus. Mikhl's example had already been superseded. The way to belong, they were telling me, was to enter "their" inner sanctum and to officiate as High Priest.

As for me, I had JEW written all over me. Here was a scholar from the *Jewish* Theological Seminary who was (supposedly) writing a biography of . . . Sholem Aleichem. (Ach, if I had only learned Russian, I could someday have written his biography. Meanwhile, I had to put on a good show.)

A reluctant court Jew, I doubled as a kind of father confessor. From one week to the next, another participant revealed to me his or her true self. Alden Gordon, working on the Marquis de Marigny, wanted me to know that he was a proud Reform Jew from the South. Then he picked my brain about the merits of the Haskalah, the Jewish Enlightenment. Michael Wreszin confided that his father was the first Jew to be admitted to the New York Stock Exchange, and in his presentation Michael spent a lot of time discussing Dwight Macdonald's hatred of Jews as a subset of his hatred of America. While there was no way that Mary Ellen W. could herself be Jewish, she let on over lunch that her husband was Israeli and that she spoke fluent Hebrew. After my presentation, which came last, we all went out for a late lunch, where Ken told the assembled that his mother had been born in Vilna, though she arrived here at a young age, and in the john, before saying goodbye, Jacques S., who taught at the United States Marine Academy at King's Point and had never exchanged a single word with me before, told me how much he enjoyed hearing Sholem Aleichem read in the Yiddish original, which he alone, among all the participants, understood, because his parents had been Polish Jews, members of the French Resistance, etc. etc.

That morning at the seminar I had presented my thesis about the life and times of Solomon Rabinovitsh, known and loved the world over as Sholem Aleichem, Mr. How-Do-You-Do. Here, I argued, was your typical upwardly mobile Russian Jew, torn between bourgeois aspirations and an inbred Jewish fatalism; a man so insecure, so manipulative, that writing stories and letters became for him a means of seduction; in short, a narcissistic personality. This last earned me a compliment over lunch from Ken Silverman. How had I arrived at such a bold thesis? That was easy. What drew me to Sholem Aleichem, I explained, were behavior patterns and family pathologies that

I recognized from home. Solomon Rabinovitsh was a male version of my mother.

"In that case," Ken asked, "have you thought about writing *her* biography?"

So as it turned out, only four out of the thirteen other scholars in my biography seminar, my big chance to enter the mainstream, were bona fide gentiles. Should I ultimately fail to become a truly cosmopolitan New York Jew, the next best thing, I concluded, was having lunch with Evelyn and reading her late husband's devilishly difficult verse.

30

Partisans' Hymn

Ask me the name of any town or townlet in Poland and I can tell you its Jewish equivalent. Góra Kalwaria? Ger. Opatów? Apt. Rzeszów? Reyshe. Tyszowce? Tishevits. Chełm? Khelm. These places are the capitals of my Yiddish
heartland. They exist on a separate plane, in their own geography, which is
why I had zealously avoided going there as long as possible.

In the spring of my forty-fourth year, I accepted an invitation from the
Polish Ministry of Culture to help decide "The Future of Auschwitz," a
bizarre and impossible assignment, which Raphael Scharf, with his Polish
manners, British wit, and Jewish heart, tried to alleviate by taking me and
Professor Khone Shmeruk on a walking tour of Kraków. Forty-four, explained Scharf after quoting a passage from Mickiewicz's poetic drama
Dziady (Forefathers' Eve), carried deep mystical significance for the Polish
national poet, whose first name was Adam, "man" in Hebrew, the numeri-
cal value of whose letters, *alef-dalet-mem,* add up to forty-five. Even Professor Shmeruk, implausibly, tried to cheer me up. "You know what they used
to say?" he asked rhetorically. "There are three impossibilities in life: A Jew
sitting in a droshky without a parcel by his side, a policeman doing his beat
with an umbrella, and a whore wearing glasses." Speaking of whores,
Scharf was quick to point out where the most famous Jewish brothel in prewar Kraków had been located: right across from the courtyard where

Gebirtig lived, on Berek Joselewicz Street. "Naturally," said Scharf, "there's no mention of it in any of his songs."

It was easy for them to conjure up the lost worlds of Polish Jewry. They'd been born here. What did I have to come back to, other than this depressing and futile conference? When again, after this impromptu pre-conference tour, would I hear Yiddish spoken in Poland? And when last I conversed in Yiddish, in Warsaw, it was too painful for words. Ruta Sakowska, who never left Poland because someone had to preside over the publication of the Warsaw Ghetto Archive, said to me, so quietly that the Director of the Institute could not possibly have heard, "*undzer eynzamkayt iz umbashrayb-lekh,* our isolation, our loneliness is indescribable." So who were they kidding with their locker-room banter? Do the arithmetic! I wanted to shout to my elderly friend and would-be mentor; forty-four means that I'm old enough to speak a fluent *mame-loshn* but too young to have ever heard it spoken here, where every tenth person once spoke Yiddish and, in the major cities, every third.

English was the lingua franca of our five-day meeting, much to the chagrin of the French delegates, because English was the language of our convener, Jonathan Webber, the language of both the American and British delegations, and the language of post-communist Poland. Hebrew, thanks to Jonathan's intervention, had recently been added to the languages that greet the visitor to the Auschwitz *Stammlager,* visitors who are assumed to be of European descent, since there are no Arabic, Chinese, or Japanese inscriptions. Wanda, with her jet-black hair and high Slavic cheekbones, gives us the standard tour in flawless English. She apologizes for her relative inexperience. Only fifteen years on the job. Yesterday, she informs us, they buried the veteran guide, a former French inmate who lived on the premises for forty-seven years.

The one word that gives Wanda trouble is HOLLOW-COST, and the reason becomes clear as we proceed through the camp, beginning at the infamous gate, with its labor-camp façade, and follow the cobblestones block by block, the mug shots of the Polish-Christian inmates displayed in Number 6 (Jews were tattooed, she explains, never photographed), to the various national exhibits, the Bulgarian so egregious that it has recently been closed, again after Jonathan protested, and from there to Death Block 11, where Wanda becomes extremely animated when showing us the execution yard with its individual hooks, the kangaroo courtroom, and the underground punishment cells, one with a perpetual candle lit by Pope John Paul in memory of Father Kolbe, and her voice starts to quiver when she recounts the "untold" story of the Home Army soldiers who were tortured and perished here. All this, including the (reconstructed) gallows next to Crematorium I where Commandant Hoess was hanged, is the manageable story of known victims whose native countries have honored them with national pavilions. The HOLLOW-COST narrative is still ragged. Only lately could Wanda speak of Jewish victims, and the final tally of how many and what proportion has still to be decided. There is more to see than to tell: the canisters of Cyclone B in Block 5, with its rooms of human hair, combs, brushes, prosthetic devices, shoes, kettles, valises, in short, the horror show that beyond naming its own objects has defied our scholarly attempts to render it in words.

Just as we enter Block 27, the only one dedicated to the "The Suffering and Struggle of the Jews," the alliteration and implicit symmetry already bespeaking late Stalinist doublespeak, someone comes running to say that an official Israeli delegation has just arrived, the first ever. Jonathan complains that this will wreck our schedule, but our group decides to attend the ceremony. And indeed, just outside, between Block 27 and the wall that obscures the offending cross from the Carmelite monastery, officers from each unit of the Israeli army are taking up formation. A unit of the Polish cavalry in funny hats and quaint uniforms is there standing guard, and a group of Israeli high school students is making a lot of noise. I seek out my colleagues Alvin Rosenfeld and Michael Steinlauf, sensing that we will need each other's emotional support.

For if there *is* a language to talk about this place, Ehud Barak, heading the delegation as Chief of Staff of the Israel Defense Forces, believes Hebrew to be that language, a dense, allusive, and high-literary Hebrew. No one will translate his address, perhaps because what he is saying is less important than that he is saying it, a Jewish soldier, not a survivor—Barak himself, not a speech writer. Europe, he proclaims, was waiting for the destruction of the Jews to happen; any nation could have brought it about. And in a different voice, he informs his audience, most of whom cannot understand a word he's saying, that his army, built upon the three pillars of Might, Right, and Clearsightedness, has arrived here fifty years too late. I am having a hard time following his diction and complicated syntax. I am too busy crying.

The next day we visit Birkenau, the place that most tourists never see because there is so little to see, just the grass-covered dead-ended railroad tracks, the endless rows of chimneys—metonymic remains of the barracks that were dismantled for firewood soon after the war—a few restored watch towers and miles of rotting barbed wire. Why is it so cold here, even in April, even in my thermal undershirt and layers of clothing? Because Birkenau was built on a swamp. And why won't Jonathan allow us to wander among the chimneys, trying to imagine where the barracks dubbed "Mexico" (the place of abandon and German brothels) and "Canada" (the place of plenty, the looted goods from the incoming transports) were located? Because we must cover the inventory of relics and landmarks, like the monument to the Soviet POWs that takes forty minutes to reach through the muddy terrain. I have not thought about them for many years.

We're in bumper-to-bumper traffic driving back of a Sunday in Saint Agathe, six of us crammed into Father's Oldsmobile. Nelly and Fima, who normally don't talk about the war, get on the subject of food, and Fima tells us the story of the potato that was stolen from him in Auschwitz and how the loss of that potato, which he had carefully hidden, made him want to die, but at a wedding in Tel Aviv ten years later he got it back, from a former Katzétnik who had slept across from him in the barracks and who had stolen it to save his own life, which reminds Nelly of the Soviet POWs who were left without any food at all and tried to stay alive by eating human flesh.

So this is the monument to their memory, and it's getting colder by the minute, but Jonathan presses on, because there are mounds of forks and spoons for us to see, just lying there out in the open, which used to be so much higher before souvenir hunters started helping themselves, and the Sauna, which could become the site of a major new exhibit, or of a chapel, or of something yet to be decided, and the Auschwitz monument itself, which will occupy much of our deliberation during the coming days, and the ruins of the gas chambers, and the remains of Crematoria III, IV and V.

But Jonathan is not the only one who has spent his life devising means of commemorating the nameless dead. I have plans of my own. I have brought a *yizkor* candle in a frosted glass all the way from New York and I propose that we stop our tour of duty and find an appropriate spot to light the candle, like this spot right here, between the ruins of Crematorium IV, blown up by the members of the *Sonderkommando* led by Leyb Langfus and Zalman Gradowski on October 7, 1944, and the ash pit pond nearby, and whosoever wants to is welcome to join me in lighting the candle, but because there is no sheltered spot the candle goes out before we finish singing the Partisans' Hymn by Hirsh Glik, the lyrics to which only four of us among this august group of scholars can sing, and Jonathan has never heard this hymn before although he's heard of it, and I have chosen this song because according to Gradowski's chronicle, which I published in my massive and carefully annotated anthology, it was sung by the Czech transport inside the gas chamber, so it behooves us to sing it too, but with only four of us who know the words and the space so open to the April wind, our voices drown in the vast expanse that is Birkenau, and I am choking on the Yiddish lyrics anyway, and screaming inside me is another voice, screaming so loud that I forget to lead my choir in the penultimate stanza that sings of tomorrow's sun and the rising dawn and the coming generations that will go on singing this song forever.

The voice inside me is screaming in English.

31

The Menorah

Lublin was an oasis of femininity after Kraków. The few female delegates in Kraków, had they had something to say about The Future of Auschwitz, deferred to the men. Jonathan, representing one extreme, wanted the whole site constructed of authentic materials as a lasting memorial to the Jewish martyrs. Raphael Scharf, active in Polish-Jewish rapprochement, and Staszek Krajewski, a Jewish liason to the Polish Church, were opposed to making a fetish of the past. It was enough to preserve some part that would stand for the whole.

In Lublin, I was immediately surrounded not by one doting woman but by five: Monika, her mother, Joanna, Agnieszka, and Ewa. The last three were single. All were non-Jews, in thrall, like me, to the Polish-Jewish past. All were in agreement that I was the most charming man who had ever visited from New York and that, in general, dark-haired Jewish males were irresistible. What I couldn't get over was the melody of their English. All but Monika's mother, who spoke English haltingly, had the same singsong way of raising their voice at the end of a sentence. How come Moses Herzog, a Bellow character whose descriptive abilities I've always admired, never took note of how Wanda, his Polish lover, spoke to him in French?

Their English fluency bore witness to years spent abroad in exile or in study and to a freedom of spirit, evinced most keenly by their fascination with all things Jewish. Monika had come to the States to study Yiddish, which was how I'd met her, and she now introduced me to her family and friends. Her hair seemed a bit too streaked this time—the second pregnancy had made it dry as straw—but the glint of her gray-green eyes were still as I remembered them from her going-away party in Washington Heights.

While Monika's mother fed me her incredible chocolate cheese cake and gefilte fish made from a traditional Jewish recipe, Monika and her friends nourished me with stories, from which there emerged one archetypal tale, tailored, perhaps, to its addressee: the tale of how each of them had discovered the missing Jews of Poland.

At her perfunctory interview with the secret police before being allowed to spend a month doing research in Oxford on *Winnie the Pooh* and other British children's classics, Monika was not forewarned that, at her second tea-time discussion in the common room, her British hosts, despite their careful breeding and stiff upper lip, would cite the dismal record of Polish anti-Semitism and the dastardly behavior of Poles during the Holocaust. What anti-Semitism? she asked, her voice rising an octave higher than usual. Poland had always been a beacon of tolerance! Why, back in the sixteenth century, when there were autos-da-fé elsewhere in Europe, Poland was a safe haven for the Jews. We're not asking you about the sixteenth century, her hosts replied; we're talking about the twentieth. Monika returned to Poland deeply troubled. A year later, her British pen-pal came to Lublin for a visit and they were comparing notes.

"Who's your favorite author?" Monika wanted to know.

"Isaac Bashevis Singer."

"Who's he?" asked Monika.

"Don't you know? He writes a lot about demons and the Jews of Poland."

"Really? Perhaps you could send me some of his books."

And that's how it all started.

For Ewa, the revelation happened much closer to home. Ewa was born and raised in Warsaw, the daughter of a class enemy, her father having fought with the Home Army in the doomed Warsaw Uprising. She was eight years old and they were out taking a walk. "Here," he informed her, "is where the trolley tracks ended—at the walls of the ghetto." Ewa was afraid of her father and knew enough not to ask: What was the ghetto and who lived there? This she would discover on her own during her years of exile in Detroit.

The first big fight Agnieszka remembers having with *her* father was about the Jews. Over dinner one evening he recalled an incident that had occurred in his native town right after the war. A Jew returned and was killed that very night. And although everyone knew who did it, no one turned him in. Agnieszka, who was studying to become a lawyer, was outraged. The man was guilty of murder. Sure, life was cheap, and there was a civil war going on, but murder is murder, and for this murder the Poles bore sole responsibility. Her father got up from the table and walked out of the room.

Maybe another reason they're so fond of me is that I don't remind them of their fathers. Monika, for example, married Chris, the polar opposite of her muscular, fanatically goal-oriented father, her father, who sets out for Hanover the day I arrive wearing a T-shirt and khaki shorts, as if he intended to walk all the way. Come to think of it, Monika met Chris at the first public lecture on a Jewish theme ever held in Lublin, at the Catholic University; Chris, whose unusual path of return led him from a mining town in Ontario, where he was born and raised, to Poland, and from a family of lapsed church-goers to a deeply personal Roman Catholic faith.

Joanna makes fun of his grammatical mistakes, but she is jealous, because Chris worships the ground that Monika treads on. Chris takes me for a long walk, to see the yard and house where Monika grew up, her grandparents' house. And the table at which we eat our meals, Chris tells me with pride, was built by her great-grandfather, as was the massive credenza. Chris has adopted her forbears in the same way as my women friends have adopted the Jews.

They vie with each other over who can show me more. Did Monika take me to see the model of the Jerusalem Temple inside the former Lublin Yeshiva? Joanna wants to know. Of course not! For his part, Chris thinks it was foolish of Joanna to take me to Under the Devil's Paw, a popular tavern just inside the gate of Old Town. Why fill my head with these stupid local legends? Agnieszka, who is not particularly fond of Joanna, invites me home for lunch. Home is in the first postwar housing project, known as Osiedle, the Settlement, from which almost everyone of her generation has emigrated to the four corners of the earth, like her brother, who defected back in the 1970s and now lives in Denver. But when her parents died and their apartment reverted to her, Agnieszka thought, Why not? What's wrong with going back to the place where I grew up? I can still spend my sabbaticals at Rutgers if I want.

Ewa writes for the local edition of the *Gazeta Wyborcza,* Poland's largest daily. She very much wants me to meet Mr. Honig, one of the last remaining Jews in Lublin. She once did a story about him, comparing him to Lazarus, risen from the dead, because Mr. Honig survived Majdanek, Belzec, and Trawniki. We speak in Yiddish, so Ewa won't understand. They're two men shy of a quorum, he laments, in Lublin, a great Jewish center, which sustained thirty-eight shuls before the war, not counting innumerable shtibls. He shows me around the Old Jewish Cemetery, of which he is the caretaker, and complains bitterly that his plans for restoration have been thwarted. By whom? I cannot figure it out. Yes, he remembers Jacob Glatstein's visit in 1934 to bury his mother. Not much left of that cemetery, though. The Germans used the tombstones to pave the roads.

Włodek, another friend of Monika's, has offered to take me to his dacha in a place called Górecko, close to nature, but Monika insists that we do a quick tour of Singer's Poland. She has become the preeminent translator of Singer from Yiddish into Polish; the only one, in fact, because Singer's American publisher insists that all translations be made from the English and not from the Yiddish original. There's no point visiting Kreshev, spelled "Krzeszów" (for future reference), because a curse still hangs over the town, just as Singer described it in his story.

"You and Chris should lead I. B. Singer Tours through Historic Poland," I suggest from the back seat. "See the attic where Itchele Singer first read Spinoza! See where Rechele's demon was exorcised! Visit the town where Singer's father once served as rabbi. Spend a day at the dacha where Singer laid his many lovers!" Instead of laughing, Monika starts crying.

In most small towns, there's nothing to see, except for a parking lot or commons where the marketplace used to be. All the surrounding houses, we know in advance, once belonged to the Jews. Monika has brought along a book with the relevant statistics:

Biłgoraj (1921): 3,715 Jews out of 5,603 total population
Frampol (1921): 1,465 Jews out of 2,720
Goraj (1921): only 394 Jews out of 2,331

Tishevitz (Tyszowce), with its 4,420 inhabitants in 1921, of whom 2,451 were Jews, 1,592 Poles, and 377 Ukrainians, we must leave for another trip, because it is far off the beaten track. The real, unspoken reason is that I have written a book about this shtetl, and know its every house of learning, study, and defecation, and Monika is being protective of me. I would recognize nothing.

We settle on a lengthier visit to Józefów Lubelski, because there is still a synagogue left standing there and a bigger surprise yet: one remaining Jew.

January 4, 1993
Chief Librarian
Józefów Municipal Library
Józefów, Poland

Dear Madame:

Last April, as you may recall, I visited your library in the company of my friends Chris and Monika G., from Lublin. On that occasion you were kind enough to introduce us to Mrs. Maria Danuta Bil, the last surviving Jew in Józefów. We very much enjoyed meeting her. Before taking leave of you, I also promised to donate a Hanukkah lamp ("menorah") to your library. It was my hope that when seeing the menorah, visitors would realize that the building, one of the largest and oldest in town, once served as a synagogue, and that Józefów itself was once a thriving Jewish community. Here is that menorah.

Allow me, however, to add a personal note. Upon returning home, I, David Roskies, learned that my maternal grandfather, Israel Welczer, was a native of Józefów. What's more, my own mother, Masza Welzcer, had her birth registered in your town (end of December, 1906), although, in point of fact, she was born in Wilno-Vilnius. In addition, on my father's side, the Weintraub family and my late Aunt Malcia (b. 1889) were originally from Józefów! And so, when you place the menorah in the niche where the Torah scroll used to stand (and where a portrait of a woman hung when we visited you in April), we ask that the following inscription be posted nearby, in Polish and in English:

"IN MEMORY OF ISRAEL BEN AARON WELCZER (1862–1925), BORN IN JÓZEFÓW. Donated by his daughter, MASZA WELCZER-ROSKIES (Montreal, Canada), and by his grandson, DAVID G. ROSKIES (New York City)."

Though this menorah is neither an antique nor a valuable treasure, it was used in our home in Montreal, Canada, for fifty years. My mother, who fled Europe in 1940, asked that I donate it to you in our name.

Sincerely,
David G. Roskies

32

Dream House

It was Mother's dream house, and mine too. A three-story house made of red brick with the front door painted a bright blue. Thirteen rooms, not counting the laundry room, pantry, wine cellar, and capacious closets. In some rooms, like the sun porch and basement, she never ventured, which made them the perfect refuge, for she was always "on," from the moment the creak of the floorboards gave me away to the last *a gute nakht*. The basement was the safest bet, escaping to my electric train, printing press, recording studio, or imaginary playmates. To this day, the house on Pagnuelo is where I seduce every woman I've ever desired, ever betrayed. It's amazing how they all end up here: Esther, Leah, Ilana, Abby, Miri, even Tami Azzulai from Kiryat Hayyim. Once, years after the divorce, I dreamt of Miri lying on Mother's side of the bed, drenched in menstrual blood, and in another dream, I insisted on Abby letting me get behind the wheel of her sports car, parked in our long driveway, despite my never having learned to use a stick shift.

Each floor had its own character. Upstairs, only Mother walked around in the nude. The rest of us kept our doors closed. It was forbidden, however, to let anyone sit on your bed—a superstitious relic perhaps, or a display of domestic modesty. On the ground floor every table was Mother's stage: the white enamel kitchen table, the breakfast room table, cluttered with

Yiddish periodicals and old New Year's cards, and the fancy dining room table where, after Father died, she insisted on serving all her guests.

Who was Malvina compared to her? Who for that matter was I—no more than a prompter, feeding her cues if ever the conversation lagged, which wasn't often. And how she could ad-lib! No two performances were ever the same. I once tried to do the math. Say there were 150 separate skits in her repertoire, five times the number of chapters in this book, but each time she combined them anew, because each time there was something else to jog her memory, to inspire rage or indignation, then the performative possibilities were virtually endless. The way her eyes would sparkle and her head tilt slightly to the side the moment the soliloquy began, as garrulous as Sholem Aleichem, as grand as Jacob Gordin.

When her energy finally began to flag, it was time for me to learn her technique, the Masha Method, the way all encounters, if properly scripted, flow into each other. That visit I came alone, because my son Aryeh was still afraid of her, and my wife, Shana, would forever remain a stranger. Without my spare set of keys, I had to ring the doorbell and through the panel of stained glass could make her out hobbling out of the kitchen. Not until she unlocked the front door did I notice her hair. "Boris Kletzkin!" I blurted out. She had allowed her hair to go completely white. The allusion, calculated to be a little off, hit the mark, and she laughed. Then I gave her a big hug and said, more gently this time, *"Got tsu danken, groy gevorn,* thank God, turned gray."

The Boris Kletzkin Story goes like this:

Anything published by the Vilna press of Boris Kletzkin, which specialized in modern Yiddish literature and scholarship, was especially coveted, not only because of the high-quality paper, the distinctive typeface, and the covers embossed in tin with the portraits of Joseph Opatoshu, David Bergelson, H. Leivick, and Moyshe Kulbak, but also because Kletzkin was a good friend of Mother's; actually, not so much Kletzkin himself as his lover Esther Notik, her favorite Hebrew teacher from the Yehudia School for Girls. Kletzkin took up with her during World War I, when he sent his wife and child off to the interior of Russia, and were it not for her several abortions, Esther, his *pilégesh,* or concubine, might have borne him children too, for Kletzkin was the son of landed gentry and had money to burn. Once, when Mother went around collecting for the Jewish Student Organization, he pulled a twenty-zloty note out of his pocket without a second thought;

then again, when visiting Fradl in her summer dacha, Kletzkin would take a walk in the forest and send Esther to go in by herself, so as not to offend Fradl's religious sensibilities. So the Kletzkin edition of the modern Yiddish classics was a prized possession, and when brother Grisha established a bookshelf in Nyonya's memory at Stefan Batory University, Mother donated a complete deluxe set of Leivick and Opatoshu, which cost a fortune. But Kletzkin's glory days were just about over, and when he crashed, everyone knew it, because he appeared on Small Stefan Street with his bushy black beard turned completely grey. The owner of the Kletzkin Publishing House could no longer afford to dye his hair.

How clever of me to link these two illustrious Vilners, both known for their contributions to Yiddish culture and their freewheeling lifestyle, and to award Mother the prize, for while Kletzkin went broke, Masha was still solvent and had merely decided that the time had come to show her age.

The second reference was more direct and contextual.

A small circle of friends had gathered at Grisha's in honor of Mother's sixteenth birthday.

"So what do you see, Masha," they ask her, "what do you see your future to be?"

Accustomed to performing in front of important people from the age of three, she said, "I see myself with a *vander-shtekn*, a staff of exile, in my hand. A long road lies ahead. I make it through, and reach the age of sixty. Then I take a look at myself in the mirror and say, *Got tsu danken, groy gevorn*, thank God, turned gray!"

This was vintage Mother, completely self-referential. No one but she could measure her own triumph. At the time, it was pure bravado, since reaching sixty seemed an impossible goal, given that her own mother had only just died, at the age of fifty-eight. Lo these many years later, however, Mother's turning officially white at the age of eighty-three was cause for rejoicing.

Then again, were Mother to look at herself in the mirror, she would see that a few of her teeth were missing, not on account of those nasty Bundists who got her saintly mother clapped in prison, but because she took such lousy care of them, and she would note that while Fradl had wasted away with TB, her daughter grew more ample over the years, so much so that it was hard to imagine how, living alone, she managed to hook up her corset. Even to climb the stairs before bedtime was a major feat.

Since all meals were now served in the dining room, the table was always set. The paintings, by Alexander Bercovitch, Sylvia Ary, and Yosl Bergner, were still crooked, and I couldn't help but smile at Bergner's still-life of the cut-open fish, remembering the story of how he had gone to buy the fish at the Carmel Market in Tel Aviv.

"Young man," the fish monger asked him in Yiddish, "what do you need it for?"

"*Ikh darf es af tsu moln,*" he replied, by which he meant, "I need it for painting."

"*Fish,*" she scoffed, thinking he meant *moln,* as in "grind," "*fish darf men preglen, nit moln,* fish are for frying, not for grinding."

There was fresh mushroom-barley soup to start on, made especially by Xenia and brought over only yesterday by Eva in honor of my visit.

"No one will disturb us this afternoon," Mother promised.

Lately, she admitted, her father had been much on her mind. How badly he had been treated by her half-sisters and half-brothers, particularly by Grisha! They were so obviously jealous, jealous both of him and of her, the only child born out of love, the product of a mixed marriage between a Polish Hasid and a pureblood Litvak. How they made fun of her, always sending her on meaningless errands, just to get her out of the house. She wouldn't even tell me the names they used to call her.

And here's what she was thinking. After Fradl died, she stayed with her father and his chambermaid. Once, she came back very late from a rendezvous with Seidman. It must have been around 12:30. The janitor opened the entrance to the courtyard, but the chambermaid had gone to sleep, so Mother couldn't get into the apartment. There was a ledge to sit on (where? how?) that looked into her father's bedroom, so she decided to sit there until daybreak. And the hours passed quickly—that's how taken she was with her father's *hadres-ponem,* his stately, regal, appearance. At 7:00, the servant awoke, saw her sitting there, and let her in, and Mother went to bed and slept and slept.

"Wait a minute!" I almost shouted. "What language did you and he speak? Did you still speak to him in Russian? Still call him 'Uncle'? Use the formal form of address?"

"How can you ask such a thing? When it was just the two of us, freed of their poisonous hatred, we spoke Yiddish. My father could barely speak Russian."

"So it was he who taught you to speak Yiddish!"

"Ach, leave me alone!"

The main course was *hálushkes,* stuffed cabbage, another of Xenia's specialties, served with potatoes and beets. Heavy on carbohydrates, the way I liked it.

"How many years do you think we spent together?" she asked defiantly. "Papa had his first heart attack soon after Mother died. But I was determined to live. I possessed a special power, *ikh hob gehat aza keyakh,* to overcome all obstacles.

"After the heart attack, I was desperately lonely. So one day I sat down to write a letter, to Misha Yossipovitsh."

"To whom?"

"To Misha Yossipovitsh, my first love."

"You mean, even before Seidman?"

"Yes. I never told you about him before. My sister Mina rented an apartment from the Rosengartens, and Misha was their nephew. He had recently left Moscow and would visit them occasionally, from Lodz. He was my height. We came from the same background. He spoke a beautiful Russian."

"How did you meet him?"

"I just told you. I would come to Mina's to play the piano, and he would visit the Rosengartens.

"So I sat down and wrote him a letter. And the very next day, before the letter arrived, I look out, and there, standing under the chestnut tree opposite my window, is Misha. My angel. He doffs his hat, I run downstairs and rush into his arms. We go straightaway to Mina's, where I play for him all afternoon."

"Why did you break up?"

"I was seventeen and he was twenty-one, raring to go. He wanted me to sleep with him. I couldn't go that route. My mother had warned me."

"Because you were annointed."

"That's right. So I broke up with him, also through a letter."

"Why write to him if he could read your desire without a letter?"

"*Af nisht tsu badarfn.* Just in case."

"Maybe you'll play for me, too?"

"Oh, my Dovidl, you've given me inspiration. You know, I haven't played for such a long time. There *is* something I want to play for you, a Russian song that Binyomin loved so much that he invited me to Israel just to hear me play it. Louise has asked me for the music, but I haven't given it to her yet."

Slowly, she got up from the table and hobbled into the living room, though not before stopping in front of me to say, *"Host nokh di kompot nisht gegesn,* you haven't eaten your compote yet."

Judging by her labored gait I understood that her travels were over—no more hikes and skiing trips with the Know-Your-Land movement; no more shopping expeditions into Zakopane; no more escapes to the pine forests of Cape Cod. Though no place, of course, could ever replace Vilna, Montreal had by now become a true city of refuge. Let her children seek their sanctuary elsewhere; she would not even follow. Here, in this dream house, she reigned supreme, her sovereignty over the past unchallenged. We, her three surviving children, could hitch a ride on the travelogue of her mind. Or we could sample her repertoire of songs, in six languages, on a set of twelve cassettes locked away for now in the closet adjacent to Eva's room. Or we could listen to her play.

For the next twenty minutes, as I remained seated at the dining-room table, not eating my compote but scribbling notes on a pale-blue napkin, she played: for Misha, her first love; for Benjamin, her firstborn; for Fradl, who bequeathed to them the gift of music despite the husband who had suffered no music; for Grisha, the brother she had forgiven for everything; for sister Annushka, who had taught her how to play; for Papale, the student with the elbow patches on his jacket, who was seduced by her songs. She played by ear on a piano that hadn't been tuned in years, her fingers stiffened by arthritis, as she hummed the Russian lyrics to herself, seeing as her youngest, the one who had been gifted by God, couldn't understand them anyway.

Genealogy

ANSKY, S. [pen name of Shloyme-Zanvl Rappoport] (1863, Vitebsk–1920, Warsaw). Revolutionary, ethnographer, Russian-Yiddish poet, playwright, and prose writer. His *Between Two Worlds or The Dybbuk*, which premiered in Vilna in 1920, became the most famous play in the Yiddish repertoire. My mother's class welcomed Ansky to her school upon his escape from Petrograd in 1918.

ASTOUR, MIKHL [formerly Chernikhov] (1916, Kharkov–2004, St. Louis). After a brief tenure as Professor of Yiddish and Russian Literature at Brandeis University, Astour served for many years as Professor of Classical Cultures and Ancient Near East at Southern Illinois University (Edwardsville). A lifelong Territorialist and a close boyhood friend of Avrom Sutzkever in Vilna, he adopted the nom de guerre Astur, meaning "hawk," in 1933.

BERCOVITCH, ALEXANDER (1891, Kherson–1951, Montreal). Painter and set designer who trained in Jerusalem, St. Petersburg, Munich, and Central Asia before settling in Montreal in 1926. He was the father of the noted literary scholar Sacvan Bercovitch and the painter Sylvia Ary.

BERGNER, YOSL (1920, Vienna–). Major Israeli painter and son of the
Yiddish poet Melekh Ravitch. He spent his childhood in Warsaw, emigrated to Australia in 1937, and, after serving in the Australian army,
settled in Israel in 1950.

BERNSHTEYN, MORDECAI (Matvey) (1905, Bitten, White Russia–1966,
New York). Lifelong Bundist who spent most of the postwar years in
Argentina.

BRODERZON, MOYSHE (1890, Moscow–1956, Warsaw). Prolific expressionist poet, popular song writer, and a central figure in Yiddish
Lodz between the two world wars. He was reburied in Haifa in
1970.

CHOSID, MORDECAI (1909, Sekuran, Bessarabia–1988, Montreal).
Yiddish-Hebrew pedagogue in Montreal since 1950 and a Yiddish
poet.

DAWANG, SIMA (1907, Vilna–1986, Montreal). Vilna-trained Yiddish pedagogue and Holocaust survivor. She relocated to Montreal in 1951, the
year she began teaching at the Jewish People's School.

DREYER, SHMUEL (1895, near Bialystok–1941, near Bialystok). From 1921
a staff writer of *Vilner tog*. In 1924 he received his law degree in Vilna,
where he was active in Jewish communal life.

DREYER-SFARD, REGINA/RIVTSHE (1910, Bialystok–1991, Jerusalem).
Founder of the Maydim Yiddish Marionette Theater in Vilna. She stud-
ied with Sergei Eisenstein in Moscow and taught film history at the
Lodz Film School, and, after being expelled from Poland in 1968, at Tel
Aviv University.

DUNSKY, SHIMSHEN (1899, Yashinovke, near Bialystok–1981, Montreal).
Judaic scholar, beloved pedagogue, and lifelong Labor Zionist. He
served from 1927 to 1969 as vice-principal of the Jewish People's School,
and published a bilingual scholarly edition of Midrash Rabba on the
Five Scrolls.

DVORZHETSKI (DWORZECKI) MARK (1908, Vilna–1975, Tel Aviv). Medical doctor and a leading chronicler and scholar of the Holocaust who testified at the Eichmann trial in 1961.

ELBERG, YEHUDA (1912, Zniersz, near Lodz–2003, Montreal). Yiddish novelist and short-story writer who survived the Warsaw ghetto and settled in Montreal in 1951.

ERIK, MAX [pen name of Zalmen Merkin] (1898, Sosnowiec–1937, the Gulag). Polish officer, lawyer, literary critic, and scholar. He taught my mother Yiddish literature and married her classmate Ida Rosenshein. The major historian of Old Yiddish literature, Erik assumed a professorship in the Belorussian Acadamy of Sciences in Minsk and later became Professor of Yiddish Literature and Literary Criticism in Kiev. He was arrested on April 10, 1936.

FEINBERG, LEYB (1897 Kadima, Ukraine–1969, New York). Yiddish poet and translator of Russian literature.

FIBICH, FELIX (1917, Warsaw–). Dancer and choreographer who was married to the choreographer and dancer Judith Berg.

GEBIRTIG, MORDECAI (1877, Kraków–1942, Kraków ghetto). The most popular Yiddish songwriter of interwar Poland and perhaps of all time.

GILINSKY, SHLOYME-FAYVISH (1888, Lingmian, Lithuania–1961, Lexington, New York). According to his official biography, he was a Zionist Socialist agitator in the first decade of the twentieth century who only joined the Bund in 1921. I prefer my mother's version.

GLATSTEIN, JACOB/YANKEV (1896, Lublin–1971, New York). A founding member of the Introspectivist school in Yiddish poetry and a Yiddish novelist, journalist, and literary critic.

GLIK, HIRSH (1922, Vilna–1944, Estonian forests). Poet and partisan, author of the "Partisans' Hymn."

GORDIN, JACOB (1853, Mirgorod–1909, New York). Russian-language journalist and communitarian. He emigrated to the United States in 1891, the same year he launched the reform of the Yiddish theater with his play *Siberia*, after which he dominated the Yiddish theater worldwide until his death.

GREEN, ARTHUR (1941, Patterson, N.J.–). Scholar of Jewish mysticism and theologian. He studied Yiddish with Mikhl Astour at Brandeis University and Hasidism with Abraham Joshua Heschel at the Jewish Theological Seminary, where he received Rabbinic ordination in 1967. He was the driving force of Havurat Shalom, which he helped found in 1968.

GROBER, KHAYELE (1898, Bialystok–1978, Haifa). A founding member of the Moscow Habimah, thereafter, a perpipatetic Yiddish actress.

GROSSBARD, HERTZ (1892, Lodz–1994, Holon, Israel). A founding member of the Vilna Troupe. Also acted on the German stage. Master of the one-man Yiddish "word concert." Lived in Montreal from 1951 to 1971.

HOROWITZ, BER (1895, a village in the Carpathians–1942, Stanislawów). Neo-romantic poet and short-story writer. During a visit to Czernowitz, he painted a portrait of my brother, Ben, in which he was made to resemble the young Pushkin.

HRUSHOVSKI, BENJAMIN (1928, Vilna–). Founder and chief theoretician of the Tel Aviv School of Poetics and Semiotics, and a Hebrew-Yiddish poet. He changed his name to Harshav when he left Israel in 1986 and assumed a professorship in Hebrew and Comparative Literature at Yale University.

KACZERGINSKI, SHMERKE (1908, Vilna–1954, Mendossa, Argentina). Poet and partisan, a founding member of the group *Yung Vilne*, and a member of the Polish Communist Party.

KAMIEN, YOYSEF (1900, Vilna–Uralsk, 1942). Joined the Vilna Troupe in 1921, with which he continued to perform after having a leg amputated in 1935.

KLETZKIN, BORIS (1875, Horodishtsh, White Russia–1937, Vilna). After settling in Vilna in 1885, he dedicated his sizable fortune to furthering Yiddish secular culture. The Kletzkin Publishing House, founded in 1910, set the gold standard for Yiddish literary and academic publishing.

KON, PINKHES (?–1941, Vilna ghetto). Settled in Vilna in 1919, where he trained and practiced as a lawyer. He published numerous scholarly articles on the history and culture of Vilna Jewry.

KORN, RACHEL (1898, Podliski, a village in East Galicia–1982, Montreal). Poet and prose writer who specialized in the rural Galician landscape, and mother of Dr. Irene (Renia) Kupferszmidt, our family physician.

LEIVICK, H. [Leyvik Halpern] (1888, Ihumin, White Russia–1962, New York). Considered the prophetic voice of Yiddish literature.

LIBO, ALEXANDER (1890, Vilna–1970, Tel Aviv). Began his medical career in Vilna in 1913. He survived the Vilna ghetto and immigrated to Israel in 1958.

LICHT, EVELYN [née Markul] (1905, New York–1993, New York). Painter and art instructor.

LICHT, MIKHL (1893 in a village in Volhynia–1953, New York). A member of the Introspectivist circle in New York. He kept a low profile on account of a severe heart condition and his uncompromising commitment to high modernism.

MANGER, ITZIK (1901, Czernowitz–1969, Tel Aviv). *Enfant terrible* and a major lyric poet, famous for his ballads and *Bible Poems*.

MARKISH, ESTHER [née Lazebnikov] (1912, Yekaterinoslav–). The daughter of a wealthy oil dealer from Baku who married Peretz Markish in 1929. A graduate of the Moscow Institute for Foreign Languages, she became a leading translator of French literature into Russian. After a two-year-long struggle with the Soviet authorities, she was allowed to immigrate to Israel with her son David in November 1972, where she lives in Bat Yam.

MARKISH, PERETZ (1895, Polonoyye–12 August, 1952, in the Lubianka Prison, Moscow). A founder of the Expressionist movement in Yiddish poetry. He was awarded the Order of Lenin.

MATZ, FRADL [née Polachek] (1863, Minsk–1921, Vilna). An accomplished singer who was married off to Judah Leib Matz in 1878, their marriage immortalized in song by the famed wedding bard Elyokum Zunser. She bore him many children, ten of whom survived. They were, roughly in this order, Alexander, Helena, Mina, Rosa, Nyonya (Benjamin), Annushka, Lisa, Maria, Grisha, and Nathan. Helena's fate is unknown. Mina, Rosa, and Maria perished in the Vilna ghetto. Nathan was committed to an asylum in Koidonov. Masha, my mother, was the sole surviving offspring of Fradl's second marriage, to Yisroel Welczer, a marriage out of love.

MATZ, GRISHA [Hirsh] (1899, Vilna–1941, Vilna). A founding member of the Vilna TOZ, the Society for the Protection of Health, which he directed after the death of Dr. Zemach Szabad in 1935. He briefly ran the printing press of Fradl Matz, published *Health Resorts and Tourism in Poland* (Warsaw, 1935), the first work of its kind in Yiddish, and chaired the Yiddish Theater Society of Vilna. He married Nadia Vinisky, a banker's daughter, and was murdered in the first weeks of the German occupation of Vilna.

MATZ, JUDAH LEIB (1832, Vilna–1902, Vilna). Son of Eliezer Lipmann Matz, creator of the Hebrew font that was used throughout Eastern Europe and the Americas. The Matz Publishing House, founded by Judah Leib in 1869, specialized in Hebrew prayer books and didactic storybooks in Yiddish. The Matz family had no link to the Gaon of Vilna (despite Mother's claims to the contrary).

MAZEH, MORDECAI (1880, Borisov–1942, Treblinka). Instructor of gymnastics in Vilna Jewish schools, director of the Yehudia School for Girls.

Founding director of the Vilna Troupe. Headed the Theater Department of the Jewish Self-Help organization in the Warsaw ghetto.

PERETZ, ISAAC LEYB (ca. 1852, Zamość–1915, Warsaw). Yiddish-Hebrew poet, prose writer, playwright, and a chief ideologue of Jewish cultural renewal in and through the Yiddish language.

RABINOVITSH, ISRAEL (1894, Bitten, White Russia–1964, Montreal). Ethnomusicologist and editor of the *Keneder odler*, Canada's only Yiddish daily, from 1932 to 1952.

RAN, LEYZER (1912, Vilna–1995, New York). Survivor of the Gulag who memorialized Jewish Vilna. He moved to New York in 1953.

RAPPEL, MALVINA (1901–1987, New York). Born into a family of Yiddish actors: her father, Leyzer, was a lead actor and co-director of the Elysseum Theater in Warsaw; her mother, Zina, a leading actress; and her three younger sisters Esther, Zila, and Anja also acted and sang.

RAVITCH, MELEKH [pen name of Zekharye Bergner] (1893, Radymno, Galicia–1976, Montreal). Expressionist poet, secretary of the Yiddish Writer's Club in Warsaw who settled in Montreal in 1940. He is best known for his multi-volume memoir *Dos mayse-bukh fun mayn lebn*. Until Mother's terrible falling out with him during my sophomore year in college, Ravitch's bronze bust stood in our living room. It has since been bequeathed to the Jewish Public Library.

REISEN, AVROM (1876, Keidany, White Russia–1953, New York). A modern folk bard who introduced the Chekhovian short story into Yiddish. A member of Peretz's inner circle, he settled permanently in America after the outbreak of World War I.

ROCHMAN, LEYB (1918, Minsk Mazowiecki—1978, Jerusalem). Raised in a Hasidic environment, he was one of the few survivors of the Holocaust from his hometown. He is best known for his chronicle of survival *Un in dayn blut zolstu lebn* (1949), translated as *The Pit and the Trap*. He later became the Israel correspondent for the *Jewish Daily Forward* and the editor of Yiddish news programs for Kol Yisrael.

ROSENFARB, CHAVA (1923, Lodz–). Yiddish literature's leading woman novelist, she survived the Lodz ghetto and eventually settled in Montreal in 1950.

ROSKES, DOVID (1860, Zabludowo–1943, Bialystok ghetto). Youngest child of Hershl and Feygl Rojzkes who married Odl Nay (1863–1932) in 1880. He was the blind patriarch who foresaw the German invasion and masterminded my family's escape from Europe. Their surviving children were Shiye (1884–1961), Itshe (Isaac) (1895–1955), Perele (1897–1943), Henakh (Enoch) (1900–1985), and Leybl (Leo, my father) (1905–1976).

ROSKIES, BENJAMIN (1931, Krosno–1974, Montreal). Eldest son of Masha and Leybl, he was an accomplished musician, a poet, and a textile manufacturer.

ROSKIES, MASHA [née Welczer] (1906, Vilna–1999, Montreal). Only surviving child of Fradl Matz and Yisroel Welczer. She married Leybl Roskes on February 13–14, 1930, and bore him five children, four of whom survived.

SCHAECHTER, MORDKHE (1927, Czernowitz–2007, New York). Scholar and ideologue of the Yiddish language. He immigrated in 1951 to New York, where he raised a Yiddish-speaking family and instilled a love of Yiddish in several generations of students.

SCHARF, RAPHAEL (1914, Kraków–2003, London). Trained as a lawyer. He left Poland in 1938 for England, where he worked as a journalist and became active in Polish-Jewish rapprochement.

SEGAL, J. I. (1896, Solobkovtsy, Ukraine–1954, Montreal). The dean of Yiddish poets in Montreal, where he settled in 1911.

SEIDMAN, BORIS (1895, Vilna–1961, New York). Not his real name, but everything attributed to him has been faithfully recorded. His grand-daughter lives in Newton, Massachusetts.

SHMERUK, KHONE (1921, Warsaw–1997, Warsaw). Professor of Yiddish literature at the Hebrew University. He is one of the few people in my story to die in the same city where he was born.

SHOLEM ALEICHEM [pen name of Solomon Rabinovitsh] (1859, Pereyaslav–1916, New York). One of the great comic writers in world literature and the best reason for a person to learn Yiddish.

SINGER, ISAAC BASHEVIS (1904, Leoncin–1991, New York). Awarded the Nobel Prize in Literature in 1978. Like the author of this book, Singer spent most of his life in Manhattan, dreaming of other cities.

STEINBARG, ELIEZER (1880, Lipkany, Bessarabia–1932, Czernowitz). Master of the fable.

STOTSKY, LEYB (1902, Vilna–ca. 1941, Siberia). Poet, polyglot, and journalist.

SUTZKEVER, AVROM (Abrasha) (1913, Smorgon–). The major Yiddish poet of the twentieth century, founder and editor of *Di goldene keyt* (1949–1995). "The First Poem" appears in his *Poetishe verk* 2 (Tel Aviv, 1963): 503–505. He has lived in Tel Aviv since 1947.

VAYTER, A. [pen name of Isaac Meyer Devenishski] (1878, Benyakon, near Vilna–1919, Vilna). Yiddish playwright. He was active in the Bund under the nom-de-guerre Comrade Aaron. His murder at the hands of Polish Legionnaires who dragged him out of his apartment galvanized the Jewish intellectual elite of Vilna.

WARSHAWSKI, ANNA [née Matz] (ca. 1890, Vilna–1943, Estonia). Settled in Kovno with her second husband, Lyova, after graduating from the Berlin Conservatory of Music. In Kovno, she ran a kindergarten and performed Yiddish songs both as soloist and member of Engel's Choir.

With her two daughters, Bella and Fifa, she and her husband were deported from the Kovno ghetto on October 26, 1943.

WASSERMAN, DORA [née Goldfarb] (1919, Zhitomir–2003, Montreal). Studied with Solomon Mikhoels at the Jewish State Theater School (GOSET) from 1935 to 1939. After the war she was repatriated with her Polish-born husband and arrived in Montreal in January 1950. She founded and was the director of the Yiddish Theater Group in 1957, first under the auspices of the Jewish People's School and, since 1967, at the Saidye Bronfman Centre. She also ran a Yiddish Youth Theater at the Jewish Public Library. After Dora suffered a severe stroke, the Group was taken over by her younger daughter, Bryna.

WEINREICH, MAX (1894, Goldingen, Kurland–1969, New York). The leading scholar of the Yiddish language, and a founder and director of the YIVO Institute.

WELCZER, YISROEL (1859, Juzefów Lubelski–1925, Vilna). An Orthodox-Hasidic bookseller. He had four children by his first wife, whom he divorced to marry my grandmother. He refused all offers of marriage after Fradl died.

WISEMAN, SHLOYME (1899, Dinovitz/Dunayevtsky, Ukraine–1985, Montreal). Hebrew-Yiddish writer, translator, and pedagogue par excellence. He came to Canada in 1913, where he served as principal of the Jewish People's School from 1920 to 1969.

Masha Roskies Sings

LINER NOTES

The original reel-to-reel recordings, made in August 1973, are housed at the YIVO Institute for Jewish Research in New York. A complete copy was donated to the United States Memorial Holocaust Museum in Washington, D.C., where they were digitized.

1. "Der rebe Elimeylekh" (The Rebbe Elimeylekh). Moyshe Nadir 00:36
   Chapter 1, "The Rebbe Elimeylekh." Masha recorded only part of the song.

2. "Kh'vil nit zayn keyn rebe" (Save me from becoming a Rebbe). 01:52
   Chapter 7, "Malvina's Roses." The song ends with a delicious parody of *lernen*, Jewish textual study. Presumably, this was the part that gave Malvina the most trouble and required Masha's tutoring.

3. "In a shtetele nit vayt fun danen" (In a little shtetl not far from here). 01:14
   Chapter 8, "The Watercarrier." Sung in Yiddish with a Polish chorus, the meaning of which was never explained.

4. "Song of Mashleyb." 01:40
   Chapter 11, "The Black Canopy." Composed by Masha's circle of friends, in particular one "Dr. Alk."

Children, alas, Masha the bride has decided to abandon us.
But let's sing and be merry, for Masha the Queen is off to the King.
Yes, Leybele will live it up, when Masha cooks him a song in a broth.
A song is her life, Mashke means: Spirits. So let her sing us a *lekhayim*.
Song is her life, her very essence. So let's all drink a toast!

5. "Loz dayne zorgn" (Cast your cares away). Moyshe Broderzon. 01:19
Chapter 12, "May Day."

6. "Keyft, keyft kinderlekh nartsizn" (Children, buy my daffodils). 00:33
Chapter 12, "May Day."

7. "Kum Leybke tantsn" (Come Leybke, dance with me). Mordecai Gebirtig.
03:42
Chapter 13, "The Wooden Box." Masha performs a middle stanza that
does not appear in any edition or recording of Gebirtig's songs.

8. "Di zhiduvkes" (The Jew-girls). Set to a popular Polish melody. 01:00
Chapter 18, "Cape Cod."

9. "Di shenste lidgezangen" (The loveliest songs). Avrom Reisen/Felix
Mendelssohn. 01:42
Chapter 18, "Cape Cod."

10. "Pei, moya devochka" (Drink, my girl). Aleksandr Vertinsky/Leyb Stotsky. 02:14
Chapter 18, "Cape Cod."

The CD ends, as does the memoir, with Masha singing in Russian, her
mother tongue.

Acknowledgments

This book could not have been written but for the help of the following people: Monika Adamczyk-Garbowska, Bonny Fetterman, Joel Rosenberg, Hillel Schwartz, Michael Swirsky, Hana Wirth-Nesher, and Shoshana Zonderman. My thanks to Danny O'Brien for composing and scanning the images and to Mazebright Music of New Jersey for producing the CD.